The Faber Book of Modern Verse

THE FABER BOOK OF
Modern Verse

Edited by
MICHAEL ROBERTS

FOURTH EDITION
Revised by
PETER PORTER

faber and faber

First published in 1936
by Faber and Faber Limited
3 Queen Square London WC1N 3AU
This fourth edition published in 1982
Printed in Great Britain by
Fakenham Press Limited, Fakenham, Norfolk

British Library Cataloguing in Publication Data

The Faber book of modern verse.—4th ed.
1. English poetry—20th century
I. Roberts, Michael II. Porter, Peter
821′.912′08 PR1225

ISBN 0–571–18055–8
ISBN 0–571–18017–5 Pbk

Poets

Contents

CONTENTS

Introduction to the First Edition

More often than prose or mathematics, poetry is received in a hostile spirit, as if its publication were an affront to the reader; yet most of the poetry which is published probably appears because, at the time of writing, it delighted the writer and convinced him that it held some profound significance or some exact description which he hoped that others, too, might see. One might expect that any poetry depending upon a very personal experience or a relatively private use of words would be ignored; and certainly a great deal of new poetry does meet with indifference because it seems private and incomprehensible. There remains, however, a considerable body of poetry which excites an active animosity, not because it states opinions and expresses feelings which are repugnant to the ordinary man, but because the reader feels compelled to argue that it is not poetry at all: many of the poems in this book aroused that animosity on their first appearance. Much of that hostility has now vanished: it is seen that these poets were saying things which were true, and important, and which could not be said as well in any other way. In that sense, it might be claimed that this collection represents the most significant poetry of this age; but the omission of Charles Sorley, Walter de la Mare, Edmund Blunden, Edwin Muir, William Plomer, Roy Campbell, all of whom seem to me to have written good poems without having been compelled to make any notable development of poetic technique, is sufficient evidence that this is not intended to be a comprehensive anthology of the best poems of our age.

The poems in the book were, with few exceptions, first printed after 1910. This date is arbitrary, and so are some of the inclusions and omissions. I have included only poems which seem to me to add to the resources of poetry, to be likely to influence the future development of poetry and language, and to please me for reasons neither personal nor idiosyncratic. But the capacity to provoke controversy has been ncither a necessary nor a sufficient condition for inclusion. Mr Yeats is included, although the breadth of his appeal has always placed him beyond controversy, but it is worth noting that in his images, approximations to ordinary speech rhythms, political implications and private references, and in his strictly poetic[1] use of myth and legend, he has anticipated many of the devices of the younger men. The earlier poems of some of the older poets are omitted, and the later included, when it is in the later work that a significant development appears. A number of young poets who have written good poems are included, although the full significance of their innovations is not yet wholly clear. Perhaps the most general characteristic of the poems in this book is that they seldom record a recognized "poetical" experience.

To most readers it will not be surprising that an anthology of modern poetry should begin with Hopkins: but I do not mean to suggest that his poetry made a complete break with the poetry of the past and marked the inauguration of a new age. In rhythm and in imagery, as well as in the thoughts and feelings which he intended to express, he differed from most of the English poets of his time, but there was no sharp discontinuity. Doughty, born only a year before Hopkins, resembled him in his inversions, his alliteration, the violence of his syntax, and above all in the emphasis which he succeeded in placing on accumulated masses of nouns, verbs, adjectives and adverbs, often unleavened by prepositions or conjunctions. Doughty's poetry is massive and uneven: a strong case could have been made out for including it; but it lacks the intensity which, in the poetry of Hopkins, was the expression of an important moral conflict, related to an outer social and intellectual conflict.

It is not possible to compile an anthology of serious poetry without reflecting the social and moral problems of our time; but writing may be poetic without being either moral or didactic. Poetry may be intended to amuse, or to ridicule, or to persuade, or to produce an effect which we feel to be more valuable than amusement and different from instruction; but primarily poetry is an exploration of the possibilities of language. It does not aim

[1] The word "poetic" is here used to describe a special concentration of sensuous impression, idea and evocation in a word or phrase. The word "poetical" is used to describe an attempted evocation by conventional symbols, of a state of mind sometimes called mystical.

directly at consolation or moral exhortation, nor at the expression of exquisite moments, but at an extension of significance; and it might be argued that a too self-conscious concern with "contemporary" problems deflects the poet's effort from his true objective. The technical merit of a poem is measured by its accuracy, not by the importance of a rough approximation to what is being said, nor by the number of people to whom it is immediately intelligible. If a poet is incomprehensible to many people, but clearly intelligible to a few, as Hopkins appeared to be when his collected poems were first published, it may be because he is speaking of things not commonly experienced and is using subtleties of rhythm and imagery not used in ordinary speech, and therefore not widely understood. If it can be shown that a poet's use of language is valid for some people, we cannot dismiss his way of speaking as mere "obscurity" and idiosyncrasy, though we may regret the necessity for such a rhetoric as we may regret the necessity for scientific jargon and mathematical notation.

The significant point about Hopkins was, however, not that he invented a style different from the current poetic style, but that, working in subterranean fashion, he moulded a style which expressed the tension and disorder that he found inside himself. Good poetry is more likely to be written about subjects which are, to the writer, important, than about unimportant subjects, because only on subjects of personal importance to himself does he feel the need for that accuracy of speech which itself lessens the tension which it describes. Deliberately to imitate a style arising from one poet's crisis would be absurd, but something similar is likely to appear when a crisis of a general kind arouses a personal conflict in many poets. The conflict may be the product of a fractured personality or a decaying society, or, like some of the "problems" of academic philosophy, a result of the deficiencies of language. The terms of the conflict may be intellectual, when people are torn between conflicting systems of ideas. They may be theological, when people argue that they themselves should be perfect, being the children of God, but are perplexed by the recognition that they are evil. The terms may be political and aesthetic, when people cling to some features of the existing state, but see that there can be no good future until that state is overthrown. Sometimes, as in Donne, several of these terminologies are superimposed, serving as metaphors for each other, and concentrating, intensifying, and ultimately simplifying the problems by this poetic identification. For "problems" of this kind are seldom independent; there is a relation between the personal and moral problem and the political and intellectual.

To those who have not felt some adumbration of such a crisis, the expression and resolution of conflict and disorder must appear like the strained muscles and distorted features of a strong man pretending to lift stupendous but non-existent weights. But for those who have come near to feeling the crisis themselves, the poetry is important. Words do something more than call up ideas and emotions out of a lumber-room: they call them up, but they never replace them exactly where they were. A good descriptive poem may enable us to be more articulate, to perceive more clearly, and to distinguish more readily between sensitive and sentimental observation, than before. But a poem may do more than that: even though we may not accept the poet's explicit doctrine, it may change the configuration of the mind and alter our responses to certain situations: it may harmonize conflicting emotions just as a good piece of reasoning may show the fallacy of an apparent contradiction in logic.

But the poetic use of language can cause discord as easily as it can cure it. A bad poem, a psychologically disordered poem, if it is technically effective may arouse uneasiness or nausea or anger in the reader. A sentimental poem, which deals with a situation by ignoring some of the factors, is offensive in this way; and a poem is equally confusing if it takes into account greater complexities of thought and intricacies of feeling than the reader has ever noticed. It unsettles the mind—and by the mind I mean more than the conscious mind; and the reader expends the energy he originally brought to the poem in trivial irritation with the poet.

It is very natural that this should be the first response of many readers to "new" poetry, but in so far as the poet is a good poet, the situation will remedy itself. The problem which worried the poet will worry other people, or the new grounds which he saw for delight and hope will become apparent to them too: perhaps their recognition of the new element will be accelerated by his writing. But in either case they will welcome the way of speech which makes them articulate. Sometimes, as in the case of Hopkins, the problem which is his today is the world's tomorrow. Sometimes his writing is significant primarily for only a few of each generation, as when it is evoked by some remote place or rare experience or an intricate thought which few can follow. Sometimes it expresses only the problem of few or many people at one particular moment. But in each case, if the writer is a good poet, good in the sense of being rhetorically effective, his writing has a value over and above that of its immediate appeal: he has added to the possibilities of speech, he has discovered evocative rhythms and image-sequences unknown before. It may happen that in some future state of society there will be no people in the position of Mr Eliot's Prufrock, and therefore no people for whom the poem is actual. But the rhetorical merit of the poem remains: it has said something which could not be said in ordinary speech, and said it exactly, and people who are interested in effective expression will read it. Pope and Erasmus Darwin both wrote poems which were chiefly of didactic interest in their own time, but the elegance of Pope's writing keeps it alive today, whereas the poetry of Erasmus Darwin is almost forgotten. Chaucer has influenced English poetry and English language more than Langland, though Langland was, and is, the nearer to the thought and feeling of the common people.

In contrast to the previous twenty years, when the "decadence" of the content of certain poems was continually discussed, critical discussion for the past thirty years has been concerned most often with the form, or alleged formlessness, of modern poetry. In the narrow sense, the word "form" is used to describe special metrical and stanzaic patterns: in a wider sense it is used for the whole set of relationships involving the sensuous imagery and the auditory rhetoric of a poem. A definite "form" in the narrower (and older) sense is not an asset unless it is an organized part of the "form" in the wider sense, for the final value of a poem always springs from the inter-relation of form and content. In a good poet a change or development of technique always springs from a change or development of subject-matter.

If, then, we are to discuss technical innovations effectively, we must also discuss content; and here, at once, an important point appears. Roughly speaking, the poets in this book may be divided into two classes: those whose poetry is primarily a defence and vindication of existing cultural values, and those who, using the poetic qualities of the English language, try to build up poetry out of the realities implicit in the language, and which they find in their own minds rather than base it upon humanistic learning and memories of other poetry. The poets of the first kind possess what might be called a "European" sensibility: they are aware of Baudelaire, Corbière, Rimbaud, Laforgue and the later Symbolists (it is notable that German poetry has had little influence upon them), they turn to Dante or Cavalcanti more readily than to Milton, they are more likely to be interested in a Parisian movement in poetry, such as Surrealism, than in the corresponding tendency in *Alice Through the Looking Glass* or Young's *Night Thoughts*. Most of them are Americans by birth, but their appeal is as much to the English as to the American reader. Among their English predecessors they might number Donne, Crashaw and Pope.

Poets in whose work the "English" element predominates take the language as they find it, developing the implications of its idioms, metaphors and symbols. They are "first order" poets: that is to say, it is not necessary to have a wide acquaintance with European literature, or even with English literature, to appreciate their work. They may be given an ancestry in Langland, Skelton, Doughty, on the one hand, and Blake, Shelley and perhaps Edward Lear, on the other, but their work does not depend upon a knowledge of literary history: it is an intensification of qualities inherent in the English language itself, and for this reason it is less easy to translate than that of the "European" poets, in whose poems the specific properties of the language they are using is a more casual element.

These classes are not exclusive: they represent two moods of poetry rather than two kinds of poet. The poetry of W. B. Yeats, for example, must be considered under both headings: but the work of Ezra Pound and T. S. Eliot is clearly "European" in cast. Robert Graves for a time hesitated between the two, then identified himself with that view of poetry which Laura Riding has increasingly emphasized—poetry as the final residue of significance in language, freed from extrinsic decoration, superficial contemporaneity, and didactic bias.

The "European" poet is acutely aware of the social world in which he lives, he criticizes it, but in a satirical rather than in an indignant manner, he adjusts himself to it, he is interested in its accumulated store of music, painting, sculpture, and even in its bric-à-brac. There is something of the dandy, something of the dilettante, in his make-up, but he is aware of the futility and evanescence of all this, and of the irresponsibility of big business, conventional politics and mass education. He is witty, and acutely self-conscious. His attitude is the outcome of a genuine care for much that is valuable in the past, and it gains its strength from a desire to preserve these things: to preserve them, not by violence, but by exercise, for they are not "things" at all, but certain attitudes and activities.

Every vital age, perhaps, sees its own time as crucial and full of perils, but the problems and difficulties of our own age necessarily appear more urgent to us than those of any other, and the need for an evaluating, clarifying poetry has never been greater than it appears to be today. Industrial changes have broken up the old culture, based on an agricultural community in which poor and wealthy were alike concerned, and on a Church which bore a vital relation to the State. Parallel with this, and related to it, there has been a decay of the old moral and religious order, and a change in the basis of education, which has become more and more strictly scientific. Religion and classical learning, which once provided myths and legends symbolizing the purposes of society and the role of the individual, have declined, and the disorder weighs heavily upon the serious poet, whether in England or America.

It is the theme of many of the poems of Mr Pound, and of Mr Eliot's *Waste Land*. We find the American poets, Hart Crane and Allen Tate, seeing the situation in these terms:

"The Parthenon in stucco, art for the sake of death".

And the poets—Mr Yeats among them—have attempted to clarify their own vision by expressing the disorder which they see about them, and by finding and defining those things in the older tradition which they hold to be valuable and necessary:

> Things fall apart; the centre cannot hold;
> Mere anarchy is loosed upon the world,
> The blood-dimmed tide is loosed, and everywhere
> The ceremony of innocence is drowned;
> The best lack all conviction, while the worst
> Are full of passionate intensity.

If the poet is in the "European" tradition, he describes the elements of civilization wherever he finds them: in Rome, in Greece, in Confucius, or in the Church of the Middle Ages; and against these he contrasts the violence and disorder of contemporary life. It is inevitable that poetry concerned with such issues should have political implications; but the poet is not arguing for one party against another: he is remodelling the basis upon which political creeds are founded, though sometimes immediate implications may appear in his poems.

Younger poets than Mr Eliot and Mr Pound may feel more acutely the inter-relation of culture and politics, but nevertheless they would agree with Mr Auden that "poetry is not concerned with telling people what to do, but with extending our knowledge of good and evil, perhaps making the necessity for action more urgent and its nature more clear, but only leading us to the point where it is possible for us to make a rational and moral choice".

The problem, as we see on turning to Clough's *Amours de Voyage* (1849), is not wholly new. Clough had, as Bagehot says, "an unusual difficulty in forming a creed as to the unseen world; he could not get the visible world out of his head; his strong grasp of plain facts and obvious matters was a difficulty to him. . . . He has himself given us in a poem, now first published, a very remarkable description of this curious state of mind. He has prefixed to it the characteristic motto, *"Il doutait de tout même de l'amour"*. It is the delineation of a certain love-passage in the life of a hesitating young gentleman, who was in Rome at the time of the revolution of 1848; who could not make up his mind about the revolution, who could not make up his mind whether he liked Rome, who could not make up his mind whether he liked the young lady, who let her go away without him, who went in pursuit of her and could not make out which way to look for her, who, in fine, has some sort of religion but cannot tell himself what it is. . . ."

Amours de Voyage was written in conversational hexameter, in a tone of semi-satire and half-belief,

> Rome disappoints me much; I hardly as yet understand, but
> *Rubbishy* seems the word that most exactly would suit it.
>
> * * *
>
> Luther, they say, was unwise; like a half-taught German, he
> could not
> See that old follies were passing most tranquilly out of
> remembrance;
> Leo the Tenth was employing all efforts to clear out abuses;
> Jupiter, Juno, and Venus, Fine Arts, and Fine Letters, the
> Poets,
> Scholars, and Sculptors, and Painters, were quietly clearing
> away the
> Martyrs, and Virgins, and Saints, or at any rate Thomas
> Aquinas:
> He must forsooth make a fuss and distend his huge
> Wittenberg lungs, and
> Bring back Theology once yet again in a flood upon Europe.

The resemblance to Mr Pound's *Cantos*, in tone and intention, is obvious, and there is the same detachment, the same denial of commonly-accepted responsibility that is found in *Mauberley* and *Prufrock*:

> *Dulce* it is, and *decorum* no doubt, for the country to fall,—to
> Offer one's blood an oblation to Freedom, and die for the
> Cause; yet
> Still, individual culture is also something. . . .

and the detachment passes easily into a kind of semi-serious raillery, which springs from a feeling that the generally accepted code is all wrong, and yet that there is no other to take its place:

Am I prepared to lay down my life for the British female?
Really, who knows? One has bowed and talked, till, little by little,
All the natural heat has escaped of the chivalrous spirit.
Oh, one conformed, of course; but one doesn't die for good manners,
Stab or shoot, or be shot, by way of graceful attention.
No, if it should be at all, it should be on the barricades there. . . .
Sooner far by the side of the damned and dirty plebeians.
Ah, for a child in the street I could strike; for the full-blown lady—
Somehow, Eustace, alas! I have not felt the vocation.

There is the same introspection, the same self-mockery that is found in the poetry of Jules Laforgue, the same dissatisfaction with ready-made analysis, and the same intense conviction that there is an underlying problem which is not to be laughed away:

I am in love, meantime, you think; no doubt you would think so.
I am in love, you say; with those letters, of course, you would say so.
I am in love, you declare. . . .
I am in love, you say: I do not think so, exactly.

There are lines which recall the more "metaphysical" passages of T. S. Eliot with their echoes of Chapman and Webster:

I do not like being moved: for the will is excited; and action
Is a most dangerous thing; I tremble for something factitious,
Some malpractice of heart and illegitimate process;
We are so prone to these things, with our terrible notions of duty.

and there are passages of lyrical fine writing, such as we find in *The Waste Land* and the *Cantos*:

> Tibur is beautiful, too, and the orchard slopes, and the Anio
> Falling, falling yet, to the ancient lyrical cadence;
> Tibur and Anio's tide; . . .

There are obvious technical resemblances (I am not denying the obvious differences) in tempo, pitch and rhythm, but Eliot and Pound differ from Clough in their greater compression and intensity. Although Clough's poem sustains its narrative interest, his hexameters, however freely handled, become irritating, and his imagery is often diffuse and unexciting. Browning and Walt Whitman, both of whom anticipated many of the habits of the modern poets, suffer from the same long-windedness. They do not compress a situation into a single memorable image, and Clough did not feel the problem of his young man as intensely as Ezra Pound and T. S. Eliot felt it in 1912. Clough suspected that the *malaise* was due to a fault in himself, and Bagehot, a sensitive critic, agreed with him; but for Pound and Eliot the problem was external: it was society and its standards that were crumbling. A culture adapted to the older aristocratic system of landed proprietors was falling to pieces in a world governed by big business. Civilization was becoming "a few score of broken statues, an old bitch gone in the teeth" or "a heap of broken images". It was necessary to sift out from the mass of habits, institutions and conventions the traditions which were worth preserving.

For the moment all that the poet could do was to concentrate upon surfaces: in a world in which moral, intellectual and aesthetic values were all uncertain, only sense impressions were certain and could be described exactly. From such minute particulars perhaps something could be built up. In 1913 a few poets, shocked at the vagueness and facility of the poetry of the day, determined:

1. To use the language of common speech, but to employ always the *exact* word, not the merely decorative word.
2. To create new rhythms—as the expression of new moods.

We do not insist upon "Free-verse" as the only method of writing poetry. . . . We do believe that the individuality of a poet may often be better expressed in free verse than in conventional forms.

3. To allow absolute freedom in the choice of subject.

4. To present an image. We are not a school of painters, but we believe that poetry should render particulars exactly and not deal with vague generalities.

5. To produce poetry that is hard and clear, never blurred or indefinite.

6. Finally, most of us believe that concentration is the very essence of poetry.

Edited by Ezra Pound, a number of "Imagist" anthologies appeared; T. E. Hulme wrote some of the earliest Imagist poems. Amy Lowell, F. S. Flint, H.D., J. G. Fletcher, Richard Aldington, T. S. Eliot and Ezra Pound himself at one time or other were members of the group, and the later development of the movement appears in the work of Marianne Moore. T. S. Eliot had been influenced by Baudelaire, Laforgue and Rimbaud. Ezra Pound was impressed by the work of Villon and the Provençal and early Italian poets. F. S. Flint was interested in the later Symbolists—Samain, Kahn, Jammes, Rodenbach and the earlier Verhaeren—as well as more recent writers, Vildrac, Romains, Duhamel. The name "Imagist" itself recalls "Symbolist", and the Imagists themselves sometimes confused the image, the clear evocation of a material thing, with the symbol, the word which stirs subconscious memories. Such, indeed, was their intention: their poetry was meant to widen outwards like the ripples from a stone dropped in clear water. But the scope of "pure" Imagist poetry was limited to clear renderings of visual experience: the poetry of H.D. shows both the possibilities and the limitations of the method.

It was natural that there should be a movement away from poeticality of subject and from the direct expression of emotion when the poets were in doubt about standards of art and morals: for the moment *any* emotion seemed sentimental to their realism.

But the realism itself was often deceptive. Wallace Stevens in *The Emperor of Ice-Cream* writes a poem to insist that only the commonplace is real: let "be" be the end of "seem"; but the reality he describes is itself highly-coloured, and the poem contains more than a clear visual image. When he writes:

Take from the dresser of deal,
Lacking the three glass knobs, that sheet
On which she embroidered fantails once
And spread it so as to cover her face.
If her horny feet protrude, they come
To show how cold she is, and dumb—

I am fairly sure that he is writing with some vague memory of Mantegna's picture of the dead Christ and certainly that recollection makes the image more impressive.

The poetry of Wallace Stevens and Miss Sitwell still shows the Imagist concentration upon the sensuous surface of things, but even with the latitude which they allow themselves, Imagism is limited in scope; and as Mr Pound has recorded: "at a particular date in a particular room, two authors, neither engaged in picking the other's pocket, decided that the dilution of *vers libre*, Amygism, Lee Masterism, general floppiness had gone too far and that some counter-current must be set going. Parallel situation centuries ago in China. Remedy prescribed *Emaux et Cameés* (or the Bay State Hymn Book). Rhyme and regular strophes.

"Results: Poems in Mr Eliot's *second* volume, not contained in his first *Prufrock* (Egoist, 1917), also *H. S. Mauberley*."

Between 1920 and 1926, many poets were trying to write long poems which would present a unified view of the social crisis as they saw it, and imply their criticism of it. Conrad Aiken, who had been for a brief time influenced by the ideals of the Imagists, began to work for something which would lead to more profound and more highly organized poems, and turned to music. The predominant pattern of his poems is musical, whereas the more important pattern of some poems, as St. J. Perse's *Anabase* (translated by T. S. Eliot), is one of vivid visual and tactile images.

Conrad Aiken's *Senlin* (1918), T. S. Eliot's *The Waste Land*

(1922), Richard Aldington's *Fool i' the Forest* (1925), and Archibald MacLeish's *Hamlet of A. MacLeish* (1928), were all poems of this kind. *The Waste Land* is the most concise, the most evocative, the widest in scope, and the most highly organized of these poems. It possesses "imaginative order", by which I mean, that to some minds it is cogent even before its narrative and argumentative continuity is grasped. This "imaginative order" is not something arbitrary, specific and inexplicable. If the images which are used to denote complex situations were replaced by abstractions, much of the apparent incoherence of the poem would vanish. It would become a prose description of the condition of the world, a restatement of a myth and a defence of the tragic view of life. But being a poem it does more than this; a poem expresses not merely the idea of a social or scientific fact, but also the sensation of thinking or knowing, and it does not merely defend the tragic view, it may communicate it.

The images and rhythms of *The Waste Land* are not conventionally poetical: their aura of suggestion radiates from a definite meaning relating to the ordinary world, and their full significance is not seen until the essentially tragic attitude of the poem is grasped. The omission of explanatory connecting matter when contrasting a "modern" situation with an old or the life of one class with that of another may be puzzling at first, but given a general understanding of the poem it becomes clear. Thus one situation may be described in the terms and rhythms appropriate to another, so that both the similarities and the differences are illuminated.

It is not only the "European" poets who are concerned with these problems, nor are they the only poets who aim at poetic concentration and whose work therefore presents initial difficulties. These spring from several sources. There is the intellectual difficulty which arises from the poet's use of some little-known fact, or some idea hard to grasp; there is the difficulty which comes from the unusual use of metaphor; and there is the difficulty which arises when the poet is making a deliberately fantastic use of words.

The obscurity which arises from the use of little-known or intricate ideas is easily removed. Some of the obscurity of Mr Eliot's poetry and Mr Empson's is of this kind: it needs only elucidatory notes to make it vanish, and it should be remembered that, because the ideas of science are widely known and generally believed, the poet who uses them is on safer ground than the man who makes classical allusions which, although they are accepted as poetical, are neither exactly appreciated nor fully understood.

The difficulty which arises from an unusual use of metaphor is less easy to remove: it depends far more upon the goodwill of the reader. Metaphor and simile are fundamental to civilized speech: but they have one serious disadvantage, the moment you say one thing is "like" another, you remind the reader that the two things are, after all, different; and there may be an effect of dilution and long-windedness which is inimical to poetry. The poet, therefore, condenses his metaphor. Hart Crane in *Voyages*, III, referring to the rhythm of the motion of a boat through a thickly clustered archipelago, speaks of "adagios of islands". Similarly, in *Faustus and Helen*, III, the speed and altitude of an aeroplane are suggested by the idea of "nimble blue plateaus". This kind of compressed metaphor is also found in the poetry of Stephen Spender:

Eye, gazelle, delicate wanderer,
Drinker of horizon's fluid line.

This condensation may demand an initial effort of understanding in the reader, but once the meaning is understood, the aptness and convenience of the phrase is obvious; it becomes part of one's habit of thought, and the understanding of these compressed analogies becomes, after a time, no more difficult than the understanding of a simile or a more prosaic and long-winded metaphor.

The condensation of metaphor involves no denial of logic: it is simply an extension of the implications of grammar, the development of a notation which, being less cumbersome, enables us to think more easily. It may be compared to the invention of a new notation, say that of Leibnitz or Hamilton, in mathematics: the new is defined in terms of the old, it is a shorthand which must be learned by patient effort, but, once learnt, it makes possible the solution of problems which were too complicated to attack before. The human head can only carry a certain amount of notation at any one moment, and poetry takes up less space than prose.

The third difficulty, that which springs from a deliberately fantastic use of words, is less than one might imagine. We accept, willingly, the fantastic sequences of nursery-rhyme and fairy-tale; and only a confusion of thought makes us demand, as we grow older, that poetry should always give us enlightenment or high moral doctrine. The poet has a right to play, and the reader to enjoy that play. The solemn attacks on the more riotously comic of Mr Cummings' poems are themselves ridiculous. There is in all poetry an element of verbal play; and in nonsense verses, in the poetry of Mr Cummings, in Mr Madge's *Lusty Juventus* and in the early poetry of Miss Sitwell, this element often predominates. It is found in Miss Riding's *Tillaquils* which, because it actualizes a strange experience of a kind which the reader has been accustomed to regard as "abstract", tends to be read, like her better-known poem, *The Quids*, as a satire upon academic metaphysics.

Verbal play is a form of fantasy, and when we relax and abandon ourselves to such poetry we find that some of it makes too deep an impression on our minds to be called "play" at all. In the joke-poem we may give ourselves up to the casual association of words, but many readers find this abandonment difficult when something more serious appears to be involved. They are prepared to enjoy poetry which tells a story or states a moral, but they distrust the abandonment of common sense and accepted habits of language, believing, rightly, that if common sense is abandoned, then the way is open to all nonsense, incoherence and private fantasy.

"There is a mental existence within us . . . which is not less energetic than the conscious flow, an absent mind which haunts us like a ghost or a dream and is an essential part of our lives. Incidentally . . . the unconscious life of the mind bears a wonderful resemblance to the supposed feature of imagination. . . . To lay bare the automatic or unconscious action of the mind is indeed to unfold a tale which outvies the romances of giants and ginns, wizards in their palaces, and captives in the Domdaniel roots of the sea."[1]

There are no rules to guide us, no histories to enable us to check our facts: but it is a simple experimental fact that certain people do agree that "imaginative order" is found in certain specified poems, and not in others. In so far as those people are normal, it therefore seems that the poem, though "subjective" in the old sense, is "objective" in so far as it describes something which is part of the experience of a number of people. Poetry changes in its emphasis from one time to another, and just as, in recent years, there has been a decline in the writing of descriptive poetry (a decline which the Imagists attempted to check), so in the near future we may see greater emphasis placed on poetry as a means of appealing directly to the subconscious mind, and less on poetry as a conscious criticism of life.

As we see from the quotation from Dallas, the critical theory appropriate to such poetry is not new. Hints of its method are found in the older critics, and in Shelley. "Poetry", said Shelley, "differs in this respect from logic, that it is not subject to the control of the active powers of the mind, and that its birth and recurrence have no necessary connexion with the consciousness or will." Sometimes the reason for the order of the images of such poems and the cause of their effectiveness are fairly obvious. Their power and order may come from casual memory, or from the make-up of the mind, from the deep impressions of early childhood, or from the influence of the birth trauma, or from the structure of the language itself. The meaning of a word is never a simple thing, a "standing-for" an object or relation: it is the whole complex set of grammatical habits and associations of ideas which have grown up from our first hearing of it, and the poet exploits this symbolism of words as he exploits the more directly "psychological" symbolism or substitution value of images. It is possible, therefore, for a poem to be professedly realistic and yet to have the vigour and insistence of a dream or nightmare. Good poetry always has something of this quality, but the nightmare may be directly verbal, rather than visual. Robert Graves is, I

[1] E. S. Dallas, *The Gay Science* (1866).

think, a poet whose poetry is mainly verbal. That is to say, although there is often a visual picture corresponding to his poems, the effect of the poem depends upon the direct evocative effect of the words, not on the visual stimulus.

Among the poems which deliberately free themselves from logic there are not only the joke-poems, which are simply an exercise of poetic energy showing the word-sense of the poet; but also the relaxation-poems, which range from those in which words associate themselves mainly according to relations and similarities of sound (as in Miss Sitwell's *Hornpipe*), to those which are day-dream narratives. Of these, one of the more obvious types is the wandering-ego poem in which the "I"—"On a bat's back I do fly"—paces beside the ocean, passes through caves and dismal gorges, is prisoned in miserable dungeons, rises to craggy heights and is carried upon the wind. A poem of this kind has often a tremendous self-importance which becomes inflated until the ego dominates the entire world and we arrive at the great passages in Whitman, where, Charles Madge has pointed out, the ego passes over all the earth and eventually "dissolves in lacy jags".

Then again, there are the poems which, like *Kubla Khan* or, to take a modern example, Dylan Thomas's "*Light breaks where no sun shines*", correspond to dream-fantasies of a sexual type. The woods, the hills, the rushing stream—all become substitutes for other things, and the reader (and perhaps the poet), unaware of what is happening in his own mind, is puzzled at the strange excitement which he finds in the succession of images.

In some poems, the dream-quality is exaggerated and the structure which is believed to characterize the fantasies of the deeper levels in sleep is deliberately made the model for the structure of the poem. The *Parade Virtues for a Dying Gladiator* of Sacheverell Sitwell is of that kind, and so, too, are the poems which the Surrealists, and their English admirer, David Gascoyne, aim at producing. Such poems, if they are the product of a normal mind, may become fascinating when we get over their initial strangeness; but the "order" of such poems is not necessarily identical with the "imaginative order" of myth and legend. The poem may be a good one without being specifically poetic. It might, for example, be more effective as a film than it is in printed words.

But although good poems may sometimes be shown to correspond to standard types of dream, good poetry is not likely to be written by working to fit a standard pattern. Even allegory, which would seem to require constant reference to a preconceived design, cannot be written in cold blood: the writer must be interested in the story itself, not merely in the underlying "meaning", and the story must develop with the overpowering inevitability of a dream. There are some writers who might say that if a poem has this kind of inevitability, it need not have common-sense logic or narrative sense as well. Certainly good poems of this kind have been written, though personally I prefer poems in which the compulsion of the image sequence is matched by a natural development of argument or narrative. *Kubla Khan* owes its force to its image-order, but it owes its popularity to the fact that it possesses a loose narrative order which saves the reader from the awkward fear of being taken in by nonsense. Furthermore, the two currents, the narrative and the fantastic, reinforce each other, just as the coalescence of narrative and imaginative pattern gives life and force to myth and legend.

To myths, rather than to dreams, many poets still turn for the content of their poems, and the researches of Sir James Frazer and other anthropologists have provided the *motif* of a few good poems and many bad ones. Myths are more than fumbling attempts to explain historical and scientific facts: they control and organize the feeling, thought and action of a people: their function is symbolic as well as significant. But often the stories have become the conventional material of second-rate poetry, and have become perverted so that the symbolism has been lost, and we are left with the mere husk of a story, a story easily discredited by scientific and historical research. When Mr Yeats turned to the myth as a means of giving shape and significance to his vision of the world, he was returning to the essential purpose of the myth and setting an example which Mr Eliot, among others, has followed. But the modern reader cannot be expected to be influenced by a myth whose plain narrative sense is counter to his everyday beliefs.

Either the poet must break away from any such direct narrative, or he must attempt, as I think Mr Day Lewis has attempted in his *Flight* poem, to present a story credible in the ordinary everyday sense. If the poet turns to an existing myth or legend, however shop-soiled, and sees in it a profound significance, he will see the legend itself exemplified and symbolized in the world about him.

"So", says Hart Crane, in an unpublished manuscript, "I found 'Helen' sitting in a street car; the Dionysian revels of her court and her seduction were transferred to a Metropolitan roof garden with a jazz orchestra: and the *katharsis* of the fall of Troy I saw approximated in the recent world war. . . .

"It is a terrific problem that faces the poet today—a world that is so in transition from a decayed culture toward a reorganization of human evaluations that there are few common terms, general denominators of speech, that are solid enough or that ring with any vibration or spiritual conviction. The great mythologies of the past (including the Church) are deprived of enough façade even to launch good raillery against. Yet much of their traditions are operative still—in millions of chance combinations of related and unrelated detail, psychological reference, figures of speech, precepts, etc. These are all part of our common experience and the terms, at least partially, of that very experience when it defines or extends itself.

"The deliberate program, then, of a 'break' with the past or tradition seems to me to be a sentimental fallacy. . . . The poet has a right to draw on whatever practical resources he finds in books or otherwise about him. He must tax his sensibility and his touchstone of experience for the proper selections of these themes and details, however,—and that is where he either stands, or falls into useless archaeology.

"I put no particular value on the simple objective of 'modernity'. . . . It seems to me that a poet will accidentally define his time well enough simply by reacting honestly and to the full extent of his sensibilities to the states of passion, experience and rumination that fate forces on him, first hand. He must, of course, have a sufficiently universal basis of experience to make his imagination selective and valuable. . . .

"I am concerned with the future of America . . . because I feel persuaded that here are destined to be discovered certain as yet undefined spiritual quantities, perhaps a new hierarchy of faith not to be developed so completely elsewhere. And in this process I like to feel myself as a potential factor; certainly I must speak in its terms. . . .

"But to fool one's self that definitions are being reached by merely referring frequently to skyscrapers, radio antennae, steam whistles, or other surface phenomena of our time is merely to paint a photograph. I think that what is interesting and significant will emerge only under the conditions of our submission to, and examination and assimilation of the organic effects on us of these and other fundamental factors of our experience. It can certainly not be an organic expression otherwise. And the expression of such values may often be as well accomplished with the vocabulary and blank verse of the Elizabethans as with the calligraphic tricks and slang used so brilliantly at times by an impressionist like Cummings."

If a poet is to give new life to a legend, if indeed he is to write good poetry at all, he must charge each word to its maximum poetic value. It must appeal concurrently to all the various levels of evocation and interpretation: experiments in new rhythms and new images, if they are not used in this specifically poetic way, are of no more than technical interest. In discussing new technical devices a distinction must be drawn between those which produce an effect upon the reader even before he has noticed them, and those which, like some of the devices of Mr Cummings, attract the reader's attention and lead him to infer, by ordinary reasoning, what effect the poet intended to produce. There are, I think, many examples of the first kind in this book, and of the many auditory devices of this kind, none, perhaps, are more effective, or have had greater effect upon later poets, than those of Wilfred Owen.

In Owen's poetry, the use of half-rhymes is not merely the result of an attempt to escape from the over-obviousness of rhyme-led poetry, though Owen probably discovered its possibilities in that way. His innovations are important because his sound-effects directly reinforce the general effect which he is trying to produce. In Owen's war poetry, the half-rhymes almost invariably fall from a vowel of high pitch to one of low pitch, producing an effect of frustration, disappointment, hopelessness. In other poets, rising half-rhymes are used, which produce the opposite effect, without reaching out to the full heartiness of rhyme. Full end-rhyme itself is felt by many modern poets to be too arbitrary and too noisy for serious poetry, unless modified, as Hopkins modifies it, by taking some of the stress of the last syllable of the line either by stressing earlier syllables, or by placing the emphasis of meaning, as distinct from metre, elsewhere. If they use end-rhymes at all, it is often for satiric purposes, or in a modified form, rhyming stressed with unstressed syllables, as Sacheverell Sitwell has done, and thus producing an uncertain, tentative, hesitating effect in keeping with the poet's purpose.

Nevertheless rhyme, like meaning and metre, is one of the possible elements in a verbal pattern, and few poets abandon it entirely. The sense of order in complication is part of the fascination of poetry, and often, as in the poetry of C. Day Lewis, internal rhymes, carefully but not obviously placed, are used to produce a pattern running counter to sense and rhythm and to add that intricacy and richness which marks the difference between part-song and unison.

Even when the poet writes, apparently, in a regular metre, he may use effects ignored in the formal rules of prosody and grammar. Thus Owen, in the second stanza of *Futility*, retards the movement of the first four lines by punctuation and intricacy of syntax, so that the fifth line, unimpeded, comes out with a terrific force, continued, though less vigorously and a little more slowly, as though one added a conclusive afterthought, in the final couplet. Similarly, in William Empson's *Note on Local Flora* the first seven lines form a single intricate sentence, retarding the pace, so that the eighth line, again an unimpeded sentence, is stamped with the emphasis of conviction, and the concluding couplet comes strongly, but comparatively quietly, as a conclusive deduction might do.

Often an effect of logic in a poem which, when examined,

proves illogical, is due to auditory rhetoric[1] rather than to fantasy. The poetry of Edith and Sacheverell Sitwell shows, for example, not only an unusually vivid use of sensuous impressions, and of image-patterns based, like nursery rhymes, on the compelling force of dreams, but also an effective use of sound-patterns having this convincing facility of speech. The poetry of Edith Sitwell, like the poetry of Vachel Lindsay and E. E. Cummings, needs to be read aloud, with careful changes of rhythm, volume, pitch and tempo. A practised reader will be able to determine these variations for himself: in a good poem they are usually implied, but the pointing of the *Psalms* is an example of the use of typography to help the reader. Similarly, Hopkins, in his effort to extract the utmost poetic value from the varied stress of words, resorts to a system of accents and markings; and Mr Cummings takes a great deal of trouble to show, by typographical devices, how his poems should be read. More conventional poets are less violent in their fluctuations, and less helpful in their methods. To read poetry as it should be read requires considerable practice. Most people tend to over-emphasize any regular metrical pattern which may be the background to the rhythm of the poem, and at the same time they raise the voice to a deliberately "poetical" key and make use of fluctuations of pitch which bring their reading nearer to singing than to talking. It is characteristic of modern poets in general that they fight as hard as they can against this tendency, which seems to them not to increase the significance of the poetry, but to diminish it by asserting an arbitrary music at the expense of meaning, and to read their poems as songs, and necessarily bad songs, is to misread them completely.

When in pre-war days a few poets began to write, not in regular metres, but in cadences, as Whitman and the translators of the Bible had done, it was objected that this practice would destroy the art of verse entirely. It is true that a more delicate sensibility and a more careful training are necessary if we are to appreciate cadenced verse, and it is true that the existence of cadenced verse blurs the distinction between prose and poetry; but the critical

[1] I use the word "rhetoric" here, as elsewhere, in the technical, not the popular sense. There is good rhetoric and bad rhetoric, and there is rhetoric used in a good cause and in a bad, but rhetoric itself is not necessarily bad.

vocabulary must be revised to fit the facts: to deny the facts and close your ears to the rhythms is to behave like the Inquisitor who refused to look through Galileo's telescope. Every discovery creates disorder: it is not the duty of the critic to prevent discovery or to deny it, but to create new order to replace the older. Today, the quarrel over cadenced verse has died down, and it is very hard to draw a sharp line, or to see any purpose in trying to draw a sharp line, between "free" verse and *varied* regular verse. One or two points may be noted, however. There is verse which is intended to be "free": that is to say, whose rhythm is composed to please the ear alone; there is verse which is quantitative, depending on a recurrent pattern of long and short syllables; there is verse which is accentual, depending on a recurrent pattern of accented and unaccented syllables; and there is syllabic verse. In the last (some of the poems of Marianne Moore and Herbert Read are examples) the lines are evaluated by the number of syllables they contain, and the pattern will be something like this—11:11:11:6. It is not very difficult to train the ear to recognize and enjoy syllabic patterns, and if it is objected that this training is "unnatural" it must be pointed out that all training is "unnatural" and yet inevitable. Even the writer of "free" verse has been trained to enjoy and detect certain patterns, and his "free" verse often shows the skeleton of a "regular" pattern underneath.

These effects are not felt by every reader: to some, the devices are merely evidence of technical incompetence. It is, however, demonstrable that some people respond to them without having them pointed out; the only possible conclusion is that these people are more sensitive to language than the others. The only objection to such devices is that it would never be possible to teach everyone to respond to them, therefore they tend to cut off one section of the community from another. But the same objection could be brought against the theory of tensors, and it is as necessary that some members of the community should explore the possibilities of language and use it to control and clarify emotional, spiritual and sensuous experience, as it is that others should use their mathematical notation to codify and organize our scientific knowledge.

* * *

Modern poets have been decreasingly concerned with sound-effects as independent entities, and today the auditory rhetoric of poetry is dictated, not by its own rules, but by the central impulse of the poem. Perhaps for this reason, no adequate study of auditory rhetoric exists. Prosody is little more than an enumeration and naming of all the possible combinations of stressed and unstressed syllables. It takes no account of the variety of stresses, or of the quantitative patterns interwoven with accentual patterns, and it ignores the "laws" of consonant and vowel sequences. It becomes useless if it loses sight of its original purpose and erects itself into a system of unchanging orthodoxy. In criticism all general rules and classifications are elucidatory: and new discoveries or the introduction of matters previously thought to be irrelevant may compel us to amend them or admit their limitations.

The critic tries to make distinctions and to discover rules valid for the widest possible variety of purpose; but for different purposes different classifications may be necessary, and this is true not only of the classifications which we use in discussing the technique of poetry, but also of those which we use when speaking of the poets. Where, as in the criticism of poetry, we are dealing with something as complex as personalities, any division must be arbitrary. An historical or categorical label never prescribes the ultimate achievements of the poet, it merely tells us where to look for them; and from time to time, if we are to recognize the poet as a mobile force, new categories are needed.

Often the new dividing line between the categories may not be far removed from the old; and it may be objected that the classification which results from a distinction between the "English" sensibility and "European" sensibility does not differ very much from the distinction between "romantic" and "classic" writers, or between "pure" poetry and "didactic and descriptive" poetry. There is, however, a difference in the points on which it focuses our attention. Any distinction in terms of schools and tendencies is misleading if we use it for any purpose beyond concentrating our attention for a moment on one aspect of the work of one or two selected writers; and if for the moment I have classified poets, it is merely as a shop-window arrangement, a tactful use of contrasts to focus attention on certain qualities, and to lessen some of the difficulty which readers find when they approach modern poetry for the first time.

New poetry is never popular unless it accepts the prejudices of the immediate past, and, giving an aura of heroism to actions which are already inevitable, stifles those misgivings out of which the real decisions of the present are to grow. Often in reading poems for this anthology, I have come upon one which, though its beginning seemed to show an apprehension beyond the commonplace, lapsed at the end into a false simplicity: a statement in familiar terms which had been given no new significance and depth. I have found Mr Aldington's poems, in spite of their innovations, disappointing in that way; the earlier poems of Mr Monro, and many of the poems of Mr Cummings affect me similarly. The poet has seen something, and almost seen it clearly; and then at the end, unable to say it, he has been content to say some lesser thing, and the true poem remains unwritten.

For a time, the false poem may be more popular than the true one could have been. "The poet", Johnson said, "must divest himself of the prejudice of his age and country; he must consider right and wrong in their abstracted and invariable state; he must disregard present laws and opinions, and rise to general and transcendental truths, which will always be the same. He must, therefore, content himself with the slow progress of his name, contemn the praise of his own time, and commit his claims to the justice of posterity."

Sometimes it is argued that readers, too, must leave the judgment of contemporary literature to posterity; but the judgment of posterity is only another name for the accumulated judgments of those who read most carefully and with least prejudice and preconception. To read merely to concur in the judgments of our ancestors is to inhibit all spontaneous response and to miss the pleasure of that reading which moulds the opinions, tastes and actions of our time. The first important thing about contemporary literature is that it *is* contemporary: it is speaking to us and for us, here, now. Judgment can only follow an act of sympathy and understanding, and to let our appreciation grow outwards from that which immediately appeals to us is both wiser and more enjoyable than to echo the judgments of others or to restrict and sour our appreciation by hastily attacking anything which at first seems difficult or irritating.

MICHAEL ROBERTS, 1936

Introduction to the Fourth Edition

With more than 1100 poets classified in the St James Press *Dictionary of Contemporary Poets of the English Language* (to say nothing of those who have died since Michael Roberts's selection), the task of adding to *The Faber Book of Modern Verse* is a daunting one. I am opposed temperamentally to the hard line of many commentators who, faced with such a poetic downpour, say that only one or two names matter and that posterity will inevitably consign the rest to oblivion. Such an attitude encourages laziness and unthinking orthodoxy. There is a great deal of fine poetry from the past forty years to be considered, and I do not regret the time I have spent, both as a reader and as a reviewer, getting to know it. But, in adding to Roberts's original book, I have had to take into account both the very different circumstances governing the writing of poetry today, and also the serious limits imposed upon me by the space available. Although many poets in Britain and the United States would not concede the point, we are, I believe, in the middle of a period of Post-Modernity, or perhaps Late Modernity. The world of Late Modernity is a pluralistic one, and its constituent parts view each other with scant favour. This can be shown by considering the career of W. H. Auden, now alas completed. In 1936, when the Faber book was first printed, Auden, though recognizably different from his great Modernist predecessors, seemed a fully revolutionary artist. At the time of his death, he had become the most celebrated and successful Anti-Modernist and traditionalist poet of the age. This change is not an example of the "lost leader" pattern, but of the maturing of a highly individual creator. Auden remains modern in my view because he celebrates the mixed sensibility of our present age. His brilliantly original early poems are one side of his reaction to the moral and artistic climate of the century: his later Horatian and lexically-sweetened poetry is another. But Auden's public stance was to be against official "Modernism". Pound's, of course, was to be father to it. Yet Pound's work is full of archaism and stained-glass medievalism, but nobody calls Pound a reactionary. To concentrate on Auden's revival of formal devices to the exclusion of his radical way with sensibility is to be guilty of a mechanistic simplification. But critics are always happier dealing with details of surface style, which are themselves frequently misleading. Too many polemicists want the history of modern poetry to be a straightforward story of progress, and choose their heroes and villains accordingly. More sensitive appreciation of the poetry written since 1936 reveals that drastic change exists side by side with deliberate reclamation, and that each way may be as modern as the other. In much of the most brilliant poetry of this century, the outline of past forms can be recognized. Wallace Stevens seems to me the most original aesthetician among the poets of the last hundred years, and nobody would deny him the accolade of modernity, yet his handling of stanza, syntax and rhythm is decidedly traditional. I also find the presence of Robert Browning in John Ashbery's dense and closed-circuit forms. I do not suggest that there is nothing new under the sun, only that Late Modernity is far too inchoate to permit historical imperatives or evangelical injunctions. We are in a Permanent Museum, whether we like it or not.

In going back over the earlier part of the book, I have modified Michael Roberts's original selection to accommodate a few foundation figures who have now swum more sharply into ken (William Carlos Williams, Hugh MacDiarmid, and Basil Bunting) and to bring the representation of others up to date. In general, however, I have stuck to my brief: no poem has been chosen which was available to Roberts and was not selected by him. Thus, while I am not happy with Roberts's representation of Wallace Stevens, I have not added poems from *Harmonium*, but only two beautiful and characteristic works published after 1936. To make space for the new arrivals I have trimmed the original selection, though only Vachel Lindsay, Sacheverell Sitwell, Peter Quennell, James Reeves and Clifford Dyment have been left out entirely. Some of the leading poets in the original went on to produce arresting work after 1936, and here I have sometimes elected to omit well-known early poems and substitute later pieces. Examples will be found in the selections from Pound,

Eliot, H. D., Graves, Auden, MacNeice and George Barker. Though a doctrinaire Modernist will, on a cursory inspection, conclude that I am a deep-dyed reactionary, I expect to be more often challenged for the omission of many excellent more-traditional poets whose writings have become prominent since the war. I have not always chosen poems for their weight or their solemnity. For instance, I have found a place for Gavin Ewart's playful extensions of traditional modes, for Lawrence Durrell's brilliant early excursions into the domestic surreal, for Christopher Middleton's fantasy icons and for James Fenton's revival of the political pastoral. There is a shortage of the vatic and the confessional, and no Beats, Minnesota Peruvian, West Coast Sienese (Duncan) or Zen. The line I have followed is predominantly social, but it honours verbal audacity as well. Just to reel off the names of all the movements and styles which have come to the fore in the past forty years is depressing: instead of trying to represent each, I have chosen to extend the line of modernity in only one direction—towards poetry as fiction, poetry as verbal and philosophical speculation. It is surprising how much of the real world this allows into the book. Finally, I have preferred to keep the text in one continuous, unfolding line, and have not marked off the newcomers from Michael Roberts's original contents-list. I think supplements produce a nasty gear-change in their readers, but to anyone who wants to know where the original names stop and my introduced figures start, I would point out that all after David Gascoyne are new. I have been happy to follow Donald Hall in some of his selections for the anthology's previous revision.

PETER PORTER, 1981

Gerard Manley Hopkins

The Wreck of the Deutschland

To the
happy memory of five Franciscan Nuns
exiles by the Falk Laws
drowned between midnight and morning of
Dec. 7th, 1875

Part the First

1

Thou mastering me
God! giver of breath and bread;
World's strand, sway of the sea;
Lord of living and dead;
Thou hast bound bones and veins in me, fastened me flesh,
And after it almost unmade, what with dread,
Thy doing: and dost thou touch me afresh?
Over again I feel thy finger and find thee.

2

I did say yes
O at lightning and lashed rod;
Thou heardst me truer than tongue confess
Thy terror, O Christ, O God;
Thou knowest the walls, altar and hour and night:
The swoon of a heart that the sweep and the hurl of thee trod
Hard down with a horror of height:
And the midriff astrain with leaning of, laced with fire of
stress.

3

The frown of his face
Before me, the hurtle of hell
Behind, where, where was a, where was a place?
I whirled out wings that spell
And fled with a fling of the heart to the heart of the Host.
My heart, but you were dovewinged, I can tell,
Carrier-witted, I am bold to boast,
To flash from the flame to the flame then, tower from the grace to the grace.

4

I am soft sift
In an hourglass—at the wall
Fast, but mined with a motion, a drift,
And it crowds and it combs to the fall;
I steady as a water in a well, to a poise, to a pane,
But roped with, always, all the way down from the tall
Fells or flanks of the voel, a vein
Of the gospel proffer, a pressure, a principle, Christ's gift.

5

I kiss my hand
To the stars, lovely-asunder
Starlight, wafting him out of it; and
Glow, glory in thunder;
Kiss my hand to the dappled-with-damson west:
Since, tho' he is under the world's splendour and wonder,
His mystery must be instressed, stressed;
For I greet him the days I meet him, and bless when I understand.

6

Not out of his bliss
Springs the stress felt
Nor first from heaven (and few know this)
Swings the stroke dealt—
Stroke and a stress that stars and storms deliver,
That guilt is hushed by, hearts are flushed by and melt—
But it rides time like riding a river
(And here the faithful waver, the faithless fable and miss).

7

It dates from day
Of his going in Galilee;
Warm-laid grave of a womb-life grey;
Manger, maiden's knee;
The dense and the driven Passion, and frightful sweat;
Thence the discharge of it, there its swelling to be,
Though felt before, though in high flood yet—
What none would have known of it, only the heart, being hard
at bay.

8

Is out with it! Oh,
We lash with the best or worst
Word last! How a lush-kept plush-capped sloe
Will, mouthed to flesh-burst,
Gush!—flush the man, the being with it, sour or sweet,
Brim, in a flash, full!—Hither then, last or first,
To hero of Calvary, Christ's feet—
Never ask if meaning it, wanting it, warned of it—men go.

9

Be adored among men,
God, three-numberèd form;
Wring thy rebel, dogged in den,
Man's malice, with wrecking and storm.
Beyond saying sweet, past telling of tongue,
Thou art lightning and love, I found it, a winter and warm;
Father and fondler of heart thou hast wrung:
Hast thy dark descending and most art merciful then.

10

With an anvil-ding
And with fire in him forge thy will
Or rather, rather then, stealing as Spring
Through him, melt him but master him still:
Whether at once, as once at a crash Paul,
Or as Austin, a lingering-out sweet skill,
Make mercy in all of us, out of us all
Mastery, but be adored, but be adored King.

Part the second

11

"Some find me a sword; some
The flange and the rail; flame,
Fang, or flood" goes Death on drum,
And storms bugle his fame.
But wé dream we are rooted in earth—Dust!
Flesh falls within sight of us, we, though our flower the same,
Wave with the meadow, forget that there must
The sour scythe cringe, and the blear share come.

12

On Saturday sailed from Bremen,
American-outward-bound,
Take settler and seamen, tell men with women,
Two hundred souls in the round—
O Father, not under thy feathers nor ever as guessing
The goal was a shoal, of a fourth the doom to be drowned;
Yet did the dark side of the bay of thy blessing
Not vault them, the millions of rounds of thy mercy not reeve even them in?

13

Into the snows she sweeps,
Hurling the haven behind,
The Deutschland, on Sunday; and so the sky keeps,
For the infinite air is unkind,
And the sea flint-flake, black-backed in the regular blow,
Sitting Eastnortheast, in cursed quarter, the wind;
Wiry and white-fiery and whirlwind-swivellèd snow
Spins to the widow-making unchilding unfathering deeps.

14

She drove in the dark to leeward,
She struck—not a reef or a rock
But the combs of a smother of sand: night drew her
Dead to the Kentish Knock;
And she beat the bank down with her bows and the ride of her keel:
The breakers rolled on her beam with ruinous shock;
And canvas and compass, the whorl and the wheel
Idle for ever to waft her or wind her with, these she endured.

15

Hope had grown grey hairs,
Hope had mourning on,
Trenched with tears, carved with cares,
Hope was twelve hours gone;
And frightful a nightfall folded rueful a day
Nor rescue, only rocket and lightship, shone,
And lives at last were washing away:
To the shrouds they took,—they shook in the hurling and horrible airs.

16

One stirred from the rigging to save
The wild woman-kind below,
With a rope's end round the man, handy and brave—
He was pitched to his death at a blow,
For all his dreadnought breast and braids of thew:
They could tell him for hours, dandled the to and fro
Through the cobbled foam-fleece, what could he do
With the burl of the fountains of air, buck and the flood of the wave?

17

They fought with God's cold—
And they could not and fell to the deck
(Crushed them) or water (and drowned them) or rolled
With the sea-romp over the wreck.
Night roared, with the heart-break hearing a heart-broke rabble,
The woman's wailing, the crying of child without check—
Till a lioness arose breasting the babble,
A prophetess towered in the tumult, a virginal tongue told.

18

Ah, touched in your bower of bone
Are you! turned for an exquisite smart,
Have you! make words break from me here all alone,
Do you!—mother of being in me, heart.
O unteachably after evil, but uttering truth,
Why, tears! is it? tears; such a melting, a madrigal start!
Never-eldering revel and river of youth,
What can it be, this glee? the good you have there of your own?

19

Sister, a sister calling
A master, her master and mine!—
And the inboard seas run swirling and hawling;
The rash smart sloggering brine
Blinds her; but she that weather sees one thing, one;
Has one fetch in her: she rears herself to divine
Ears, and the call of the tall nun
To the men in the tops and the tackle rode over the storm's brawling.

20

She was first of a five and came
Of a coifèd sisterhood.
(O Deutschland, double a desperate name!
O world wide of its good!
But Gertrude, lily, and Luther, are two of a town,
Christ's lily and beast of the waste wood:
From life's dawn it is drawn down,
Abel is Cain's brother and breasts they have sucked the same.)

21

Loathed for a love men knew in them,
Banned by the land of their birth,
Rhine refused them. Thames would ruin them;
Surf, snow, river and earth
Gnashed: but thou art above, thou Orion of light;
Thy unchancelling poising palms were weighing the worth,
Thou martyr-master: in thy sight
Storm flakes were scroll-leaved flowers, lily showers—sweet heaven was astrew in them.

22

Five! the finding and sake
And cipher of suffering Christ.
Mark, the mark is of man's make
And the word of it Sacrificed.
But he scores it in scarlet himself on his own bespoken,
Before-time-taken, dearest prizèd and priced—
Stigma, signal, cinquefoil token
For lettering of the lamb's fleece, ruddying of the rose flake.

23

Joy fall to thee, father Francis,
Drawn to the Life that died;
With the gnarls of the nails in thee, niche of the lance, his Lovescape crucified
And seal of his seraph-arrival! and these thy daughters
And five-livèd and leavèd favour and pride,
Are sisterly sealed in wild waters,
To bathe in his fall-gold mercies, to breathe in his all-fire glances.

24

Away in the loveable west,
On a pastoral forehead of Wales,
I was under a roof here, I was at rest,
And they the prey of the gales;
She to the black-about air, to the breaker, the thickly
Falling flakes, to the throng that catches and quails
Was calling "O Christ, Christ, come quickly":
The cross to her she calls Christ to her, christens her
wild-worst Best.

25

The majesty! what did she mean?
Breathe, arch and original Breath.
Is it love in her of the being as her lover had been?
Breathe, body of lovely Death.
They were else-minded then, altogether, the men
Woke thee with a *we are perishing* in the weather of
Gennesareth.
Or is it that she cried for the crown then,
The keener to come at the comfort for feeling the combating
keen?

26

For how to the heart's cheering
The down-dugged ground-hugged grey
Hovers off, the jay-blue heavens appearing
Of pied and peeled May!
Blue-beating and hoary-glow height; or night, still higher,
With belled fire and the moth-soft Milky Way,
What by your measure is the heaven of desire,
The treasure never eyesight got, nor was ever guessed what for
the hearing?

27

No, but it was not these.
The jading and jar of the cart,
Time's tasking, it is fathers that asking for ease
Of the sodden-with-its-sorrowing heart,
Not danger, electrical horror; then further it finds
The appealing of the Passion is tenderer in prayer apart:
Other, I gather, in measure her mind's
Burden, in wind's burly and beat of endragonèd seas.

28

But how shall I . . . make me room there:
Reach me a . . . Fancy, come faster—
Strike you the sight of it? look at it loom there,
Thing that she . . . there then! the Master,
Ipse, the only one, Christ, King, Head:
He was to cure the extremity where he had cast her;
Do, deal, lord it with living and dead;
Let him ride, her pride, in his triumph, despatch and have
done with his doom there.

29

Ah! there was a heart right!
There was single eye!
Read the unshapeable shock night
And knew the who and the why;
Wording it how but by him that present and past,
Heaven and earth are word of, worded by?—
The Simon Peter of a soul! to the blast
Tarpeian-fast, but a blown beacon of light.

30

Jesu, heart's light,
Jesu, maid's son,
What was the feast followed the night
Thou hadst glory of this nun?—
Feast of the one woman without stain.
For so conceivèd, so to conceive thee is done;
But here was heart-throe, birth of a brain,
Word, that heard and kept thee and uttered thee outright.

31

Well, she has thee for the pain, for the
Patience; but pity of the rest of them!
Heart, go and bleed at a bitterer vein for the
Comfortless unconfessed of them—
No not uncomforted: lovely-felicitous Providence
Finger of a tender of, O of a feathery delicacy, the breast of the
Maiden could obey so, be a bell to, ring of it, and
Startle the poor sheep back! is the shipwreck then a harvest, does tempest carry the grain for thee?

32

I admire thee, master of the tides,
Of the Yore-flood, of the year's fall;
The recurb and the recovery of the gulf's sides,
The girth of it and the wharf of it and the wall;
Stanching, quenching ocean of a motionable mind;
Ground of being, and granite of it: past all
Grasp God, throned behind
Death with a sovereignty that heeds but hides, bodes but abides;

33

With a mercy that outrides
The all of water, an ark
For the listener; for the lingerer with a love glides
Lower than death and the dark;
A vein for the visiting of the past-prayer, pent in prison,
The-last-breath penitent spirits—the uttermost mark
Our passion-plungèd giant risen,
The Christ of the Father compassionate, fetched in the storm of his strides.

34

Now burn, new born to the world,
Double-naturèd name,
The heaven-flung, heart-fleshed, maiden-furled
Miracle-in-Mary-of-flame,
Mid-numbered He in three of the thunder-throne!
Not a dooms-day dazzle in his coming nor dark as he came;
Kind, but royally reclaiming his own;
A released shower, let flash to the shire, not a lightning of fire hard-hurled.

35

Dame, at our door
Drowned, and among our shoals,
Remember us in the roads, the heaven-haven of the Reward:
Our King back, oh, upon English souls!
Let him easter in us, be a dayspring to the dimness of us, be a crimson-cresseted east,
More brightening her, rare-dear Britain, as his reign rolls,
Pride, rose, prince, hero of us, high-priest,
Our hearts' charity's hearth's fire, our thoughts' chivalry's throng's Lord.

Felix Randal

Felix Randal the farrier, O he is dead then? my duty all ended,
Who have watched his mould of man, big-boned and
hardy-handsome
Pining, pining, till time when reason rambled in it and some
Fatal four disorders, fleshed there, all contended?

Sickness broke him. Impatient he cursed at first, but mended
Being anointed and all; though a heavenlier heart began some
Months earlier, since I had our sweet reprieve and ransom
Tendered to him. Ah well, God rest him all road ever he
offended!

This seeing the sick endears them to us, us too it endears.
My tongue had taught thee comfort, touch had quenched thy
tears,
Thy tears that touched my heart, child, Felix, poor Felix
Randal;

How far from then forethought of, all thy more boisterous
years,
When thou at the random grim forge, powerful amidst peers,
Didst fettle for the great grey drayhorse his bright and
battering sandal!

Pied Beauty

Glory be to God for dappled things—
For skies of couple-colour as a brinded cow;
For rose-moles all in stipple upon trout that swim;
Fresh-firecoal chestnut-falls; finches' wings;
Landscape plotted and pieced—fold, fallow, and plough;
And áll trádes, their gear and tackle and trim.

All things counter, original, spare, strange;
  Whatever is fickle, freckled (who knows how?)
    With swift, slow; sweet, sour; adazzle, dim;
He fathers-forth whose beauty is past change:
      Praise him.

Andromeda

Now Time's Andromeda on this rock rude,
With not her either beauty's equal or
Her injury's, looks off by both horns of shore,
Her flower, her piece of being, doomed dragon's food.
  Time past she has been attempted and pursued
By many blows and banes; but now hears roar
A wilder beast from West than all were, more
Rife in her wrongs, more lawless, and more lewd.

  Her Perseus linger and leave her tó her extremes?—
Pillowy air he treads a time and hangs
His thoughts on her, forsaken that she seems,
  All while her patience, morselled into pangs,
Mounts; then to alight disarming, no one dreams,
With Gorgon's gear and barebill, thongs and fangs.

The Candle Indoors

Some candle clear burns somewhere I come by.
I muse at how its being puts blissful back
With yellowy moisture mild night's blear-all black,
Or to-fro tender trambeams truckle at the eye.
By that window what task what fingers ply,
I plod wondering, a-wanting, just for lack
Of answer the eagerer a-wanting Jessy or Jack
There—God to aggrándise, God to glorify.—

Come you indoors, come home; your fading fire
Mend first and vital candle in close heart's vault:
You there are master, do your own desire;
What hinders? Are you beam-blind, yet to a fault
In a neighbour deft-handed? are you that liar
And, cast by conscience out, spendsavour salt?

Inversnaid

This darksome burn, horseback brown,
His rollrock highroad roaring down,
In coop and in comb the fleece of his foam
Flutes and low to the lake falls home.

A windpuff-bonnet of fáwn-fróth
Turns and twindles over the broth
Of a pool so pitchblack, féll-frówning,
It rounds and rounds Despair to drowning.

Degged with dew, dappled with dew
Are the groins of the braes that the brook treads through,
Wiry heathpacks, flitches of fern,
And the beadbonny ash that sits over the burn.

What would the world be, once bereft
Of wet and of wildness? Let them be left,
O let them be left, wildness and wet;
Long live the weeds and the wilderness yet.

GERARD MANLEY HOPKINS

The Windhover

To Christ our Lord

I caught this morning morning's minion, king-
    dom of daylight's dauphin, dapple-dawn-drawn
        Falcon, in his riding
    Of the rolling level underneath him steady air, and striding
High there, how he rung upon the rein of a wimpling wing
In his ecstasy! then off, off forth on swing,
    As a skate's heel sweeps smooth on a bow-bend: the hurl and
            gliding
    Rebuffed the big wind. My heart in hiding
Stirred for a bird,—the achieve of, the mastery of the thing!

Brute beauty and valour and act, oh, air, pride, plume, here
    Buckle! AND the fire that breaks from thee then, a billion
Times told lovelier, more dangerous, O my chevalier!

    No wonder of it: shéer plód makes plough down sillion
Shine, and blue-bleak embers, ah my dear,
    Fall, gall themselves, and gash gold-vermilion.

"As kingfishers catch fire, dragonflies draw flame"

As kingfishers catch fire, dragonflies dráw fláme;
As tumbled over rim in roundy wells
Stones ring; like each tucked string tells, each hung bell's
Bow swung finds tongue to fling out broad its name;
Each mortal thing does one thing and the same:
Deals out that being indoors each one dwells;
Selves—goes itself; *myself* it speaks and spells,
Crying *Whát I do is me: for that I came.*

I say móre: the just man justices;
Kéeps gráce: thát keeps all his goings graces;
Acts in God's eye what in God's eye he is—
Chríst—for Christ plays in ten thousand places,
Lovely in limbs, and lovely in eyes not his
To the Father through the features of men's faces.

Harry Ploughman

Hard as hurdle arms, with a broth of goldish flue
Breathed round; the rack of ribs; the scooped flank; lank
Rope-over thigh; knee-nave; and barrelled shank—
  Head and foot, shoulder and shank—
By a grey eye's heed steered well, one crew, fall to;
Stand at stress. Each limb's barrowy brawn, his thew
That onewhere cuddled, onewhere sucked or sank—
  Soared or sank—,
Though as a beechbole firm, finds his, as at a roll-call, rank
And features, in flesh, what deed he each must do—
  His sinew-service where do.
He leans to it, Harry bends, look. Back, elbow, and liquid
    waist
In him, all quail to the wallowing o' the plough: 's cheek
    crimsons; curls
Wag or crossbridle, in a wind lifted, windlaced—
  See his wind- lilylocks-laced;
Churlsgrace, too, child of Amansstrength, how it hangs or
    hurls
Them—broad in bluff hide his frowning feet lashed! raced
With, along them, cragiron under and cold furls—
  With-a-fountain's shining-shot furls.

GERARD MANLEY HOPKINS

"No worst, there is none. Pitched past pitch of grief"

No worst, there is none. Pitched past pitch of grief,
More pangs will, schooled at forepangs, wilder wring.
Comforter, where, where is your comforting?
Mary, mother of us, where is your relief?
My cries heave, herds-long; huddle in a main, a chief
Woe, world-sorrow; on an age-old anvil wince and sing—
Then lull, then leave off. Fury had shrieked "No lingering!
Let me be fell: force I must be brief".

O the mind, mind has mountains; cliffs of fall
Frightful, sheer, no-man-fathomed. Hold them cheap
May who ne'er hung there. Nor does long our small
Durance deal with that steep or deep. Here! creep,
Wretch, under a comfort serves in a whirlwind: all
Life death does end and each day dies with sleep.

Spelt from Sibyl's Leaves

Earnest, earthless, equal, attuneable, | vaulty, voluminous, . . . stupendous
Evening strains to be tíme's vást, | womb-of-all, home-of-all, hearse-of-all night.
Her fond yellow hornlight wound to the west, | her wild hollow hoarlight hung to the height
Waste; her earliest stars, earl-stars, | stárs principal, overbend us,
Fíre-féaturing heaven. For earth | her being has unbound, her dapple is at an end, as-
tray or aswarm, all throughther, in throngs; | self ín self steepèd and páshed—qúite

Disremembering, dísmémbering | áll now. Heart,
you round me right
With: Óur évening is over us; óur night | whélms,
whélms, ánd will end us.
Only the beak-leaved boughs dragonish | damask the
tool-smooth bleak light; black,
Ever so black on it. Óur tale, O óur oracle! | Lét life,
wáned, ah lét life wind
Off hér once skéined stained véined varíety | upon, áll
on twó spools; párt, pen, páck
Now her áll in twó flocks, twó folds—black, white; |
right, wrong; reckon but, reck but, mind
But thése two; wáre of a wórld where bút these | twó
tell, each off the óther; of a rack
Where, selfwrung, selfstrung, sheathe- and shelterless, |
thóughts agaínst thoughts ín groans grínd.

"My own heart let me more have pity on; let"

My own heart let me more have pity on; let
Me live to my sad self hereafter kind,
Charitable; not live this tormented mind
With this tormented mind tormenting yet.
I cast for comfort I can no more get
By groping round my comfortless, than blind
Eyes in their dark can day or thirst can find
Thirst's all-in-all in all a world of wet.

Soul, self; come, poor Jackself, I do advise
You, jaded, let be; call off thoughts awhile
Elsewhere; leave comfort root-room; let joy size
At God knows when to God knows what; whose smile
's not wrung, see you; unforeseen times rather—as skies
Betweenpie mountains—lights a lovely mile.

GERARD MANLEY HOPKINS

That Nature is a Heraclitean Fire and of the Comfort of the Resurrection

Cloud-puffball, torn tufts, tossed pillows | flaunt forth, then chevy on an air-
built thoroughfare: heaven-roysterers, in gay-gangs | they throng: they glitter in marches.
Down roughcast, down dazzling whitewash, | wherever an elm arches,
Shivelights and shadowtackle in long | lashes lace, lance, and pair.
Delightfully the bright wind boisterous | ropes, wrestles, beats earth bare
Of yestertempest's creases; in pool and rut peel parches
Squandering ooze to squeezed | dough, crust, dust; stanches, starches
Squadroned masks and manmarks | treadmire toil there
Footfretted in it. Million-fuelèd, | nature's bonfire burns on.
But quench her bonniest, dearest | to her, her clearest-selvèd spark
Man, how fast his firedint, | his mark on mind, is gone!
Both are in an unfathomable, all is in an enormous dark
Drowned. O pity and indig | nation! Manshape, that shone
Sheer off, disseveral, a star, | death blots black out; nor mark
Is any of him at all so stark
But vastness blurs and time | beats level. Enough! the Resurrection,
A heart's-clarion! Away grief's gasping, | joyless days, dejection.
Across my foundering deck shone
A beacon, an eternal beam. | Flesh fade, and mortal trash

Fall to the residuary worm; | world's wildfire, leave
    but ash:
        In a flash, at a trumpet crash,
I am all at once what Christ is, | since he was what I am,
    and
This Jack, joke, poor potsherd, | patch, matchwood,
    immortal diamond,
        Is immortal diamond.

W. B. Yeats

An Irish Airman Foresees His Death

I know that I shall meet my fate
Somewhere among the clouds above;
Those that I fight I do not hate,
Those that I guard I do not love;
My country is Kiltartan Cross,
My countrymen Kiltartan's poor,
No likely end could bring them loss
Or leave them happier than before.
Nor law, nor duty bade me fight,
Nor public men, nor cheering crowds,
A lonely impulse of delight
Drove to this tumult in the clouds;
I balanced all, brought all to mind,
The years to come seemed waste of breath,
A waste of breath the years behind
In balance with this life, this death.

Easter, 1916

I have met them at close of day
Coming with vivid faces
From counter or desk among grey
Eighteenth-century houses.
I have passed with a nod of the head
Or polite meaningless words,
Or have lingered awhile and said
Polite meaningless words,
And thought before I had done

Of a mocking tale or a gibe
To please a companion
Around the fire at the club,
Being certain that they and I
But lived where motley is worn:
All changed, changed utterly;
A terrible beauty is born.

That woman's days were spent
In ignorant good-will,
Her nights in argument
Until her voice grew shrill.
What voice more sweet than hers
When, young and beautiful,
She rode to harriers?
This man had kept a school
And rode our wingèd horse;
This other his helper and friend
Was coming into his force;
He might have won fame in the end,
So sensitive his nature seemed,
So daring and sweet his thought.
This other man I had dreamed
A drunken, vanglorious lout.
He had done most bitter wrong
To some who are near my heart,
Yet I number him in the song;
He, too, has resigned his part
In the casual comedy;
He, too, has been changed in his turn,
Transformed utterly:
A terrible beauty is born.

Hearts with one purpose alone
Through summer and winter seem
Enchanted to a stone
To trouble the living stream.
The horse that comes from the road,

The rider, the birds that range
From cloud to tumbling cloud,
Minute by minute they change;
A shadow of cloud on the stream
Changes minute by minute;
A horse-hoof slides on the brim,
And a horse plashes within it;
The long-legged moor-hens dive,
And hens to moor-cocks call;
Minute by minute they live:
The stone's in the midst of all.

Too long a sacrifice
Can make a stone of the heart.
O when may it suffice?
That is Heaven's part, our part
To murmur name upon name,
As a mother names her child
When sleep at last has come
On limbs that had run wild.
What is it but nightfall?
No, no, not night but death;
Was it needless death after all?
For England may keep faith
For all that is done and said.
We know their dream; enough
To know they dreamed and are dead;
And what if excess of love
Bewildered them till they died?
I write it out in a verse—
MacDonagh and MacBride
And Connolly and Pearse
Now and in time to be,
Wherever green is worn,
Are changed, changed utterly:
A terrible beauty is born.

September 25, 1916

The Second Coming

Turning and turning in the widening gyre
The falcon cannot hear the falconer;
Things fall apart; the centre cannot hold;
Mere anarchy is loosed upon the world,
The blood-dimmed tide is loosed, and everywhere
The ceremony of innocence is drowned;
The best lack all conviction, while the worst
Are full of passionate intensity.

Surely some revelation is at hand;
Surely the Second Coming is at hand.
The Second Coming! Hardly are those words out
When a vast image out of *Spiritus Mundi*
Troubles my sight: somewhere in sands of the desert
A shape with lion body and the head of a man,
A gaze blank and pitiless as the sun,
Is moving its slow thighs, while all about it
Reel shadows of the indignant desert birds.
The darkness drops again; but now I know
That twenty centuries of stony sleep
Were vexed to nightmare by a rocking cradle,
And what rough beast, its hour come round at last,
Slouches towards Bethlehem to be born?

A Dialogue of Self and Soul

I

MY SOUL. I summon to the winding ancient stair;
Set all your mind upon the steep ascent,
Upon the broken, crumbling battlement,
Upon the breathless starlit air,
Upon the star that marks the hidden pole;
Fix every wandering thought upon
That quarter where all thought is done:
Who can distinguish darkness from the soul?

MY SELF. The consecrated blade upon my knees
Is Sato's ancient blade, still as it was,
Still razor-keen, still like a looking-glass
Unspotted by the centuries;
That flowering, silken, old embroidery, torn
From some court-lady's dress and round
The wooden scabbard bound and wound,
Can, tattered, still protect, faded adorn.

MY SOUL. Why should the imagination of a man
Long past his prime remember things that are
Emblematical of love and war?
Think of ancestral night that can,
If but imagination scorn the earth
And intellect its wandering
To this and that and t'other thing,
Deliver from the crime of death and birth.

MY SELF. Montashigi, third of his family, fashioned it
Five hundred years ago, about it lie
Flowers from I know not what embroidery—
Heart's purple—and all these I set
For emblems of the day against the tower
Emblematical of the night,
And claim as by a soldier's right
A charter to commit the crime once more.

MY SOUL. Such fullness in that quarter overflows
And falls into the basin of the mind
That man is stricken deaf and dumb and blind,
For intellect no longer knows
Is from the *Ought*, or *Knower* from the *Known*—
That is to say, ascends to Heaven;
Only the dead can be forgiven;
But when I think of that my tongue's a stone.

II

MY SELF. A living man is blind and drinks his drop.
What matter if the ditches are impure?
What matter if I live it all once more?
Endure that toil of growing up;
The ignominy of boyhood; the distress
Of boyhood changing into man;
The unfinished man and his pain
Brought face to face with his own clumsiness;

The finished man among his enemies?—
How in the name of Heaven can he escape
That defiling and disfigured shape
The mirror of malicious eyes
Casts upon his eyes until at last
He thinks that shape must be his shape?
And what's the good of an escape
If honour find him in the wintry blast?

I am content to live it all again
And yet again, if it be life to pitch
Into the frog-spawn of a blind man's ditch,
A blind man battering blind men;
Or into that most fecund ditch of all,
The folly that man does
Or must suffer, if he woos
A proud woman not kindred of his soul.

I am content to follow to its source,
Every event in action or in thought;
Measure the lot; forgive myself the lot!
When such as I cast out remorse
So great a sweetness flows into the breast
We must laugh and we must sing,
We are blest by everything,
Everything we look upon is blest.

W. B. YEATS

Byzantium

The unpurged images of day recede;
The Emperor's drunken soldiery are abed;
Night resonance recedes, night-walker's song
After great cathedral gong;
A starlit or a moonlit dome disdains
All that man is,
All mere complexities,
The fury and the mire of human veins.

Before me floats an image, man or shade,
Shade more than man, more image than a shade;
For Hades' bobbin bound in mummy-cloth
May unwind the winding path;
A mouth that has no moisture and no breath
Breathless mouths may summon;
I hail the superhuman;
I call it death-in-life and life-in-death.

Miracle, bird or golden handiwork,
More miracle than bird or handiwork,
Planted on the star-lit golden bough,
Can like the cocks of Hades crow,
Or, by the moon embittered, scorn aloud
In glory of changeless metal
Common bird or petal
And all complexities of mire and blood.

At midnight on the Emperor's pavement flit
Flames that no faggot feeds, nor steel has lit,
Nor storm disturbs, flames begotten of flame,
Where blood-begotten spirits come
And all complexities of fury leave,
Dying into a dance,
An agony of trance,
An agony of flame that cannot singe a sleeve.

Astraddle on the dolphin's mire and blood,
Spirit after spirit! The smithies break the flood,
The golden smithies of the Emperor!
Marbles of the dancing floor
Break bitter furies of complexity,
Those images that yet
Fresh images beget,
That dolphin-torn, that gong-tormented sea.

1930

Lapis Lazuli

For Harry Clifton

I have heard that hysterical women say
They are sick of the palette and fiddle-bow,
Of poets that are always gay,
For everybody knows or else should know
That if nothing drastic is done
Aeroplane and Zeppelin will come out,
Pitch like King Billy bomb-balls in
Until the town lie beaten flat.

All perform their tragic play,
There struts Hamlet, there is Lear,
That's Ophelia, that Cordelia;
Yet they, should the last scene be there,
The great stage curtain about to drop,
If worthy their prominent part in the play,
Do not break up their lines to weep.
They know that Hamlet and Lear are gay;
Gaiety transfiguring all that dread.
All men have aimed at, found and lost;
Black out; Heaven blazing into the head:
Tragedy wrought to its uttermost.
Though Hamlet rambles and Lear rages,
And all the drop-scenes drop at once
Upon a hundred thousand stages,
It cannot grow by an inch or an ounce.

On their own feet they came, or on shipboard,
Camel-back, horse-back, ass-back, mule-back,
Old civilisations put to the sword.
Then they and their wisdom went to rack:
No handiwork of Callimachus,
Who handled marble as if it were bronze,
Made draperies that seemed to rise
When sea-wind swept the corner, stands;
His long lamp-chimney shaped like the stem
Of a slender palm, stood but a day;
All things fall and are built again,
And those that build them again are gay.

Two Chinamen, behind them a third,
Are carved in lapis lazuli,
Over them flies a long-legged bird,
A symbol of longevity;
The third, doubtless a serving-man,
Carries a musical instrument.

Every discoloration of the stone,
Every accidental crack or dent,
Seems a water-course or an avalanche,
Or lofty slope where it still snows
Though doubtless plum or cherry-branch
Sweetens the little half-way house
Those Chinamen climb towards, and I
Delight to imagine them seated there;
There, on the mountain and the sky,
On all the tragic scene they stare.
One asks for mournful melodies;
Accomplished fingers begin to play.
Their eyes mid many wrinkles, their eyes,
Their ancient, glittering eyes, are gay.

News for the Delphic Oracle

I

There all the golden codgers lay,
There the silver dew,
And the great water sighed for love,
And the wind sighed too.
Man-picker Niamh leant and sighed
By Oisin on the grass;
There sighed amid his choir of love
Tall Pythagoras.
Plotinus came and looked about,
The salt-flakes on his breast,
And having stretched and yawned awhile
Lay sighing like the rest.

II

Straddling each a dolphin's back
And steadied by a fin,
Those Innocents re-live their death,
Their wounds open again.
The ecstatic waters laugh because
Their cries are sweet and strange,
Through their ancestral patterns dance,
And the brute dolphins plunge
Until, in some cliff-sheltered bay
Where wades the choir of love
Proffering its sacred laurel crowns,
They pitch their burdens off.

III

Slim adolescence that a nymph has stripped,
Peleus on Thetis stares.
Her limbs are delicate as an eyelid,
Love has blinded him with tears;
But Thetis' belly listens.

Down the mountain walls
From where Pan's cavern is
Intolerable music falls.
Foul goat-head, brutal arm appear,
Belly, shoulder, bum,
Flash fishlike; nymphs and satyrs
Copulate in the foam.

Long-Legged Fly

That civilisation may not sink,
Its great battle lost,
Quiet the dog, tether the pony
To a distant post;
Our master Caesar is in the tent
Where the maps are spread,
His eyes fixed upon nothing,
A hand under his head.
Like a long-legged fly upon the stream
His mind moves upon silence.

That the topless towers be burnt
And men recall that face,
Move most gently if move you must
In this lonely place.
She thinks, part woman, three parts a child,
That nobody looks; her feet
Practise a tinker shuffle
Picked up on a street.
Like a long-legged fly upon the stream
Her mind moves upon silence.

That girls at puberty may find
The first Adam in their thought,
Shut the door of the Pope's chapel,
Keep those children out.

There on that scaffolding reclines
Michael Angelo.
With no more sound than the mice make
His hand moves to and fro.
Like a long-legged fly upon the stream
His mind moves upon silence.

The Circus Animals' Desertion

I

I sought a theme and sought for it in vain,
I sought it daily for six weeks or so.
Maybe at last, being but a broken man,
I must be satisfied with my heart, although
Winter and summer till old age began
My circus animals were all on show,
Those stilted boys, that burnished chariot,
Lion and woman and the Lord knows what.

II

What can I but enumerate old themes?
First that sea-rider Oisin led by the nose
Through three enchanted islands, allegorical dreams,
Vain gaiety, vain battle, vain repose,
Themes of the embittered heart, or so it seems,
That might adorn old songs or courtly shows;
But what cared I that set him on to ride,
I, starved for the bosom of his faery bride?

And then a counter-truth filled out its play,
The Countess Cathleen was the name I gave it;
She, pity-crazed, had given her soul away,
But masterful Heaven had intervened to save it.

I thought my dear must her own soul destroy,
So did fanaticism and hate enslave it,
And this brought forth a dream and soon enough
This dream itself had all my thought and love.

And when the Fool and Blind Man stole the bread
Cuchulain fought the ungovernable sea;
Heart-mysteries there, and yet when all is said
It was the dream itself enchanted me:
Character isolated by a deed
To engross the present and dominate memory.
Players and painted stage took all my love,
And not those things that they were emblems of.

III

Those masterful images because complete
Grew in pure mind but out of what began?
A mound of refuse or the sweepings of a street,
Old kettles, old bottles, and a broken can,
Old iron, old bones, old rags, that raving slut
Who keeps the till. Now that my ladder's gone,
I must lie down where all the ladders start,
In the foul rag-and-bone shop of the heart.

T. E. Hulme

Autumn

A touch of cold in the Autumn night—
I walked abroad,
And saw the ruddy moon lean over a hedge
Like a red-faced farmer.
I did not stop to speak, but nodded,
And round about were the wistful stars
With white faces like town children.

Mana Aboda

Beauty is the marking-time, the stationary vibration, the feigned ecstasy of an arrested impulse unable to reach its natural end.

Mana Aboda, whose bent form
The sky in archèd circle is,
Seems ever for an unknown grief to mourn.
Yet on a day I heard her cry:
"I weary of the roses and the singing poets—
Josephs all, not tall enough to try".

Above the Dock

Above the quiet dock in midnight,
Tangled in the tall mast's corded height,
Hangs the moon. What seemed so far away
Is but a child's balloon, forgotten after play.

T. E. HULME

The Embankment

The fantasia of a fallen gentleman on a cold, bitter night.

Once, in finesse of fiddles found I ecstasy,
In a flash of gold heels on the hard pavement.
Now see I
That warmth's the very stuff of poesy.
Oh, God, make small
The old star-eaten blanket of the sky,
That I may fold it round me and in comfort lie.

Conversion

Light-hearted I walked into the valley wood
In the time of hyacinths,
Till beauty like a scented cloth
Cast over, stifled me. I was bound
Motionless and faint of breath
By loveliness that is her own eunuch.

Now pass I to the final river
Ignominiously, in a sack, without sound,
As any peeping Turk to the Bosphorus.

William Carlos Williams

The Semblables

The red brick monastery in
the suburbs over against the dust-
hung acreage of the unfinished
and all but subterranean

munitions plant: those high
brick walls behind which at Easter
the little orphans and bastards
in white gowns sing their Latin

responses to the hoary ritual
while frankincense and myrrh
round out the dark chapel making
an enclosed sphere of it

of which they are the worm:
that cell outside the city beside
the polluted stream and dump
heap, uncomplaining, and the field

of upended stones with a photo
under glass fastened here and there
to one of them near the deeply
carved name to distinguish it;

that trinity of slate gables
the unembellished windows piling
up, the chapel with its round
window between the dormitories

peaked by the bronze belfry
peaked in turn by the cross,
verdegris—faces all silent
that miracle that has burst sexless

from between the carrot rows.
Leafless white birches, their
empty tendrils swaying in
the all but no breeze guard

behind the spiked monastery fence
the sacred statuary. But ranks
of brilliant car-tops row on row
give back in all but glory the

late November sun and hushed
attend, before that tumbled
ground, those sightless walls
and shovelled entrances where no

one but a lonesome cop swinging
his club gives sign, that agony
within where the wrapt machines
are praying . . .

Philomena Andronico

With the boys busy
at ball
in the worn lot
nearby

She stands in
the short street
reflectively bouncing
the red ball

Slowly
practiced
a little awkwardly
throwing one leg over

(Not as she had done
formerly
screaming and
missing

But slowly
surely) then
pausing throws
the ball

With a full slow
very slow
and easy motion
following through

With a slow
half turn—
as the ball flies
and rolls gently

At the child's feet
waiting—
and yet he misses
it and turns

And runs while she
slowly
regains her former
pose

Then shoves her fingers
up through
her loose short hair
quickly

Draws one stocking
tight and
waiting
tilts

Her hips and
in the warm still
air lets
her arms
            Fall

Fall
loosely
(waiting)
at her sides

From Asphodel, that Greeny Flower

Book II

Approaching death,
        as we think the death of love,
                no distinction
any more suffices to differentiate
        the particulars
                of place and condition
with which we have been long
        familiar.
                All appears
as if seen
        wavering through water,
                We start awake with a cry
of recognition
        but soon the outlines
                become again vague.

If we are to understand our time,
        we must find the key to it,
                not in the eighteenth
and nineteenth centuries,
        but in earlier, wilder
                and darker epochs . . .
So to know, what I have to know
        about my own death,
                if it be real,
I have to take it apart.
        What does your generation think
                of Cézanne?
I asked a young artist.
        The abstractions of Hindu painting,
                he replied,
is all at the moment which interests me.
        He liked my poem
                about the parts
of a broken bottle,
        lying green in the cinders
                of a hospital courtyard.
There was also, to his mind,
        the one on gay wallpaper
                which he had heard about
but not read.
        I was grateful to him
                for his interest.
Do you remember
        how at Interlaken
                we were waiting, four days,
to see the Jungfrau
        but rain had fallen steadily.
                Then
just before train time
        on a tip from one of the waitresses
                we rushed
to the Gipfel Platz
        and there it was!

in the distance
covered with new-fallen snow.
When I was at Granada,
I remember,
in the overpowering heat
climbing a treeless hill
overlooking the Alhambra.
At my appearance at the summit
two small boys
who had been playing
there
made themselves scarce.
Starting to come down
by a new path
I at once found myself surrounded
by gypsy women
who came up to me,
I could speak little Spanish,
and directed me,
guided by a young girl,
on my way.
These were the pinnacles.
The deaths I suffered
began in the heads
about me, my eyes
were too keen
not to see through
the world's niggardliness.
I accepted it
as my fate.
The wealthy
I defied
or not so much they,
for they have their uses,
as they who take their cues from them.
I lived
to breathe above the stench
not knowing how I in my own person

would be overcome
finally. I was lost
failing the poem.
But if I have come from the sea
it is not to be
wholly
fascinated by the glint of waves.
The free interchange
of light over their surface
which I have compared
to a garden
should not deceive us
or prove
too difficult a figure.
The poem
if it reflects the sea
reflects only
its dance
upon that profound depth
where
it seems to triumph.
The bomb puts an end
to all that.
I am reminded
that the bomb
also
is a flower
dedicated
howbeit
to our destruction.
The mere picture
of the exploding bomb
fascinates us
so that we cannot wait
to prostrate ourselves
before it. We do not believe
that love
can so wreck our lives.

The end
        will come
                in its time.
Meanwhile
        we are sick to death
                of the bomb
and its childlike
        insistence.
                Death is no answer,
no answer—
        to a blind old man
                whose bones
have the movement
        of the sea,
                a sexless old man
for whom it is a sea
        of which his verses
                are made up.
There is no power
        so great as love
                which is a sea,
which is a garden—
        as enduring
                as the verses
of that blind old man
        destined
                to live forever.
Few men believe that
        nor in the games of children.
                They believe rather
in the bomb
        and shall die by
                the bomb.
Compare Darwin's voyage of the *Beagle*,
        a voyage of discovery if there ever was one,
                to the death
incommunicado
        in the electric chair

of the Rosenbergs.
It is the mark of the times
that though we condemn
what they stood for
we admire their fortitude.
But Darwin
opened our eyes
to the gardens of the world,
as *they* closed them.
Or take that other voyage
which promised so much
but due to the world's avarice
breeding hatred
through fear,
ended so disastrously;
a voyage
with which I myself am so deeply concerned,
that of the *Pinta*,
the *Niña*
and the *Santa María*.
How the world opened its eyes!
It was a flower
upon which April
had descended from the skies!
How bitter
a disappointment!
In all,
this led mainly
to the deaths I have suffered.
For there had been kindled
more minds
than that of the discoverers
and set dancing
to a measure,
a new measure!
Soon lost.
The measure itself
has been lost

and we suffer for it.
We come to our deaths
in silence.
The bomb speaks.
All suppressions,
from the witchcraft trials at Salem
to the latest
book burnings
are confessions
that the bomb
has entered our lives
to destroy us.
Every drill
driven into the earth
for oil enters my side
also.
Waste, waste!
dominates the world.
It is the bomb's work.
What else was the fire
at the Jockey Club in Buenos Aires
(*malos aires*, we should say)
when with Perón's connivance
the hoodlums destroyed,
along with the books
the priceless Goyas
that hung there?
You know how we treasured
the few paintings
we still cling to
especially the one
by the dead
Charlie Demuth.
With your smiles
and other trivia of the sort
my secret life
had been made up,
some baby's life

which had been lost
        had I not intervened.
                But the words
made solely of air
        or less
                that came to me
out of the air
        and insisted
                on being written down,
I regret most—
        that there has come an end
                to them.
For in spite of it all,
        all that I have brought on myself,
                grew that single image
that I adore
        equally with you
                and so
it brought us together.

Ezra Pound

Near Perigord

A Perigord, pres del muralh
  Tan que i puosch' om gitar ab malh.

You'd have men's hearts up from the dust
And tell their secrets, Messire Cino,
Right enough? Then read between the lines of Uc St. Circ,
Solve me the riddle, for you know the tale.

Bertrans, En Bertrans, left a fine canzone:
"Maent, I love you, you have turned me out.
The voice at Montfort, Lady Agnes' hair,
Bel Miral's stature, the viscountess' throat,
Set all together, are not worthy of you . . ."
And all the while you sing out that canzone,
Think you that Maent lived at Montaignac,
One at Chalais, another at Malemort
Hard over Brive—for every lady a castle,
Each place strong.

          Oh, *is* it easy enough?
Tairiran held hall in Montaignac,
His brother-in-law was all there was of power
In Perigord, and this good union
Gobbled all the land, and held it later for some hundred years.
And our En Bertrans was in Altafort,
Hub of the wheel, the stirrer-up of strife,
As caught by Dante in the last wallow of hell—
The headless trunk "that made its head a lamp",
For separation wrought out separation,
And he who set the strife between brother and brother
And had his way with the old English king,
Viced in such torture for the "counterpass".

How would you live, with neighbours set about you—
Poictiers and Brive, untaken Rochecouart,
Spread like the finger-tips of one frail hand;
And you on that great mountain of a palm—
Not a neat ledge, not Foix between its streams,
But one huge back half-covered up with pine,
Worked for and snatched from the string-purse of
  Born—
The four round towers, four brothers—mostly fools:
What could he do but play the desperate chess,
And stir old grudges?
        "Pawn your castles, lords!
Let the Jews pay."
        And the great scene—
(That, maybe, never happened!)
        Beaten at last,
Before the hard old king:
        "Your son, ah, since he died
My wit and worth are cobwebs brushed aside
In the full flare of grief. Do what you will."

  Take the whole man, and ravel out the story.
He loved this lady in castle Montaignac?
The castle flanked him—he had need of it.
You read to-day, how long the overlords of Perigord,
The Talleyrands, have held the place; it was no transient
  fiction.
And Maent failed him? Or saw through the scheme?

  And all his net-like thought of new alliance?
Chalais is high, a-level with the poplars.
Its lowest stones just meet the valley tips
Where the low Dronne is filled with water-lilies.
And Rochecouart can match it, stronger yet,
The very spur's end, built on sheerest cliff,
And Malemort keeps its close hold on Brive,
While Born, his own close purse, his rabbit warren,
His subterranean chamber with a dozen doors,

A-bristle with antennae to feel roads,
To sniff the traffic into Perigord.
And that hard phalanx, that unbroken line,
The ten good miles from there to Maent's castle,
All of his flank—how could he do without her?
And all the road to Cahors, to Toulouse?
What would he do without her?

"Papiol,
Go forthright singing—Anhes, Cembelins.
There is a throat; ah, there are two white hands;
There is a trellis full of early roses,
And all my heart is bound about with love.
Where am I come with compound flatteries—
What doors are open to fine compliment?"
And every one half jealous of Maent?
He wrote the catch to pit their jealousies
Against her; give her pride in them?

Take his own speech, make what you will of it—
And still the knot, the first knot, of Maent?

Is it a love poem? Did he sing of war?
Is it an intrigue to run subtly out,
Born of a jongleur's tongue, freely to pass
Up and about and in and out the land,
Mark him a craftsman and a strategist?
(St Leider had done as much at Polhonac,
Singing a different stave, as closely hidden.)
Oh, there is precedent, legal tradition,
To sing one thing when your song means another,
"*Et albirar ab lor bordon*—"
Foix' count knew that. What is Sir Bertrans' singing?
Maent, Maent, and yet again Maent,
Or war and broken heaumes and politics?

II

End fact. Try fiction. Let us say we see
En Bertrans, a tower-room at Hautefort,
Sunset, the ribbon-like road lies, in red cross-light,
Southward toward Montaignac, and he bends at a table
Scribbling, swearing between his teeth; by his left hand
Lie little strips of parchment covered over,
Scratched and erased with *al* and *ochaisos*.
Testing his list of rhymes, a lean man? Bilious?
With a red straggling beard?
And the green cat's-eye lifts towards Montaignac.

Or take his "magnet" singer setting out,
Dodging his way past Aubeterre, singing at Chalais
In the vaulted hall,
Or, by a lichened tree at Rochecouart
Aimlessly watching a hawk above the valleys,
Waiting his turn in the midsummer evening,
Thinking of Aelis, whom he loved heart and soul . . .
To find her half alone, Montfort away,
And a brown, placid, hated woman visiting her,
Spoiling his visit, with a year before the next one.
Little enough?
Or carry him forward. "Go through all the courts,
My Magnet," Bertrans had said.

We came to Ventadour
In the mid love court, he sings out the canzon,
No one hears save Arrimon Luc D'Esparo—
No one hears aught save the gracious sound of compliments.
Sir Arrimon counts on his fingers, Montfort,
Rochecouart, Chalais, the rest, the tactic,
Malemort, guesses beneath, sends word to Cœur-de-Lion:
The compact, de Born smoked out, trees felled
About his castle, cattle driven out!
Or no one sees it, and En Bertrans prospered?

And ten years after, or twenty, as you will,
Arnaut and Richard lodge beneath Chalus:
The dull round towers encroaching on the field,
The tents tight drawn, horses at tether
Farther and out of reach, the purple night,
The crackling of small fires, the bannerets,
The lazy leopards on the largest banner,
Stray gleams on hanging mail, an armourer's torch-flare
Melting on steel.

And in the quietest space.
They probe old scandals, say de Born is dead;
And we've the gossip (skipped six hundred years).
Richard shall die to-morrow—leave him there
Talking of *trobar clus* with Daniel.
And the "best craftsman" sings out his friend's song,
Envies its vigour . . . and deplores the technique,
Dispraises his own skill?—That's as you will.
And they discuss the dead man,
Plantagenet puts the riddle: "Did he love her?"
And Arnaut parries: "Did he love your sister?
True, he has praised her, but in some opinion
He wrote that praise only to show he had
The favour of your party; had been well received."
"You knew the man."
"*You* knew the man."
"I am an artist, you have tried both métiers."
"You were born near him."
"Do we know our friends?"
"Say that he saw the castles, say that he loved Maent!"
"Say that he loved her, does it solve the riddle?"
End the discussion, Richard goes out next day
And gets a quarrel-bolt shot through his vizard,
Pardons the bowman, dies,

End our discussion. Arnaut ends
"In sacred odour"—(that's apocryphal!)
And we can leave the talk till Dante writes:

Surely I saw, and still before my eyes
Goes on that headless trunk, that bears for light
Its own head swinging, gripped by the dead hair,
And like a swinging lamp that says, "Ah me!
I severed men, my head and heart
Ye see here severed, my life's counterpart."

Or take En Bertrans?

III

Ed eran due in uno, ed uno in due;
Inferno, XXVIII, 125

Bewildering spring, and by the Auvezere
Poppies and day's eyes in the green émail
Rose over us; and we knew all that stream,
And our two horses had traced out the valleys;
Knew the low flooded lands squared out with poplars,
In the young days when the deep sky befriended.
   And great wings beat above us in the twilight,
And the great wheels in heaven
Bore us together . . . surging . . . and apart . . .
Believing we should meet with lips and hands,
   High, high and sure . . . and then the counter-thrust:
"Why do you love me? Will you always love me?
But I am like the grass, I cannot love you."
Or, "Love, and I love and love you,
And hate your mind, not *you*, your soul, your hands."

So to this last estrangement, Tairiran!

There shut up in his castle, Tairiran's,
She who had nor ears nor tongue save in her hands,
Gone—ah gone—untouched, unreachable!
She who could never live save through one person,
She who could never speak save to one person,
And all the rest of her a shifting change,
A broken bundle of mirrors . . .!

EZRA POUND

Exile's Letter

To So-Kin of Rakuyo, ancient friend, Chancellor of Gen.
Now I remember that you built me a special tavern
By the south side of the bridge at Ten-Shin.
With yellow gold and white jewels, we paid for song and
laughter
And we were drunk for month on month, forgetting the kings
and princes.
Intelligent men came drifting in from the sea and from the west
border,
And with them, and with you especially
There was nothing at cross purpose,
And they made nothing of sea-crossing or of
mountain-crossing,
If only they could be of that fellowship,
And we all spoke out our hearts and minds, and without regret.
And then I was sent off to South Wei,
smothered in laurel groves,
And you to the north of Raku-hoku
Till we had nothing but thoughts and memories in common.

And then, when separation had come to its worst,
We met, and travelled into Sen-Go
Through all the thirty-six folds of the turning and twisting
waters,
Into a valley of the thousand bright flowers,
That was the first valley;
And into ten thousand valleys full of voices and pine-winds.
And with silver harness and reins of gold,
Out came the East of Kan foreman and his company.
And there came also the "True man" of Shi-yo to meet me,
Playing on a jewelled mouth-organ.
In the storied houses of San-Ko they gave us more Sennin
music,
Many instruments, like the sound of young phoenix broods.
The foreman of Kan Chu, drunk, danced
because his long sleeves wouldn't keep still

With that music playing,
And I, wrapped in brocade, went to sleep with my head on his
lap,
And my spirit so high it was all over the heavens,
And before the end of the day we were scattered like stars, or
rain.
I had to be off to So, far away over the waters,
You back to your river-bridge.

And your father, who was brave as a leopard,
Was governor in Hei Shu, and put down the barbarian rabble.
And one May he had you send for me,
despite the long distance.
And what with broken wheels and so on, I won't say it wasn't
hard going.
Over roads twisted like sheep's guts.
And I was still going, late in the year,
in the cutting wind from the North,
And thinking how little you cared for the cost,
and you caring enough to pay it.
And what a reception:
Red jade cups, food well set on a blue jewelled table,
And I was drunk, and had no thought of returning.
And you would walk out with me to the western corner of the
castle,
To the dynastic temple, with water about it clear as blue jade,
With boats floating, and the sound of mouth-organs and
drums,
With ripples like dragon-scales, going grass-green on the water,
Pleasure lasting, with courtesans, going and coming without
hindrance,
With the willow flakes falling like snow,
And the vermilioned girls getting drunk about sunset,
And the water, a hundred feet deep, reflecting green eyebrows
—Eyebrows painted green are a fine sight in young
moonlight,
Gracefully painted—
And the girls singing back at each other,

Dancing in transparent brocade,
And the wind lifting the song, and interrupting it,
Tossing it up under the clouds.
        And all this comes to an end.
        And is not again to be met with.
I went up to the court for examination,
Tried Layu's luck, offered the Choyo song,
And got no promotion,
        and went back to the East Mountains
        White-headed.

And once again, later, we met at the South bridge-head.
And then the crowd broke up, you went north to San palace,
And if you ask how I regret that parting:
It is like the flowers falling at Spring's end
        Confused, whirled in a tangle.
What is the use of talking, and there is no end of talking,
There is no end of things in the heart.
I call in the boy,
Have him sit on his knees here
        To seal this,
And send it a thousand miles, thinking.

By Rihaku

E. P. Ode pour l'Election de Son Sepulchre

I

For three years, out of key with his time,
He strove to resuscitate the dead art
Of poetry; to maintain "the sublime"
In the old sense. Wrong from the start—

No, hardly, but seeing he had been born
In a half-savage country, out of date;
Bent resolutely on wringing lilies from the acorn;
Capaneus; trout for factitious bait;

"Ἴδμεν γάρ τοι πάνθ᾽, ὅσ᾽ ἐνὶ Τροίῃ
Caught in the unstopped ear;
Giving the rocks small lee-way
The chopped seas held him, therefore, that year.

His true Penelope was Flaubert,
He fished by obstinate isles;
Observed the elegance of Circe's hair
Rather than the mottoes on sundials.

Unaffected by "the march of events",
He passed from men's memory in *l'an trentiesme*,
De son eage; the case presents
No adjunct to the Muses' diadem.

II

The age demanded an image
Of its accelerated grimace,
Something for the modern stage,
Not, at any rate, an Attic grace;

Not, not certainly, the obscure reveries
Of the inward gaze;
Better mendacities
Than the classics in paraphrase!

The "age demanded" chiefly a mould in plaster,
Made with no loss of time,
A prose kinema, not, not assuredly, alabaster
Or the "sculpture"of rhyme.

III

The tea-rose tea-gown, etc.
Supplants the mousseline of Cos,
The pianola "replaces"
Sappho's barbitos.

Christ follows Dionysus,
Phallic and ambrosial
Made way for macerations;
Caliban casts out Ariel.

All things are a flowing,
Sage Heracleitus says;
But a tawdry cheapness
Shall outlast our days.

Even the Christian beauty
Defects—after Samothrace;
We see *τὸ καλὸν*
Decreed in the market-place.

Faun's flesh is not to us,
Nor the saint's vision.
We have the Press for wafer;
Franchise for circumcision.

All men, in law, are equals.
Free of Pisistratus,
We choose a knave or an eunuch
To rule over us.

O bright Apollo,
τίν' ἄνδρα, τίν' ἥρωα, τίνα θεὸν
What god, man, or hero
Shall I place a tin wreath upon!

IV

These fought in any case,
and some believing,
        pro domo, in any case . . .

Some quick to arm,
some for adventure,
some from fear of weakness,
some from fear of censure,
some for love of slaughter, in imagination,
learning later . . .
some in fear, learning love of slaughter;

Died some, pro patria,
  non "dulce" non "et decor" . . .
walked eye-deep in hell
believing in old men's lies, then unbelieving
came home, home to a lie,
home to many deceits,
home to old lies and new infamy;
usury age-old and age-thick
and liars in public places.

Daring as never before, wastage as never before.
Young blood and high blood,
fair cheeks and fine bodies;

fortitude as never before

frankness as never before,
disillusions as never told in the old days,
hysterias, trench confessions,
laughter out of dead bellies.

V
There died a myriad,
And of the best, among them,
For an old bitch gone in the teeth,
For a botched civilization,

Charm, smiling at the good mouth,
Quick eyes gone under earth's lid,

For two gross of broken statues,
For a few thousand battered books.

EZRA POUND

Homage to Sextus Propertius: XII

Who, who will be the next man to entrust his girl to a friend?
        Love interferes with fidelities;
The gods have brought shame on their relatives;
        Each man wants the pomegranate for himself;
Amiable and harmonious people are pushed incontinent into
            duels,
A Trojan and adulterous person came to Menelaus under the
            rites of hospitium,
And there was a case in Colchis, Jason and that woman in
            Colchis;
And besides, Lynceus,
                        you were drunk.

Could you endure such promiscuity?
        She was not renowned for fidelity;
But to jab a knife in my vitals, to have passed on a swig of
            poison,
Preferable, my dear boy, my dear Lynceus,
Comrade, comrade of my life, of my purse, of my person;
But in one bed, in one bed alone, my dear Lynceus,
        I deprecate your attendance;
I would ask a like boon of Jove.

And you write of Acheloüs, who contended with Hercules,
You write of Adrastus' horses and the funeral rites of Achenor,
And you will not leave off imitating Aeschylus.
        Though you make a hash of Antimachus,
You think you are going to do Homer.
        And still a girl scorns the gods,
Of all these young women
        not one has enquired the cause of the world,
Nor the modus of lunar eclipses
        Nor whether there be any patch left of us
After we cross the infernal ripples,
        nor if the thunder fall from predestination;
Nor anything else of importance.

Upon the Actian marshes Virgil is Phoebus' chief of police,
He can tabulate Caesar's great ships.
He thrills to Ilian arms,
He shakes the Trojan weapons of Aeneas,
And casts stores on Lavinian beaches.
Make way, ye Roman authors,
clear the street O ye Greeks,
For a much larger Iliad is in the course of construction
(and to Imperial order)
Clear the streets O ye Greeks!
And you also follow him "neath Phrygian pine shade":
Thyrsis and Daphnis upon whittled reeds,
And how ten sins can corrupt young maidens;
Kids for a bribe and pressed udders,
Happy selling poor loves for cheap apples.

Tityrus might have sung the same vixen;
Corydon tempted Alexis,
Head farmers do likewise, and lying weary amid their oats
They get praise from tolerant Hamadryads.

Go on, to Ascraeus' prescription, the ancient,
respected, Wordsworthian:
"A flat field for rushes, grapes grow on the slope."

And behold me, a small fortune left in my house.
Me, who had no general for a grandfather!
I shall triumph, among young ladies of indeterminate
character,
My talent acclaimed in their banquets,
I shall be honoured with yesterday's wreaths.

And the god strikes to the marrow.

Like a trained and performing tortoise,
I would make verse in your fashion, if she should command it,
With her husband asking a remission of sentence,
And even this infamy would not attract numerous
readers

Were there an erudite or violent passion,
For the nobleness of the populace brooks nothing below its
                own altitude.
One must have resonance, resonance and sonority . . . like a
                goose.

Varro sang Jason's expedition,
        Varro, of his great passion Leucadia,
There is song in the parchment; Catullus the highly
                indecorous,
Of Lesbia, known above Helen;
And in the dyed pages of Calvus,
        Calvus mourning Quintilia,
And but now Gallus had sung of Lycoris.
        Fair, fairest Lycoris—
The waters of Styx poured over the wound:
And now Propertius of Cynthia, taking his stand among these.

Canto LXXXI

Zeus lies in Ceres' bosom
Taishan is attended of loves
        under Cythera, before sunrise
and he said: "Hay aquí mucho catolicismo—(sounded
catoli*th*ismo)
        y muy poco reliHion"
and he said: "Yo creo que los reyes desaparecen"
(Kings will, I think disappear)
That was Padre José Elizondo
                in 1906 and in 1917
or about 1917
        and Dolores said: "Come pan, niño," eat bread, me lad
Sargent had painted her
                before he descended
(i.e. if he descended
        but in those days he did thumb sketches.

impressions of the Velasquez in the Museo del Prado
and books cost a peseta,
brass candlesticks in proportion,
hot wind came from the marshes
and death-chill from the mountains.
And later Bowers wrote: "but such hatred,
I had never conceived such"
and the London reds wouldn't show up his friends
(i.e. friends of Franco
working in London) and in Alcázar
forty years gone, they said: "go back to the station to eat
you can sleep here for a peseta"
goat bells tinkled all night
and the hostess grinned: Eso es luto, *haw!*
mi marido es muerto
(it is mourning, my husband is dead)
when she gave me paper to write on
with a black border half an inch or more deep,
say 5/8ths, of the locanda
"We call *all* foreigners frenchies"
and the egg broke in Cabranez' pocket,
thus making history. Basil says
they beat drums for three days
till all the drumheads were busted
(simple village fiesta)
and as for his life in the Canaries . . .
Possum observed that the local folk dance
was danced by the same dancers in divers localities
in political welcome . . .
the technique of demonstration
Cole studied that (not G.D.H., Horace)
"You will find" said old André Spire,
that every man on that board (Crédit Agricole)
has a brother-in-law
"You the one, I the few"
said John Adams
speaking of fears in the abstract
to his volatile friend Mr Jefferson.

(To break the pentameter, that was the first heave)
or as Jo Bard says: they never speak to each other,
if it is baker and concierge visibly
        it is La Rouchefoucauld and de Maintenon audibly.
"Te cavero le budella"
                "La corata a te"
In less than a geological epoch
                said Henry Mencken
"Some cook, some do not cook
        some things cannot be altered"
'Ιυγξ. . . . . 'εμὸν ποτί δῶμα τὸν ἄνδρα
What counts is the cultural level,
        thank Benin for this table ex packing box
        "doan yu tell no one I made it"
                from a mask fine as any in Frankfurt
"It'll get you offn th' groun"
                Light as the branch of Kuanon
And at first disappointed with shoddy
the bare ram-shackle quais, but then saw the high buggy
wheels
                and was reconciled,
George Santayana arriving in the port of Boston
and kept to the end of his life that faint *thethear*
of the Spaniard
                as a grace quasi imperceptible
as did Muss the *v* for *u* of Romagna
and said the grief was a full act
        repeated for each new condoleress
working up to a climax.
and George Horace said he wd "get Beveridge" (Senator)
Beveridge wouldn't talk and he wouldn't write for the papers
but George got him by campin' in his hotel
and assailin' him at lunch breakfast an' dinner
                three articles
and my ole man went on hoein' corn
        while George was a-tellin' him,
come across a vacant lot
        where you'd occasionally see a wild rabbit

or mebbe only a loose one
        AOI!
a leaf in the current
                at my grates no Althea
libretto
        Yet
        Ere the season died a-cold
        Borne upon a zephyr's shoulder
        I rose through the aureate sky
                Lawes and Jenkyns guard thy rest
                Dolmetsch ever be thy guest,
        Has he tempered the viol's wood
        To enforce   both the grave   and the acute?
        Has he curved us the bowl of the lute?
                Lawes and Jenkyns guard thy rest
                Dolmetsch ever be thy guest
        Hast 'ou fashioned so airy a mood
          To draw up leaf from the root?
        Hast 'ou found   a cloud   so light
          As seemed neither mist nor shade?

                Then resolve me, tell me aright
                If Waller sang or Dowland played,

            Your eyen two wol sleye me sodenly
            I may the beauté of hem nat susteyne

And for 180 years almost nothing.

Ed ascoltando al leggier mormorio
        there came new subtlety of eyes into my tent,
whether of spirit or hypostasis,
        but what the blindfold hides
or at carneval
                nor any pair showed anger
        Saw but the eyes and stance between the eyes,
colour, diastasis,
        careless or unaware it had not the
    whole tent's room

nor was place for the full Ειδὼς
interpass, penetrate
        casting but shade beyond the other lights
            sky's clear
            night's sea
            green of the mountain pool
            shone from the unmasked eyes in half-mask's space.
What thou lovest well remains,
                                        the rest is dross
What thou lov'st well shall not be reft from thee
What thou lov'st well is thy true heritage
Whose world, or mine or theirs
                                        or is it of none?
First came the seen, thus the palpable
        Elysium, though it were in the halls of hell,
What thou lovest well is thy true heritage
What thou lov'st well shall not be reft from thee

The ant's a centaur in his dragon world.
Pull down thy vanity, it is not man
Made courage, or made order, or made grace,
        Pull down thy vanity, I say pull down.
Learn of the green world what can be thy place
In scaled invention or true artistry,
Pull down thy vanity,
                                Paquin pull down!
The green casque has outdone your elegance.

"Master thyself, then others shall thee beare"
        Pull down thy vanity
Thou art a beaten dog beneath the hail,
A swollen magpie in a fitful sun,
Half black half white
Nor knowst'ou wing from tail
Pull down thy vanity
                        How mean thy hates
Fostered in falsity,
                        Pull down thy vanity,

Rathe to destroy, niggard in charity,
Pull down thy vanity,
I say pull down.

But to have done instead of not doing
this is not vanity
To have, with decency, knocked
That a Blunt should open
To have gathered from the air a live tradition
or from a fine old eye the unconquered flame
This is not vanity.
Here error is all in the not done,
all in the diffidence that faltered . . .

from Canto CXV

The scientists are in terror
and the European mind stops
Wyndham Lewis chose blindness
rather than have his mind stop

Night under wind mid garofani
the petals are almost still.

Mozart, Linnaeus, Sulmona,

When one's friends hate each other
how can there be peace in the world
Their asperities diverted me in my green time.

A blown husk that is finished
but the light sings eternal
a pale flare over marshes
where the salt hay whispers to tide's change

Time, space,
    neither life nor death is the answer.

And of men seeking good,
        doing evil.

In meine Heimat
        where the dead walked
        and the living were made of cardboard

T. S. Eliot

Sweeney among the Nightingales

ὤμοι, πέπληγμαι καιρίαν πληγὴν ἔσω

Apeneck Sweeney spreads his knees
Letting his arms hang down to laugh,
The zebra stripes along his jaw
Swelling to maculate giraffe.

The circles of the stormy moon
Slide westward toward the River Plate,
Death and the Raven drift above
And Sweeney guards the horned gate.

Gloomy Orion and the Dog
Are veiled; and hushed the shrunken seas;
The person in the Spanish cape
Tries to sit on Sweeney's knees

Slips and pulls the table cloth
Overturns a coffee-cup,
Reorganised upon the floor
She jaws and draws a stocking up;

The silent man in mocha brown
Sprawls at the window-sill and gapes;
The waiter brings in oranges
Bananas figs and hothouse grapes;

The silent vertebrate in brown
Contracts and concentrates, withdraws;
Rachel *née* Rabinovitch
Tears at the grapes with murderous paws;

She and the lady in the cape
Are suspect, thought to be in league;
Therefore the man with heavy eyes
Declines the gambit, shows fatigue,

Leaves the room and reappears
Outside the window, leaning in,
Branches of wistaria
Circumscribe a golden grin;

The host with someone indistinct
Converses at the door apart,
The nightingales are singing near
The Convent of the Sacred Heart,

And sang within the bloody wood
When Agamemnon cried aloud,
And let their liquid siftings fall
To stain the stiff dishonoured shroud.

The Waste Land

"NAM Sibyllam quidem Cumis ego epse oculis meis vidi in ampulla pendere, et cum illi pueri dicerent: Σιβυλλα τί θέλεις; *respondebat illa:* ἀποθανεῖν θέλω."

For Ezra Pound
il miglior fabbro

I. The Burial of the Dead

April is the cruellest month, breeding
Lilacs out of the dead land, mixing
Memory and desire, stirring
Dull roots with spring rain.
Winter kept us warm, covering
Earth in forgetful snow, feeding
A little life with dried tubers.

Summer surprised us, coming over the Starnbergersee
With a shower of rain; we stopped in the colonnade,
And went on in sunlight, into the Hofgarten,
And drank coffee, and talked for an hour.
Bin gar keine Russin, stamm' aus Litauen, echt deutsch.
And when we were children, staying at the archduke's,
My cousin's, he took me out on a sled,
And I was frightened. He said, Marie,
Marie, hold on tight. And down we went.
In the mountains, there you feel free.
I read, much of the night, and go south in the winter.

What are the roots that clutch, what branches grow
Out of this stony rubbish? Son of man,
You cannot say, or guess, for you know only
A heap of broken images, where the sun beats,
And the dead tree gives no shelter, the cricket no relief,
And the dry stone no sound of water. Only
There is shadow under this red rock,
(Come in under the shadow of this red rock),
And I will show you something different from either
Your shadow at morning striding behind you
Or your shadow at evening rising to meet you;
I will show you fear in a handful of dust.

Frisch weht der Wind
Der Heimat zu,
Mein Irisch Kind,
Wo weilest du?

"You gave me hyacinths first a year ago;
"They called me the hyacinth girl."
—Yet when we came back, late, from the Hyacinth garden,
Your arms full, and your hair wet, I could not
Speak, and my eyes failed, I was neither
Living nor dead, and I knew nothing,
Looking into the heart of light, the silence.
Od' und leer das Meer.

Madame Sosostris, famous clairvoyante,
Had a bad cold, nevertheless
Is known to be the wisest woman in Europe,
With a wicked pack of cards. Here, said she,
Is your card, the drowned Phoenician Sailor,
(Those are pearls that were his eyes. Look!)
Here is Belladonna, the Lady of the Rocks,
The lady of situations.
Here is the man with three staves, and here the Wheel,
And here is the one-eyed merchant, and this card,
Which is blank, is something he carries on his back,
Which I am forbidden to see. I do not find
The Hanged Man. Fear death by water.
I see crowds of people, walking round in a ring.
Thank you. If you see dear Mrs Equitone,
Tell her I bring the horoscope myself:
One must be so careful these days.

Unreal City,
Under the brown fog of a winter dawn,
A crowd flowed over London Bridge, so many,
I had not thought death had undone so many.
Sighs, short and infrequent, were exhaled,
And each man fixed his eyes before his feet.
Flowed up the hill and down King William Street,
To where Saint Mary Woolnoth kept the hours
With a dead sound on the final stroke of nine.
There I saw one I knew, and stopped him, crying: "Stetson!
"You who were with me in the ships at Mylae!
"That corpse you planted last year in your garden,
"Has it begun to sprout? Will it bloom this year?
"Or has the sudden frost disturbed its bed?
"Oh keep the Dog far hence, that's friend to men,
"Or with his nails he'll dig it up again!
"You! hypocrite lecteur!—mon semblable,—mon frère!"

II. A Game of Chess

The Chair she sat in, like a burnished throne,
Glowed on the marble, where the glass
Held up by standards wrought with fruited vines
From which a golden Cupidon peeped out
(Another hid his eyes behind his wing)
Doubled the flames of sevenbranched candelabra
Reflecting light upon the table as
The glitter of her jewels rose to meet it,
From satin cases poured in rich profusion;
In vials of ivory and coloured glass
Unstoppered, lurked her strange synthetic perfumes,
Unguent, powdered, or liquid—troubled, confused
And drowned the sense in odours; stirred by the air
That freshened from the window, these ascended
In fattening the prolonged candle-flames,
Flung their smoke into the laquearia,
Stirring the pattern on the coffered ceiling.
Huge sea-wood fed with copper
Burned green and orange, framed by the coloured stone,
In which sad light a carved dolphin swam.
Above the antique mantel was displayed
As though a window gave upon the sylvan scene
The change of Philomel, by the barbarous king
So rudely forced; yet there the nightingale
Filled all the desert with inviolable voice
And still she cried, and still the world pursues,
"Jug Jug" to dirty ears.
And other withered stumps of time
Were told upon the walls; staring forms
Leaned out, leaning, hushing the room enclosed.
Footsteps shuffled on the stair.
Under the firelight, under the brush, her hair
Spread out in fiery points
Glowed into words, then would be savagely still.

"My nerves are bad to-night. Yes, bad. Stay with me.
"Speak to me. Why do you never speak. Speak.
"What are you thinking of? What thinking? What?
"I never know what you are thinking. Think."

I think we are in rats' alley
Where the dead men lost their bones.

"What is that noise?"
The wind under the door.
"What is that noise now? What is the wind doing?"
Nothing again Nothing.
"Do
"You know nothing? Do you see nothing? Do you remember
"Nothing?"
I remember
Those are pearls that were his eyes.
"Are you alive, or not? Is there nothing in your head?"
But
O O O O that Shakespeherian Rag—
It's so elegant
So intelligent
"What shall I do now? What shall I do?"
"I shall rush out as I am, and walk the street
"With my hair down, so. What shall we do tomorrow?
"What shall we ever do?"
The hot water at ten.
And if it rains, a closed car at four.
And we shall play a game of chess,
Pressing lidless eyes and waiting for a knock upon the door.

When Lil's husband got demobbed, I said—
I didn't mince my words, I said to her myself,
HURRY UP PLEASE ITS TIME
Now Albert's coming back, make yourself a bit smart.
He'll want to know what you done with that money he gave you
To get yourself some teeth. He did, I was there.

You have them all out, Lil, and get a nice set,
He said, I swear, I can't bear to look at you.
And no more can't I, I said, and think of poor Albert,
He's been in the army four years, he wants a good time,
And if you don't give it him, there's others will, I said.
Oh is there, she said. Something o' that, I said.
Then I'll know who to thank, she said, and give me a straight look.
HURRY UP PLEASE ITS TIME
If you don't like it you can get on with it, I said,
Others can pick and choose if you can't.
But if Albert makes off, it won't be for lack of telling.
You ought to be ashamed, I said, to look so antique.
(And her only thirty-one.)
I can't help it, she said, pulling a long face,
It's them pills I took, to bring it off, she said.
(She's had five already, and nearly died of young George.)
The chemist said it would be all right, but I've never been the same.
You *are* a proper fool I said.
Well, if Albert won't leave you alone, there it is, I said,
What you get married for if you don't want children?
HURRY UP PLEASE ITS TIME
Well, that Sunday Albert was home, they had a hot gammon,
And they asked me in to dinner, to get the beauty of it hot—
HURRY UP PLEASE ITS TIME
HURRY UP PLEASE ITS TIME
Goodnight Bill. Goodnight Lou. Goodnight May. Goodnight.
Ta ta. Goodnight. Goodnight.
Good night, ladies, good night, sweet ladies, good night, good night.

T. S. ELIOT

III. The Fire Sermon

The river's tent is broken: the last fingers of leaf
Clutch and sink into the wet bank. The wind
Crosses the brown land, unheard. The nymphs are departed.
Sweet Thames, run softly, till I end my song.
The river bears no empty bottles, sandwich papers,
Silk handkerchiefs, cardboard boxes, cigarette ends
Or other testimony of summer nights. The nymphs are departed.
And their friends, the loitering heirs of City directors;
Departed, have left no addresses.
By the waters of Leman I sat down and wept . . .
Sweet Thames, run softly till I end my song,
Sweet Thames, run softly, for I speak not loud or long.
But at my back in a cold blast I hear
The rattle of the bones, and chuckle spread from ear to ear.
A rat crept softly through the vegetation
Dragging its slimy belly on the bank
While I was fishing in the dull canal
On a winter evening round behind the gashouse
Musing upon the king my brother's wreck
And on the king my father's death before him.
White bodies naked on the low damp ground
And the bones cast in a little low dry garret,
Rattles by the rat's foot only, year to year.
But at my back from time to time I hear
The sound of horns and motors, which shall bring
Sweeney to Mrs. Porter in the spring.
O the moon shone bright on Mrs. Porter
And on her daughter
They wash their feet in soda water
Et O ces voix d'enfants, chantant dans la coupole!

Twit twit twit
Jug jug jug jug jug jug
So rudely forc'd.
Tereu

Unreal City
Under the brown fog of a winter noon
Mr. Eugenides, the Smyrna merchant
Unshaven, with a pocket full of currants
C.i.f. London: documents at sight,
Asked me in demotic French
To luncheon at the Cannon Street Hotel
Followed by a weekend at the Metropole.
At the violet hour, when the eyes and back
Turn upward from the desk, when the human engine waits
Like a taxi throbbing waiting,
I Tiresias, though blind, throbbing between two lives,
Old man with wrinkled female breasts, can see
At the violet hour, the evening hour that strives
Homeward, and brings the sailor home from sea,
The typist home at teatime, clears her breakfast, lights
Her stove, and lays out food in tins.
Out of the window perilously spread
Her drying combinations touched by the sun's last rays,
On the divan are piled (at night her bed)
Stockings, slippers, camisoles, and stays.
I Tiresias, old man with wrinkled dugs
Perceived the scene, and foretold the rest—
I too awaited the expected guest.
He, the young man carbuncular, arrives,
A small house agent's clerk, with one bold stare,
One of the low on whom assurance sits
As a silk hat on a Bradford millionaire.
The time is now propitious, as he guesses,
The meal is ended, she is bored and tired,
Endeavours to engage her in caresses
Which still are unreproved, if undesired.
Flushed and decided, he assaults at once;
Exploring hands encounter no defence;
His vanity requires no response,
And makes a welcome of indifference.
(And I Tiresias have foresuffered all
Enacted on this same divan or bed;

I who have sat by Thebes below the wall
And walked among the lowest of the dead.)
Bestows one final patronising kiss,
And gropes his way, finding the stairs unlit . . .

She turns and looks a moment in the glass,
Hardly aware of her departed lover;
Her brain allows one half-formed thought to pass;
"Well now that's done: and I'm glad it's over."
When lovely woman stoops to folly and
Paces about her room again, alone,
She smooths her hair with automatic hand,
And puts a record on the gramophone.

"This music crept by me upon the waters"
And along the Strand, up Queen Victoria Street.
O City city, I can sometimes hear
Beside a public bar in Lower Thames Street,
The pleasant whining of a mandoline
And a clatter and a chatter from within
Where fishmen lounge at noon: where the walls
Of Magnus Martyr hold
Inexplicable splendour of Ionian white and gold.

The river sweats
Oil and tar
The barges drift
With the turning tide
Red sails
Wide
To leeward, swing on the heavy spar.
The barges wash
Drifting logs
Down Greenwich reach
Past the Isle of Dogs.
Weialala leia
Wallala leialala

Elizabeth and Leicester
Beating oars
The stern was formed
A gilded shell
Red and gold
The brisk swell
Rippled both shores
Southwest wind
Carried down stream
The peal of bells
White towers
                Weialala leia
                Wallala leialala
"Trams and dusty trees.
Highbury bore me. Richmond and Kew
Undid me. By Richmond I raised my knees
Supine on the floor of a narrow canoe."

"My feet are at Moorgate, and my heart
Under my feet. After the event
He wept. He promised 'a new start.'
I made no comment. What should I resent?"

"On Margate Sands.
I can connect
Nothing with nothing.
The broken fingernails of dirty hands.
My people humble people who expect
Nothing."
        la la

To Carthage then I came

Burning burning burning burning
O Lord Thou pluckest me out
O Lord Thou pluckest

burning

IV. Death by Water

Phlebas and Phoenician, a fortnight dead,
Forgot the cry of gulls, and the deep sea swell
And the profit and loss.
                                        A current under sea
Picked his bones in whispers. As he rose and fell
He passed the stages of his age and youth
Entering the whirlpool.
                                        Gentile or Jew
O you who turn the wheel and look to windward,
Consider Phlebas, who was once handsome and tall as you.

V. What the Thunder Said

After the torchlight red on sweaty faces
After the frosty silence in the gardens
After the agony in stony places
The shouting and the crying
Prison and palace and reverberation
Of thunder of spring over distant mountains
He who was living is now dead
We who were living are now dying
With a little patience

Here is no water but only rock
Rock and no water and the sandy road
The road winding above among the mountains
Which are mountains of rock without water
If there were water we should stop and drink
Amongst the rock one cannot stop or think
Sweat is dry and feet are in the sand
If there were only water amongst the rock
Dead mountain mouth of carious teeth that cannot spit
Here one can neither stand nor lie nor sit
There is not even silence in the mountains
But dry sterile thunder without rain

There is not even solitude in the mountains
But red sullen faces sneer and snarl
From doors of mudcracked houses
                                                            If there were water
    And no rock
    If there were rock
    And also water
    And water
    A spring
    A pool among the rock
    If there were the sound of water only
    Not the cicada
    And dry grass singing
    But sound of water over a rock
    Where the hermit-thrush sings in the pine trees
    Drip drop drip drop drop drop drop
    But there is no water

Who is the third who walks always beside you?
When I count, there are only you and I together
But when I look ahead up the white road
There is always another one walking beside you
Gliding wrapt in a brown mantle, hooded
I do not know whether a man or a woman
—But who is that on the other side of you?

What is that sound high in the air
Murmur of maternal lamentation
Who are those hooded hordes swarming
Over endless plains, stumbling in cracked earth
Ringed by the flat horizon only
What is the city over the mountains
Cracks and reforms and bursts in the violet air
Falling towers
Jerusalem Athens Alexandria
Vienna London
Unreal

A woman drew her long black hair out tight
And fiddled whisper music on those strings
And bats with baby faces in the violet light
Whistled, and beat their wings
And crawled head downwards down a blackened wall
And upside down in air were towers
Tolling reminiscent bells, that kept the hours
And voices singing out of empty cisterns and exhausted wells.

In this decayed hole among the mountains
In the faint moonlight, the grass is singing
Over the tumbled graves, about the chapel
There is the empty chapel, only the wind's home.
It has no windows, and the door swings,
Dry bones can harm no one.
Only a cock stood on the rooftree
Co co rico co co rico
In a flash of lightning. Then a damp gust
Bringing rain.

Ganga was sunken, and the limp leaves
Waited for rain, while the black clouds
Gathered far distant, over Himavant.
The jungle crouched, humped in silence.
Then spoke the thunder
DA
Datta: what have we given?
My friend, blood shaking my heart
The awful daring of a moment's surrender
Which an age of prudence can never retract
By this, and this only, we have existed
Which is not to be found in our obituaries
Or in memories draped by the beneficient spider
Or under seals broken by the lean solicitor
In our empty rooms
DA
Dayadhvam: I have heard the key
Turn in the door once and turn once only

We think of the key, each in his prison
Thinking of the key, each confirms a prison
Only at nightfall, aethereal rumours
Revive for a moment a broken Coriolanus
DA
Damyata: The boat responded
Gaily, to the hand expert with sail and oar
The sea was calm, your heart would have responded
Gaily, when invited, beating obedient
To controlling hands

I sat upon the shore
Fishing, with the arid plain behind me
Shall I at least set my lands in order?
London Bridge is falling down falling down falling down
Poi s'ascose nel foco che gli affina
Quando fiam ceu chelidon—O swallow swallow
Le Prince d'Aquitaine à la tour abolie
These fragments I have shored against my ruins
Why then Ile fit you. Hieronymo's mad againe.
Datta. Dayadhvam. Damyata.
Shantih shantih shantih

Journey of the Magi

"A cold coming we had of it,
Just the worst time of the year
For a journey, and such a long journey:
The ways deep and the weather sharp,
The very dead of winter."
And the camels galled, sore-footed, refractory,
Lying down in the melting snow.
There were times we regretted
The summer palaces on slopes, the terraces,
And the silken girls bringing sherbet.

Then the camel men cursing and grumbling
And running away, and wanting their liquor and women,
And the night-fires going out, and the lack of shelters,
And the cities hostile and the towns unfriendly
And the villages dirty and charging high prices:
A hard time we had of it.
At the end we preferred to travel all night,
Sleeping in snatches,
With the voices singing in our ears, saying
That this was all folly.

Then at dawn we came down to a temperate valley,
Wet, below the snow line, smelling of vegetation;
With a running stream and a water-mill beating the darkness,
And three trees on the low sky,
And an old white horse galloped away in the meadow.
Then we came to a tavern with vine-leaves over the lintel,
Six hands at an open door dicing for pieces of silver,
And feet kicking the empty wine-skins.
But there was no information, and so we continued
And arrived at evening, not a moment too soon
Finding the place; it was (you may say) satisfactory.

All this was a long time ago, I remember,
And I would do it again, but set down
This set down
This: were we led all that way for
Birth or Death? There was a Birth, certainly,
We had evidence and no doubt. I had seen birth and death,
But had thought they were different; this Birth was
Hard and bitter agony for us, like Death, our death.
We returned to our places, these Kingdoms,
But no longer at ease here, in the old dispensation,
With an alien people clutching their gods.
I should be glad of another death.

Marina

Quis hic locus, quae regio, quae mundi plaga?

What seas what shores what grey rocks and what islands
What water lapping the bow
And scent of pine and the woodthrush singing through the fog
What images return
O my daughter.

Those who sharpen the tooth of the dog, meaning
Death
Those who glitter with the glory of the humming bird, meaning
Death
Those who sit in the stye of contentment, meaning
Death
Those who suffer the ecstasy of the animals, meaning
Death

Are become unsubstantial, reduced by a wind,
A breath of pine, and the woodsong fog
By this grace dissolved in place

What is this face less clear and clearer
The pulse in the arm, less strong and stronger—
Given or lent? more distant than stars and nearer than the eye
Whispers and small laughter between leaves and hurrying feet
Under sleep, where all the waters meet.

Bowsprit cracked with ice and paint cracked with heat.
I made this, I have forgotten
And remember.
The rigging weak and the canvas rotten
Between one June and another September.
Made this unknowing, half conscious, unknown, my own.
The garboard strake leaks, the seams need caulking.
This form, this face, this life
Living to live in a world of time beyond me; let me

Resign my life for this life, my speech for that unspoken,
The awakened, lips parted, the hope, the new ships.

What seas what shores what granite islands towards my timbers
And woodthrush calling through the fog
My daughter.

Little Gidding

1

Midwinter spring is its own season
Sempiternal though sodden towards sundown,
Suspended in time, between pole and tropic.
When the short day is brightest, with frost and fire,
The brief sun flames the ice, on pond and ditches,
In windless cold that is the heart's heat,
Reflecting in a watery mirror
A glare that is blindness in the early afternoon.
And glow more intense than blaze of branch, or brazier,
Stirs the dumb spirit: no wind, but pentecostal fire
In the dark time of the year. Between melting and freezing
The soul's sap quivers. There is no earth smell
Or smell of living thing. This is the spring time
But not in time's covenant. Now the hedgerow
Is blanched for an hour with transitory blossom
Of snow, a bloom more sudden
Than that of summer, neither budding nor fading,
Not in the scheme of generation.
Where is the summer, the unimaginable
Zero summer?

If you came this way,
Taking the route you would be likely to take
From the place where you would be likely to come from,
If you came this way in may time, you would find the hedges
White again, in May, with voluptuary sweetness.
It would be the same at the end of the journey,
If you came at night like a broken king,
If you came by day not knowing what you came for,
It would be the same, when you leave the rough road
And turn behind the pig-sty to the dull façade
And the tombstone. And what you thought you came for
Is only a shell, a husk of meaning
From which the purpose breaks only when it is fulfilled
If at all. Either you had no purpose
Or the purpose is beyond the end you figured
And is altered in fulfilment. There are other places
Which also are the world's end, some at the sea jaws,
Or over a dark lake, in a desert or a city—
But this is the nearest, in place and time,
Now and in England.

If you came this way,
Taking any route, starting from anywhere,
At any time or at any season,
It would always be the same: you would have to put off
Sense and notion. You are not here to verify,
Instruct yourself, or inform curiosity
Or carry report. You are here to kneel
Where prayer has been valid. And prayer is more
Than an order of words, the conscious occupation
Of the praying mind, or the sound of the voice praying.
And what the dead had no speech for, when living,
They can tell you, being dead: the communication
Of the dead is tongued with fire beyond the language of the living.
Here, the intersection of the timeless moment
Is England and nowhere. Never and always.

2

Ash on an old man's sleeve
Is all the ash the burnt roses leave.
Dust in the air suspended
Marks the place where a story ended.
Dust inbreathed was a house—
The wall, the wainscot and the mouse.
The death of hope and despair,
    This is the death of air.

  There are flood and drouth
Over the eyes and in the mouth,
Dead water and dead sand
Contending for the upper hand.
The parched eviscerate soil
Gapes at the vanity of toil,
Laughs without mirth.
    This is the death of earth.

  Water and fire succeed
The town, the pasture and the weed.
Water and fire deride
The sacrifice that we denied.
Water and fire shall rot
The marred foundations we forgot,
Of sanctuary and choir.
    This is the death of water and fire.

  In the uncertain hour before the morning
    Near the ending of interminable night
    At the recurrent end of the unending
After the dark dove with the flickering tongue
  Had passed below the horizon of his homing
  While the dead leaves still rattled on like tin
Over the asphalt where no other sound was
  Between three districts whence the smoke arose
  I met one walking, loitering and hurried

As if blown towards me like the metal leaves
   Before the urban dawn wind unresisting.
   And as I fixed upon the down-turned face
That pointed scrutiny with which we challenge
   The first-met stranger in the waning dusk
   I caught the sudden look of some dead master
Whom I had known, forgotten, half recalled
   Both one and many; in the brown baked features
   The eyes of a familiar compound ghost
Both intimate and unidentifiable.
   So I assumed a double part, and cried
   And heard another's voice cry: "What! are *you* here?"
Although we were not. I was still the same,
   Knowing myself yet being someone other—
   And he a face still forming; yet the words sufficed
To compel the recognition they preceded.
   And so, compliant to the common wind,
   Too strange to each other for misunderstanding,
In concord at this intersection time
   Of meeting nowhere, no before and after,
   We trod the pavement in a dead patrol.
I said: "The wonder that I feel is easy,
   Yet ease is cause of wonder. Therefore speak:
   I may not comprehend, may not remember."
And he: "I am not eager to rehearse
   My thought and theory which you have forgotten.
   These things have served their purpose: let them be.
So with your own, and pray they be forgiven
   By others, as I pray you to forgive
   Both bad and good. Last season's fruit is eaten
And the fullfed beast shall kick the empty pail.
   For last year's words belong to last year's language
   And next year's words await another voice.
But, as the passage now presents no hindrance
   To the spirit unappeased and peregrine
   Between two worlds become much like each other,
So I find words I never thought to speak
   In streets I never thought I should revisit

When I left my body on a distant shore.
Since our concern was speech, and speech impelled us
To purify the dialect of the tribe
And urge the mind to aftersight and foresight,
Let me disclose the gifts reserved for age
To set a crown upon your lifetime's effort.
First, the cold friction of expiring sense
Without enchantment, offering no promise
But bitter tastelessness of shadow fruit
As body and soul begin to fall asunder.
Second, the conscious impotence of rage
At human folly, and the laceration
Of laughter at what ceases to amuse.
And last, the rending pain of re-enactment
Of all that you have done, and been; the shame
Of motives late revealed, and the awareness
Of things ill done and done to others' harm
Which once you took for exercise of virtue.
Then fools' approval stings, and honour stains.
From wrong to wrong the exasperated spirit
Proceeds, unless restored by that refining fire
Where you must move in measure, like a dancer."
The day was breaking. In the disfigured street
He left me, with a kind of valediction,
And faded on the blowing of the horn.

3

There are three conditions which often look alike
Yet differ completely, flourish in the same hedgerow:
Attachment to self and to things and to persons, detachment
From self and from things and from persons; and, growing
between them, indifference
Which resembles the others as death resembles life,
Being between two lives—unflowering, between
The live and the dead nettle. This is the use of memory:
For liberation—not less of love but expanding
Of love beyond desire, and so liberation

From the future as well as the past. Thus, love of a country
Begins as attachment to our own field of action
And comes to find that action of little importance
Though never indifferent. History may be servitude,
History may be freedom. See, now they vanish,
The faces and places, with the self which, as it could, loved them,
To become renewed, transfigured, in another pattern.

Sin is Behovely, but
All shall be well, and
All manner of thing shall be well.
If I think, again, of this place,
And of people, not wholly commendable,
Of no immediate kin or kindness,
But some of peculiar genius,
All touched by a common genius,
United in the strife which divided them;
If I think of a king at nightfall,
Of three men, and more, on the scaffold
And a few who died forgotten
In other places, here and abroad,
And of one who died blind and quiet,
Why should we celebrate
These dead men more than the dying?
It is not to ring the bell backward
Nor is it an incantation
To summon the spectre of a Rose.
We cannot revive old factions
We cannot restore old policies
Or follow an antique drum.
These men, and those who opposed them
And those whom they opposed
Accept the constitution of silence
And are folded in a single party.
Whatever we inherit from the fortunate
We have taken from the defeated
What they had to leave us—a symbol:

A symbol perfected in death.
And all shall be well and
All manner of thing shall be well
By the purification of the motive
In the ground of our beseeching.

4

The dove descending breaks the air
With flame of incandescent terror
Of which the tongues declare
The one discharge from sin and error.
The only hope, or else despair
  Lies in the choice of pyre or pyre—
  To be redeemed from fire by fire.

  Who then devised the torment? Love.
Love is the unfamiliar Name
Behind the hands that wove
The intolerable shirt of flame
Which human power cannot remove.
  We only live, only suspire
  Consumed by either fire or fire.

5

What we call the beginning is often the end
And to make an end is to make a beginning.
The end is where we start from. And every phrase
And sentence that is right (where every word is at home,
Taking its place to support the others,
The word neither diffident nor ostentatious,
An easy commerce of the old and the new,
The common word exact without vulgarity,
The formal work precise but not pedantic,
The complete consort dancing together)
Every phrase and every sentence is an end and a beginning,
Every poem an epitaph. And any action

Is a step to the block, to the fire, down the sea's throat
Or to an illegible stone: and that is where we start.
We die with the dying:
See, they depart, and we go with them.
We are born with the dead:
See, they return, and bring us with them.
The moment of the rose and the moment of the yew-tree
Are of equal duration. A people without history
Is not redeemed from time, for history is a pattern
Of timeless moments. So, while the light fails
On a winter's afternoon, in a secluded chapel
History is now and England.
With the drawing of this Love and the voice of this Calling

We shall not cease from exploration
And the end of all our exploring
Will be to arrive where we started
And know the place for the first time.
Through the unknown, remembered gate
When the last of earth left to discover
Is that which was the beginning;
At the source of the longest river
The voice of the hidden waterfall
And the children in the apple-tree
Not known, because not looked for
But heard, half-heard, in the stillness
Between two waves of the sea.
Quick now, here, now, always—
A condition of complete simplicity
(Costing not less than everything)
And all shall be well and
All manner of thing shall be well
When the tongues of flame are in-folded
Into the crowned knot of fire
And the fire and the rose are one.

Harold Monro

Bitter Sanctuary

I

She lives in the porter's room; the plush is nicotined.
Clients have left their photos there to perish.
She watches through green shutters those who press
To reach unconsciousness.
She licks her varnished thin magenta lips,
She picks her foretooth with her finger nail,
She pokes her head out to greet new clients, or
To leave them (to what torture) waiting at the door.

II

Heat has locked the heavy earth,
Given strength to every sound.
He, where his life still holds him to the ground,
In anaesthesia, groaning for re-birth,
Leans at the door.
From out the house there comes the dullest flutter;
A lackey; and thin giggling from behind that shutter.

III

His lost eyes lean to find the number.
Follows his knuckled rap, and hesitating curse.
He cannot wake himself; he may not slumber;
While on the long white wall across the road
Drives the thin outline of a dwindling hearse.

IV

Now the door opens wide.

HE: "Is there room inside?"
SHE: "Are you past the bounds of pain?"
HE: "May my body lie in vain
Among the dreams I cannot keep!"
SHE: "Let him drink the cup of sleep."

V

Thin arms and ghostly hands; faint sky-blue eyes;
Long drooping lashes, lids like full-blown moons,
Clinging to any brink of floating skies:
What hope is there? What fear?—Unless to wake and see
Lingering flesh, or cold eternity.

O yet some face, half living, brings
Far gaze to him and croons—
SHE: "You're white. You are alone.
Can you not approach my sphere?"
HE: "I'm changing into stone."
SHE: "Would I were! Would *I* were!"
Then the white attendants fill the cup.

VI

In the morning through the world,
Watch the flunkeys bring the coffee;
Watch the shepherds on the downs,
Lords and ladies at their toilet,
Farmers, merchants, frothing towns.

But look how he, unfortunate, now fumbles
Through unknown chambers, and unheedful stumbles.
Can he evade the overshadowing night?
Are there not somewhere chinks of braided light?

VII

How do they leave who once are in those rooms?
Some may be found, they say, deeply asleep
In ruined tombs.
Some in white beds, with faces round them. Some
Wander the world, and never find a home.

Conrad Aiken

Prelude XIV

—You went to the verge, you say, and come back safely?
Some have not been so fortunate, —some have fallen.
Children go lightly there, from crag to crag,
And coign to coign, —where even the goat is wary,—
And make a sport of it. . . . They fling down pebbles,
Following, with eyes undizzied, the long curve,
The long slow outward curve, into the abyss,
As far as eye can follow; and they themselves
Turn back, unworried, to the here and now. . . .
But you have been there, too?—

—I saw at length
The space-defying pine, that on the last
Outjutting rock has cramped its powerful roots.
There stood I too: under that tree I stood:
My hand against its resinous bark: my face
Turned out and downward to the fourfold kingdom.
The wind roared from all quarters. The waterfall
Came down, it seemed, from Heaven. The mighty sound
Of pouring elements, —earth, air, and water,—
The cry of eagles, chatter of falling stones,—
These were the frightful language of that place.
I understood it ill, but understood.—

—You understood it? Tell me, then, its meaning.
It was an all, a nothing, or a something?
Chaos, or divine love, or emptiness?
Water and earth and air and the sun's fire?
Or else, a question, simply?—

—Water and fire were there,
And air and earth; there too was emptiness;
All, and nothing, and something too, and love.
But these poor words, these squeaks of ours, in which
We strive to mimic, with strained throats and tongues,
The spawning and outrageous elements—
Alas, how paltry are they! For I saw—

—What did you see?

—I saw myself and God.
I saw the ruin in which godhead lives:
Shapeless and vast: the strewn wreck of the world:
Sadness unplumbed: misery without bound.
Wailing I heard, but also I heard joy.
Wreckage I saw, but also I saw flowers.
Hatred I saw, but also I saw love. . . .
And thus, I saw myself.

—And this alone?

—And this alone awaits you, when you dare
To that sheer verge where horror hangs, and tremble
Against the falling rock; and, looking down,
Search the dark kingdom. It is to self you come,—
And that is God. It is the seed of seeds:
Seed for disastrous and immortal worlds.

It is the answer that no question asked,

Prelude XXIX

What shall we do—what shall we think—what shall we say—?
Why, as the crocus does, on a March morning,
With just such shape and brightness; such fragility;
Such white and gold, and out of just such earth.

Or as the cloud does on the northeast wind—
Fluent and formless; or as the tree that withers.
What are we made of, strumpet, but of these?
Nothing. We are the sum of all these accidents—
Compounded all our days of idiot trifles,—
The this, the that, the other, and the next;
What x or y said, or old uncle thought;
Whether it rained or not, and at what hour;
Whether the pudding had two eggs or three,
And those we loved were ladies. . . . Were they ladies?
And did they read the proper books, and simper
With proper persons, at the proper teas

O Christ and God and all deciduous things—
Let us void out this nonsense and be healed.

There is no doubt that we shall do, as always,
Just what the crocus does. There is no doubt
Your Helen of Troy is all that she has seen,—
All filth, all beauty, all honor and deceit.
The spider's web will hang in her bright mind,—
The dead fly died there doubly; and the rat
Find sewers to his liking. She will walk
In such a world as this alone could give—
This of the moment, this mad world of mirrors
And of corrosive memory. She will know
The lecheries of the cockroach and the worm,
The chemistry of the sunset, the foul seeds
Laid by the intellect in the simple heart. . . .
And knowing all these things, she will be she.

She will be also the sunrise on the grassblade—
But pay no heed to that. She will be also
The infinite tenderness of the voice of morning—
But pay no heed to that. She will be also
The grain of elmwood, and the ply of water,
Whirlings in sand and smoke, wind in the ferns,
The fixed bright eyes of dolls. . . . And this is all.

CONRAD AIKEN

Prelude LVI

Rimbaud and Verlaine, precious pair of poets,
Genius in both (but what is genius?) playing
Chess on a marble table at an inn
With chestnut blossom falling in blond beer
And on their hair and between knight and bishop—
Sunlight squared between them on the chess-board
Cirrus in heaven, and a squeal of music
Blown from the leathern door of Ste. Sulpice—

Discussing, between moves, iamb and spondee
Anacoluthon and the open vowel
God the great peacock with his angel peacocks
And his dependent peacocks the bright stars:
Disputing too of fate as Plato loved it,
Or Sophocles, who hated and admired,
Or Socrates, who loved and was amused:

Verlaine puts down his pawn upon a leaf
And closes his long eyes, which are dishonest,
And says "Rimbaud, there is one thing to do:
We must take rhetoric, and wring its neck!..."

Rimbaud considers gravely, moves his Queen;
And then removes himself to Timbuctoo.

And Verlaine dead, —with all his jades and mauves;
And Rimbauld dead in Marseilles with a vision,
His leg cut off, as once before his heart;
And all reported by a later lackey,
Whose virtue is his tardiness in time.

Let us describe the evening as it is:—
The stars disposed in heaven as they are:
Verlaine and Shakspere rotting, where they rot,
Rimbaud remembered, and too soon forgot;

Order in all things, logic in the dark;
Arrangement in the atom and the spark;
Time in the heart and sequence in the brain—

Such as destroyed Rimbaud and fooled Verlaine.
And let us then take godhead by the neck—

And strangle it, and with it, rhetoric.

H. D.

Evening

The light passes
from ridge to ridge,
from flower to flower—
the hypaticas, wide-spread
under the light
grow faint—
the petals reach inward,
the blue tips bend
toward the bluer heart
and the flowers are lost.

The cornel-buds are still white,
but shadows dart
from the cornel-roots—
black creeps from root to root
each leaf
cuts another leaf on the grass,
shadow seeks shadow,
then both leaf
and leaf-shadow are lost.

Sea Rose

Rose, harsh rose,
marred and with stint of petals,
meagre flower, thin,
sparse of leaf,
More precious
than a wet rose
single on a stem—
you are caught in the drift.

Stunted, with small leaf,
you are flung on the sand,
you are lifted
in the crisp sand
that drives in the wind.

Can the spice-rose
drip such acrid fragrance
hardened in a leaf?

from The Flowering of the Rod

10

It is no madness to say
you will fall, you great cities,

(now the cities lie broken);
it is not tragedy, prophecy

from a frozen Priestess,
a lonely Pythoness

who chants, who sings
in broken hexameters,

doom, doom to city-gates,
to rulers, to kingdoms;

it is simple reckoning, algebraic,
it is geometry on the wing,

not patterned, a gentian
in an ice-mirror,

yet it is, if you like, a lily
folded like a pyramid,

a flower-cone,
not a heap of skulls;

it is a lily, if you will,
each petal, a kingdom, an aeon,

and it is the seed of a lily
that having flowered,

will flower again;
it is that smallest grain,

the least of all seeds
that grows branches

where the birds rest;
it is that flowering balm,

it is heal-all,
everlasting;

it is the greatest among herbs
and becometh a tree.

Marianne Moore

The Steeple-Jack

Dürer would have seen a reason for living
  in a town like this, with eight stranded whales
to look at; with the sweet sea air coming into your house
on a fine day, from water etched
  with waves as formal as the scales
on a fish.

One by one, in two's, in three's, the seagulls keep
  flying back and forth over the town clock,
or sailing around the lighthouse without moving the wings—
rising steadily with a slight
  quiver of the body—or flock
mewing where

a sea the purple of the peacock's neck is
  paled to greenish azure as Dürer changed
the pine green of the Tyrol to peacock blue and guinea
grey. You can see a twenty-five-
  pound lobster; and fishnets arranged
to dry. The

whirlwind fife-and-drum of the storm bends the salt
  marsh grass, disturbs stars in the sky and the
star on the steeple; it is a privilege to see so
much confusion. Disguised by what
  might seem austerity, the sea-
side flowers and

trees are favoured by the fog so that you have
   the tropics at first hand: the trumpet-vine,
fox-glove, giant snap-dragon, a salpiglossis that has
spots and stripes; morning-glories, gourds,
   or moon-vines trained on fishing-twine
at the back

door. There are no banyans, frangipani, nor
   jack-fruit trees; nor an exotic serpent
life. Ring lizard and snake-skin for the foot, or crocodile;
but here they've cats, not cobras, to
   keep down the rats. The diffident
little newt

with white pin-dots on black horizontal spaced
   out bands lives here; yet there is nothing that
ambition can buy or take away. The college student
named Ambrose sits on the hill-side
   with his not-native books and hat
and sees boats

at sea progress white and rigid as if in
   a groove. Liking an elegance of which
the source is not bravado, he knows by heart the antique
sugar-bowl-shaped summer-house of
   interlacing slats, and the pitch
of the church

spire, not true, from which a man in scarlet lets
   down a rope as a spider spins a thread;
he might be part of a novel, but on the sidewalk a
sign says C. J. Poole, Steeple Jack,
   in black and white; and one in red
and white says

Danger. The church portico has four fluted
   columns, each a single piece of stone, made
modester by white-wash. This would be a fit haven for
waifs, children, animals, prisoners,
   and presidents who have repaid
sin-driven

senators by not thinking about them. There
   are a school-house, a post-office in a
store, fish-houses, hen-houses, a three-masted schooner on
the stocks. The hero, the student,
   the steeple-jack, each in his way,
is at home.

It could not be dangerous to be living
   in a town like this, of simple people,
who have a steeple-jack placing danger signs by the church
while he is gilding the solid-
   pointed star, which on a steeple
stands for hope.

Black Earth

Openly, yes,
with the naturalness
   of the hippopotamus or the alligator
   when it climbs out on the bank to experience the

sun, I do these
things which I do, which please
   no one but myself. Now I breathe and now I am sub-
   merged; the blemishes stand up and shout when the object
in view was a
renaissance; shall I say
   the contrary? The sediment of the river which
   encrusts my joints, makes me very gray but I am used

to it, it may
remain there; do away
  with it and I am myself done away with, for the
  patina of circumstance can but enrich what was

there to begin
with. This elephant-skin
  which I inhabit, fibred over like the shell of
  the cocoanut, this piece of black grass through which no
  light

can filter—cut
into checkers by rut
  upon rut of unpreventable experience—
  it is a manual for the peanut-tongued and the

hairy-toed. Black
but beautiful, my back
  is full of the history of power. Of power? What
  is powerful and what is not? My soul shall never

be cut into
by a wooden spear; through-
  out childhood to the present time, the unity of
  life and death has been expressed by the circumference

described by my
trunk; nevertheless I
  perceive feats of strength to be inexplicable after
  all; and I am on my guard; external poise, it

has its centre
well nurtured—we know
  where—in pride; but spiritual poise, it has its centre where?
  My ears are sensitized to more than the sound of

the wind. I see
and I hear, unlike the
   wandlike body of which one hears so much, which was made
   to see and not to see; to hear and not to hear;

that tree-trunk without
roots, accustomed to shout
   its own thoughts to itself like a shell, maintained intact
   by who knows what strange pressure of the atmosphere; that

spiritual
brother to the coral-
   plant, absorbed into which, the equable sapphire light
   becomes a nebulous green. The I of each is to

the I of each
a kind of fretful speech
   which sets a limit on itself; the elephant is
   black earth preceded by a tendril? Compared with those

phenomena
which vacillate like a
   translucence of the atmosphere, the elephant is
   that on which darts cannot strike decisively the first

time, a substance
needful as an instance
   of the indestructibility of matter; it
   has looked at the electricity and at the earth-

quake and is still
here; the name means thick. Will
   depth be depth, thick skin be thick, to one who can see no
   beautiful elements of unreason under it?

MARIANNE MOORE

To a Steam Roller

The illustration
is nothing to you without the application.
  You lack half wit. You crush all the particles down
    into close conformity, and then walk back and
      forth on them.

Sparkling chips of rock
are crushed down to the level of the parent block.
  Were not "impersonal judgment in aesthetic
    matters, a metaphysical impossibility", you

might fairly achieve
it. As for butterflies, I can hardly conceive
  of one's attending upon you, but to question
    the congruence of the complement is vain, if it
      exists.

To a Snail

If "compression is the first grace of style",
you have it. Contractility is a virtue
as modesty is a virtue.
It is not the acquisition of any one thing
that is able to adorn,
or the incidental quality that occurs
as a concomitant of something well said,
that we value in style,
but the principle that is hid:
in the absence of feet, "a method of conclusions";
"a knowledge of principles",
in the curious phenomenon of your occipital horn.

Silence

My father used to say,
"Superior people never make long visits,
have to be shown Longfellow's grave
or the glass flowers at Harvard.
Self-reliant like the cat—
that takes its prey to privacy,
the mouse's limp tail hanging like a shoelace from its mouth—
they sometimes enjoy solitude,
and can be robbed of speech
by speech which has delighted them.
The deepest feeling always shows itself in silence;
not in silence, but restraint".
Nor was he insincere in saying, "Make my house your inn".
Inns are not residences.

Wallace Stevens

Tea at the Palaz of Hoon

Not less because in purple I descended
The western day through what you called
The loneliest air, not less was I myself.

What was the ointment sprinkled on my beard?
What were the hymns that buzzed beside my ears?
What was the sea whose tide swept through me there?

Out of my mind the golden ointment rained,
And my ears made the blowing hymns they heard.
I was myself the compass of that sea:

I was the world in which I walked, and what I saw
Or heard or felt came not but from myself;
And there I found myself more truly and more strange.

The Emperor of Ice-Cream

Call the roller of big cigars,
The muscular one, and bid him whip
In kitchen cups concupiscent curds.
Let the wenches dawdle in such dress
As they are used to wear, and let the boys
Bring flowers in last month's newspapers.
Let be be finale of seem.
The only emperor is the emperor of ice-cream.

Take from the dresser of deal,
Lacking the three glass knobs, that sheet
On which she embroidered fantails once
And spread it so as to cover her face.
If her horny feet protrude, they come
To show how cold she is, and dumb.
Let the lamp affix its beam.
The only emperor is the emperor of ice-cream.

Asides on the Oboe

The prologues are over. It is a question, now,
Of final belief. So, say that final belief
Must be in a fiction. It is time to choose.

I

That obsolete fiction of the wide river in
An empty land; the gods that Boucher killed;
And the metal heroes that time granulates—
The philosophers' man alone still walks in dew,
Still by the sea-side mutters milky lines
Concerning an immaculate imagery.
If you say on the hautboy man is not enough,
Can never stand as god, is ever wrong
In the end, however naked, tall, there is still
The impossible possible philosophers' man,
The man who has had the time to think enough,
The central man, the human globe, responsive
As a mirror with a voice, the man of glass,
Who in a million diamonds sums us up.

II

He is the transparence of the place in which
He is and in his poems we find peace.
He sets this peddler's pie and cries in summer,
The glass man, cold and numbered, dewily cries,
"Thou art not August unless I make thee so."
Clandestine steps upon imagined stairs
Climb through the night, because his cuckoos call.

III

One year, death and war prevented the jasmine scent
And the jasmine islands were bloody martyrdoms.
How was it then with the central man? Did we
Find peace? We found the sum of men. We found,
If we found the central evil, the central good.
We buried the fallen without jasmine crowns.
There was nothing he did not suffer, no; nor we.

It was not as if the jasmine ever returned.
But we and the diamond globe at last were one.
We had always been partly one. It was as we came
To see him, that we were wholly one, as we heard
Mim chanting for those buried in their blood,
In the jasmine haunted forests, that we knew
The glass man, without external reference.

The Owl in the Sarcophagus

I

Two forms move among the dead, high sleep
Who by his highness quiets them, high peace
Upon whose shoulders even the heavens rest,

Two brothers. And a third form, she that says
Good-by in the darkness, speaking quietly there,
To those that cannot say good-by themselves.

These forms are visible to the eye that needs,
Needs out of the whole necessity of sight.
The third form speaks, because the ear repeats,

Without a voice, inventions of farewell.
These forms are not abortive figures, rocks,
Impenetrable symbols, motionless. They move

About the night. They live without our light,
In an element not the heaviness of time,
In which reality is prodigy.

There sleep the brother is the father, too,
And peace is cousin by a hundred names
And she that in the syllable between life

And death cries quickly, in a flash of voice,
Keep you, keep you, I am gone, oh keep you as
My memory, is the mother of us all,

The earthly mother and the mother of
The dead. Only the thought of those dark three
Is dark, thought of the forms of dark desire.

II

There came a day, there was a day—one day
A man walked living among the forms of thought
To see their lustre truly as it is

And in harmonious prodigy to be,
A while, conceiving his passage as into a time
That of itself stood still, perennial,

Less time than place, less place than thought of place
And, if of substance, a likeness of the earth,
That by resemblance twanged him through and through,

Releasing an abysmal melody,
A meeting, an emerging in the light,
A dazzle of remembrance and of sight.

III

There he saw well the foldings in the height
Of sleep, the whiteness folded into less,
Like many robings, as moving masses are,

As a moving mountain is, moving through day
And night, colored from distances, central
Where luminous agitations come to rest,

In an ever-changing, calmest unity,
The unique composure, harshest streakings joined
In a vanishing-vanished violet that wraps round

The giant body the meanings of its folds,
The weaving and the crinkling and the vex,
As on water of an afternoon in the wind

After the wind has passed. Sleep realized
Was the whiteness that is the ultimate intellect,
A diamond jubilance beyond the fire,

That gives its power to the wild-ringed eye.
Then he breathed deeply the deep atmosphere
Of sleep, the accomplished, the fulfilling air.

IV

There peace, the godolphin and fellow, estranged, estranged,
Hewn in their middle as the beam of leaves,
The prince of shither-shade and tinsel lights,

Stood flourishing the world. The brilliant height
And hollow of him by its brilliance calmed,
Its brightness burned the way good solace seethes.

This was peace after death, the brother of sleep,
The inhuman brother so much like, so near,
Yet vested in a foreign absolute,

Adorned with cryptic stones and sliding shines,
An immaculate personage in nothingness,
With the whole spirit sparkling in its cloth,

Generations of the imagination piled
In the manner of its stitchings, of its thread,
In the weaving round the wonder of its need,

And the first flowers upon it, an alphabet
By which to spell out holy doom and end,
A bee for the remembering of happiness.

Peace stood with our last blood adorned, last mind,
Damasked in the originals of green,
A thousand begettings of the broken bold.

This is that figure stationed at our end,
Always, in brilliance, fatal, final, formed
Out of our lives to keep us in our death,

To watch us in the summer of Cyclops
Underground, a king as candle by our beds
In a robe that is our glory as he guards.

V

But she that says good-by losing in self
The sense of self, rosed out of prestiges
Of rose, stood tall in self not symbol, quick

And potent, an influence felt instead of seen.
She spoke with backward gestures of her hand.
She held men closely with discovery,

Almost as speed discovers, in the way
Invisible change discovers what is changed,
In the way what was has ceased to be what is.

It was not her look but a knowledge that she had.
She was a self that knew, an inner thing,
Subtler than look's declaiming, although she moved

With a sad splendor, beyond artifice,
Impassioned by the knowledge that she had,
There on the edges of oblivion.

O exhalation, O fling without a sleeve
And motion outward, reddened and resolved
From sight, in the silence that follows her last word—

VI

This is the mythology of modern death
And these, in their mufflings, monsters of elegy,
Of their own marvel made, of pity made,

Compounded and compounded, life by life,
These are death's own supremest images,
The pure perfections of parental space,

The children of a desire that is the will,
Even of death, the beings of the mind
In the light-bound space of the mind, the floreate flare . . .

It is a child that sings itself to sleep,
The mind, among the creatures that it makes,
The people, those by which it lives and dies.

Hugh MacDiarmid

On the Ocean Floor

Now more and more on my concern with the lifted waves of
genius gaining
I am aware of the lightless depths that beneath them lie;
And as one who hears their tiny shells incessantly raining
On the ocean floor as the foraminifera die.

from In the Fall

Let the only consistency
In the course of my poetry
Be like that of the hawthorn tree
Which in early spring breaks
Fresh emerald, then by nature's law
Darkens and deepens and takes
Tints of purple-maroon, rose-madder and straw.

Cattle Show

I shall go among red faces and virile voices,
See stylish sheep, with fine heads and well-wooled,
And great bulls mellow to the touch,
Brood mares of marvellous approach, and geldings
With sharp and flinty bones and silken hair.

And through th'enclosure draped in red and gold
I shall pass on to spheres more vivid yet
Where countesses' coque feathers gleam and glow
And, swathed in silks, the painted ladies are
Whose laughter plays like summer lightning there.

Facing the Chair

Here under the radiant rays of the sun
Where everything grows so vividly
In the human mind and in the heart,
Love, life, and all else so beautifully,
I think again of men as innocent as I am
Pent in a cold unjust walk between steel bars,
Their trousers slit for the electrodes
And their hair cut for the cap

Because of the unconcern of men and women,
Respectable and respected and professedly Christian,
Idle-busy among the flowers of their gardens here
Under the gay-tipped rays of the sun,
And I am suddenly completely bereft
Of *la grande amitié des choses crées*,
The unity of life which can only be forged by love.

The Royal Stag

The hornless hart carries off the harem.
Magnificent antlers are nothing in love.
Great tines are only a drawback and danger
To the noble stag that must bear them.

Crowned as with an oak tree he goes,
A sacrifice for the ruck of his race,
Knowing full well that his towering points
Single him out, a mark for his foes.

Yet no polled head's triumphs since the world began
In love or war have made a high heart thrill
Like the sight of a Royal with its Rights and Crockets,
Its Pearls, and Beam, and Span.

D. H. Lawrence

End of Another Home Holiday

When shall I see the half-moon sink again
Behind the black sycamore at the end of the garden?
When will the scent of the dim white phlox
Creep up the wall to me, and in at my open window?

Why is it, the long, slow stroke of the midnight bell
(Will it never finish the twelve?)
Falls again and again on my heart with a heavy reproach?

The moon-mist is over the village, out of the mist speaks the bell,
And all the little roofs of the village bow low, pitiful, beseeching, resigned.
—Speak, you my home! What is it I don't do well?

Ah home, suddenly I love you
As I hear the sharp clean trot of a pony down the road,
Succeeding sharp little sounds dropping into silence
Clear upon the long-drawn hoarseness of a train across the valley.

* * *

The light has gone out, from under my mother's door.
That she should love me so!—
She, so lonely, greying now!
And I leaving her,
Bent on my pursuits!

Love is the great Asker.
The sun and the rain do not ask the secret
Of the time when the grain struggles down in the
dark.
The moon walks her lonely way without anguish,
Because no-one grieves over her departure.

Forever, ever by my shoulder pitiful love will linger,
Crouching as little houses crouch under the mist when I turn.
Forever, out of the mist, the church lifts up a reproachful
finger,
Pointing my eyes in wretched defiance where love hides her
face to mourn.

Oh! but the rain creeps down to wet the grain
That struggles alone in the dark,
And asking nothing, patiently steals back again!
The moon sets forth o' nights
To walk the lonely, dusky heights
Serenely, with steps unswerving;
Pursued by no sign of bereavement,
No tears of love unnerving
Her constant tread:
While ever at my side,
Frail and sad, with grey, bowed head,
The beggar-woman, the yearning-eyed
Inexorable love goes lagging.

The wild young heifer, glancing distraught,
With a strange new knocking of life at her side
Runs seeking a loneliness.
The little grain draws down the earth, to hide.
Nay, even the slumberous egg, as it labours under the
shell
Patiently to divide and self-divide,
Asks to be hidden, and wishes nothing to tell.

But when I draw the scanty cloak of silence over my eyes
Piteous love comes peering under the hood;
Touches the clasp with trembling fingers, and tries
To put her ear to the painful sob of my blood;
While her tears soak through to my breast,
  Where they burn and cauterise.

* * *

The moon lies back and reddens.
In the valley a corncrake calls
  Monotonously,
With a plaintive, unalterable voice, that deadens
  My confident activity;
With a hoarse, insistent request that falls
  Unweariedly, unweariedly,
  Asking something more of me,
    Yet more of me.

Song of a Man who Has Come Through

Not I, not I, but the wind that blows through me!
A fine wind is blowing the new direction of Time.
If only I let it bear me, carry me, if only it carry me!
If only I am sensitive, subtle, oh, delicate, a winged gift!
If only, most lovely of all, I yield myself and am borrowed

By the fine, fine wind that takes its course through the chaos of
  the world
Like a fine, an exquisite chisel, a wedge-blade inserted;
If only I am keen and hard like the sheer tip of a wedge
Driven by invisible blows,
The rock will split, we shall come at the wonder, we shall find
  the Hesperides.

Oh, for the wonder that bubbles into my soul,
I would be a good fountain, a good well-head,
Would blur no whisper, spoil no expression.

What is the knocking?
What is the knocking at the door in the night?
It is somebody wants to do us harm.

No, no, it is the three strange angels.
Admit them, admit them.

Snake

A snake came to my water-trough
On a hot, hot day, and I in pyjamas for the heat,
To drink there.

In the deep, strange-scented shade of the great dark carob-tree
I came down the steps with my pitcher
And must wait, must stand and wait, for there he was at the
 trough before me.

He reached down from a fissure in the earth-wall in the gloom
And trailed his yellow-brown slackness soft-bellied down, over
 the edge of the stone trough
And rested his throat upon the stone bottom,
And where the water had dripped from the tap, in a small
 clearness,
He sipped with his straight mouth,
Softly drank through his straight gums, into his slack long
 body,
Silently.

Someone was before me at my water-trough,
And I, like a second comer, waiting.

He lifted his head from his drinking, as cattle do,
And looked at me vaguely, as drinking cattle do,
And flickered his two-forked tongue from his lips, and mused a
    moment,
And stooped and drank a little more,
Being earth-brown, earth-golden from the burning bowels of
    the earth
On the day of Sicilian July, with Etna smoking.

The voice of my education said to me
He must be killed,
For in Sicily the black, black snakes are innocent, the gold are
    venomous.

And voices in me said, If you were a man
You would take a stick and break him now, and finish him off.

But must I confess how I liked him,
How glad I was he had come like a guest in quiet, to drink at
    my water-trough
And depart peaceful, pacified, and thankless,
Into the burning bowels of this earth?

Was it cowardice, that I dared not kill him?
Was it perversity, that I longed to talk to him?

Was it humility, to feel so honoured?
I felt so honoured.

And yet those voices:
If you were not afraid, you would kill him!

And truly I was afraid, I was most afraid,
But even so, honoured still more
That he should seek my hospitality
From out the dark door of the secret earth.

He drank enough
And lifted his head, dreamily, as one who has drunken,
And flickered his tongue like a forked night on the air, so
black,
Seeming to lick his lips,
And looked around like a god, unseeing, into the air,
And slowly turned his head,
And slowly, very slowly, as if thrice adream,
Proceeded to draw his slow length curving round
And climb again the broken bank of my wall-face.

And as he put his head into that dreadful hole,
And as he slowly drew up, snake-easing his shoulders,
and entered farther,
A sort of horror, a sort of protest against his with-
drawing into that horrid black hole,
Deliberately going into the blackness, and slowly
drawing himself after,
Overcame me now his back was turned.

I looked round, I put down my pitcher,
I picked up a clumsy log
And threw it at the water-trough with a clatter.

I think it did not hit him,
But suddenly that part of him that was left behind convulsed in
undignified haste,
Writhed like lightning, and was gone
Into the black hole, the earth-lipped fissure in the wall-front,
At which, in the intense still noon, I stared with fascination.

And immediately I regretted it.
I thought how paltry, how vulgar, what a mean act!
I despised myself and the voices of my accursed human
education.

And I thought of the albatross,
And I wished he would come back, my snake.

For he seemed to me again like a king,
Like a king in exile, uncrowned in the underworld,
Now due to be crowned again.

And so, I missed my chance with one of the lords
Of life.
And I have something to expiate;
A pettiness.

Taormina

Bavarian Gentians

Not every man has gentians in his house
in Soft September, at slow, Sad Michaelmas.

Bavarian gentians, big and dark, only dark
darkening the day-time torch-like with the smoking blueness of
  Pluto's gloom,
ribbed and torch-like, with their blaze of darkness spread blue
down flattening into points, flattened under the sweep of white
  day
torch-flower of the blue-smoking darkness, Pluto's dark-blue
  daze,
black lamps from the halls of Dio, burning dark blue,
giving off darkness, blue darkness, as Demeter's pale lamps
  give off light,
lead me then, lead me the way.

Reach me a gentian, give me a torch
let me guide myself with the blue, forked torch of this flower
down the darker and darker stairs, where blue is darkened on
  blueness.
even where Persephone goes, just now, from the frosted
  September

to the sightless realm where darkness is awake upon the dark
and Persephone herself is but a voice
or a darkness invisible enfolded in the deeper dark
of the arms Plutonic, and pierced with the passion of dense
 gloom,
among the splendour of torches of darkness, shedding darkness
 on the lost bride and her groom.

Isaac Rosenberg

Returning, We Hear the Larks

Sombre the night is:
And, though we have our lives, we know
What sinister threat lurks there.

Dragging these anguished limbs, we only know
This poison-blasted track opens on our camp—
On a little safe sleep.

But hark! Joy—joy—strange joy.
Lo! Heights of night ringing with unseen larks:
Music showering on our upturned listening faces.

Death could drop from the dark
As easily as song—
But song only dropped,
Like a blind man's dreams on the sand
By dangerous tides;
Like a girl's dark hair, for she dreams no ruin lies there,
Or her kisses where a serpent hides.

The Burning of the Temple

Fierce wrath of Solomon,
Where sleepest thou? O see,
The fabric which thou won
Earth and ocean to give thee—
O look at the red skies.

Or hath the sun plunged down?
What is this molten gold—
These thundering fires blown
Through heaven, where the smoke rolled?
Again the great king dies.

His dreams go out in smoke.
His days he let not pass
And sculptured here are broke,
Are charred as the burnt grass,
Gone as his mouth's last sighs.

Dead Man's Dump

The plunging limbers over the shattered track
Racketed with their rusty freight,
Stuck out like many crowns of thorns,
And the rusty stakes like sceptres old
To stay the flood of brutish men
Upon our brothers dear.

The wheels lurched over sprawled dead
But pained them not, though their bones crunched;
Their shut mouths made no moan.
They lie there huddled, friend and foeman,
Man born of man, and born of woman;
And shells go crying over them
From night till night and now.

Earth has waited for them,
All the time of their growth
Fretting for their decay:
Now she has them at last!
In the strength of their strength
Suspended—stopped and held.

What fierce imaginings their dark souls lit?
Earth! Have they gone into you?
Somewhere they must have gone,
And flung on your hard back
Is their souls' sack,
Emptied of God-ancestralled essences.
Who hurled them out? Who hurled?

None saw their spirits' shadow shake the grass,
Or stood aside for the half used life to pass
Out of those doomed nostrils and the doomed mouth,
When the swift iron burning bee
Drained the wild honey of their youth.

What of us who, flung on the shrieking pyre,
Walk, our usual thoughts untouched,
Our lucky limbs as on ichor fed,
Immortal seeming ever?
Perhaps when the flames beat loud on us,
A fear may choke in our veins
And the startled blood may stop.

The air is loud with death,
The dark air spurts with fire,
The explosions ceaseless are.
Timelessly now, some minutes past,
These dead strode time with vigorous life,
Till the shrapnel called "An end!"
But not to all. In bleeding pangs
Some borne on stretchers dreamed of home,
Dear things, war-blotted from their hearts.

A man's brains splattered on
A stretcher-bearer's face;
His shook shoulders slipped their load,
But when they bent to look again
The drowning soul was sunk too deep
For human tenderness.

They left this dead with the older dead,
Stretched at the cross roads.
Burnt black by strange decay
Their sinister faces lie,
The lid over each eye;
The grass and coloured clay
More motion have than they,
Joined to the great sunk silences.

Here is one not long dead.
His dark hearing caught our far wheels,
And the choked soul stretched weak hands
To reach the living word the far wheels said;
The blood-dazed intelligence beating for light,
Crying through the suspense of the far torturing wheels
Swift for the end to break
Or the wheels to break,
Cried as the tide of the world broke over his sight,
"Will they come? Will they ever come?"
Even as the mixed hoofs of the mules,
The quivering-bellied mules,
And the rushing wheels all mixed
With his tortured upturned sight.

So we crashed round the bend,
We heard his weak scream,
We heard his very last sound,
And our wheels grazed his dead face.

Break of Day in the Trenches

The darkness crumbles away—
It is the same old druid Time as ever.
Only a live thing leaps my hand—
A queer sardonic rat—

ISAAC ROSENBERG

As I pull the parapet's poppy
To stick behind my ear.
Droll rat, they would shoot you if they knew
Your cosmopolitan sympathies
(And God knows what antipathies).
Now you have touched this English hand
You will do the same to a German—
Soon, no doubt, if it be your pleasure
To cross the sleeping green between.
It seems you inwardly grin as you pass
Strong eyes, fine limbs, haughty athletes
Less chanced than you for life,
Bonds to the whims of murder,
Sprawled in the bowels of the earth,
The torn fields of France.
What do you see in our eyes
At the shrieking iron and flame
Hurled through still heavens?
What quaver—what heart aghast?
Poppies whose roots are in man's veins
Drop, and are ever dropping;
But mine in my ear is safe,
Just a little white with the dust.

Wilfred Owen

From My Diary, July 1914

Leaves
  Murmuring by myriads in the shimmering trees.
Lives
  Wakening with wonder in the Pyrenees.
Birds
  Cheerily chirping in the early day.
Bards
  Singing of summer scything thro' the hay.
Bees
  Shaking the heavy dews from bloom and frond.
Boys
  Bursting the surface of the ebony pond.
Flashes
  Of swimmers carving thro' the sparkling cold.
Fleshes
  Gleaming with wetness to the morning gold.
A mead
  Bordered about with warbling water brooks.
A maid
  Laughing the love-laugh with me; proud of looks.
The heat
  Throbbing between the upland and the peak.
Her heart
  Quivering with passion to my pressed cheek.
Braiding
  Of floating flames across the mountain brow.
Brooding
  Of stillness; and a sighing of the bough.
Stirs
  Of leaflets in the gloom; soft petal-showers;
Stars
  Expanding with the starr'd nocturnal flowers.

WILFRED OWEN

Exposure

Our brains ache, in the merciless iced east winds that knive us . . .
Wearied we keep awake because the night is silent . . .
Low, drooping flares confuse our memory of the salient . . .
Worried by silence, sentries whisper, curious, nervous,
But nothing happens.

Watching, we hear the mad gusts tugging on the wire,
Like twitching agonies of men among its brambles.
Northward, incessantly, the flickering gunnery rumbles,
Far off, like a dull rumour of some other war.
What are we doing here?

The poignant misery of dawn begins to grow . . .
We only know war lasts, rain soaks, and clouds sag stormy.
Dawn massing in the east her melancholy army
Attacks once more in ranks on shivering ranks of gray,
But nothing happens.

Sudden successive flights of bullets streak the silence.
Less deadly than the air that shudders black with snow,
With sidelong flowing flakes that flock, pause, and renew,
We watch them wandering up and down the wind's nonchalance,
But nothing happens.

Pale flakes with fingering stealth come feeling for our faces—
We cringe in holes, back on forgotten dreams, and stare, snow-dazed,
Deep into grassier ditches. So we drowse, sun-dozed,
Littered with blossoms trickling where the blackbird fusses.
Is it that we are dying?

Slowly our ghosts drag home: glimpsing the sunk fires, glozed
With crusted dark-red jewels; crickets jingle there;
For hours the innocent mice rejoice: the house is theirs;
Shutters and doors, all closed: on us the doors are closed,—
We turn back to our dying.

Since we believe not otherwise can kind fires burn;
Nor ever suns smile true on child, or field, or fruit.
For God's invincible spring our love is made afraid;
Therefore, not loath, we lie out here; therefore were born,
For love of God seems dying.

To-night, His frost will fasten on this mud and us,
Shrivelling many hands, puckering foreheads crisp.
The burying-party, picks and shovels in their shaking grasp,
Pause over half-known faces. All their eyes are ice,
But nothing happens.

Greater Love

Red lips are not so red
As the stained stones kissed by the English dead.
Kindness of wooed and wooer
Seems shame to their love pure.
O Love, your eyes lose lure
When I behold eyes blinded in my stead!

Your slender attitude
Trembles not exquisite like limbs knife-skewed,
Rolling and rolling there
Where God seems not to care;
Till the fierce Love they bear
Cramps them in death's extreme decrepitude.

Your voice sings not so soft,—
    Though even as wind murmuring through raftered loft,—
Your dear voice is not dear,
Gentle, and evening clear,
As theirs whom none now hear,
    Now earth has stopped their piteous mouths that coughed.

Heart, you were never hot,
    Nor large, nor full like hearts made great with shot;
And though your hand be pale,
Paler are all which trail
Your cross through flame and hail:
    Weep, you may weep, for you may touch them not.

Mental Cases

Who are these? Why sit they here in twilight?
Wherefore rock they, purgatorial shadows,
Drooping tongues from jaws that slob their relish,
Baring teeth that leer like skulls' teeth wicked?
Stroke on stroke of pain, —but what slow panic,
Gouged these chasms round their fretted sockets?
Ever from their hair and through their hands' palms
Misery swelters. Surely we have perished
Sleeping, and walk hell; but who these hellish?

—These are men whose minds the Dead have ravished.
Memory fingers in their hair of murders,
Multitudinous murders they once witnessed.
Wading sloughs of flesh these helpless wander,
Treading blood from lungs that had loved laughter.
Always they must see these things and hear them,
Batter of guns and shatter of flying muscles,
Carnage incomparable, and human squander,
Rucked too thick for these men's extrication.

Therefore still their eyeballs shrink tormented
Back into their brains, because on their sense
Sunlight seems a blood-smear; night comes blood-black;
Dawn breaks open like a wound that bleeds afresh
—Thus their heads wear this hilarious, hideous,
Awful falseness of set-smiling corpses.
—Thus their hands are plucking at each other;
Picking at the rope-knouts of their scourging;
Snatching after us who smote them, brother,
Pawing us who dealt them war and madness.

Futility

Move him in the sun—
Gently its touch awoke him once,
At home, whispering of fields unsown.
Always it woke him, even in France,
Until this morning and this snow.
If anything might rouse him now
The kind old sun will know.

Think how it wakes the seeds,—
Woke, once, the clays of a cold star.
Are limbs, so dear-achieved, are sides,
Full-nerved—still warm—too hard to stir?
Was it for this the clay grew tall?
—O what made fatuous sunbeams toil
To break earth's sleep at all?

Anthem for Doomed Youth

What passing-bells for these who die as cattle?
Only the monstrous anger of the guns.
Only the stuttering rifles' rapid rattle
Can patter out their hasty orisons.
No mockeries for them from prayers or bells,
Nor any voice of mourning save the choirs,—
The shrill, demented choirs of wailing shells;
And bugles calling for them from sad shires.

What candles may be held to speed them all?
Not in the hands of boys, but in their eyes
Shall shine the holy glimmers of good-byes.
The pallor of girls' brows shall be their pall;
Their flowers the tenderness of silent minds,
And each slow dusk a drawing-down of blinds.

Strange Meeting

It seemed that out of battle I escaped
Down some profound dull tunnel, long since scooped
Through granites which titanic wars had groined.
Yet also there encumbered sleepers groaned,
Too fast in thought or death to be bestirred.
Then, as I probed them, one sprang up, and stared
With piteous recognition in fixed eyes,
Lifting distressful hands as if to bless.
And by his smile, I knew that sullen hall,
By his dead smile I knew we stood in Hell.
With a thousand pains that vision's face was grained;
Yet no blood reached there from the upper ground,
And no guns thumped, or down the flues made moan.
"Strange friend", I said, "here is no cause to mourn."
"None", said the other, "save the undone years,

The hopelessness. Whatever hope is yours,
Was my life also; I went hunting wild
After the wildest beauty in the world,
Which lies not calm in eyes, or braided hair,
But mocks the steady running of the hour,
And if it grieves, grieves richlier than here.
For by my glee might many men have laughed,
And of my weeping something had been left,
Which must die now. I mean the truth untold,
The pity of war, the pity war distilled.
Now men will go content with what we spoiled.
Or, discontent, boil bloody, and be spilled.
They will be swift with swiftness of the tigress,
None will break ranks, though nations trek from progress.
Courage was mine, and I had mystery,
Wisdom was mine, and I had mastery;
To miss the march of this retreating world
Into vain citadels that are not walled
Then, when much blood had clogged their chariot-wheels
I would go up and wash them from sweet wells,
Even with truths that lie too deep for taint.
I would have poured my spirit without stint
But not through wounds; not on the cess of war.
Foreheads of men have bled where no wounds were.
I am the enemy you killed, my friend.
I knew you in this dark; for so you frowned
Yesterday through me as you jabbed and killed.
I parried; but my hands were loath and cold.
Let us sleep now. . . ."

Herbert Read

Cranach

But once upon a time
the oakleaves and the wild boars
Antonio Antonio
the old wound is bleeding.

We are in Silvertown
we have come here with a modest ambition
to know a little bit about the river
eating cheese and pickled onions on a terrace by the Thames.

Sweet Thames! the ferry glides across your bosom
like Leda's swan.
The factories ah slender graces
sly naked damsels nodding their downy plumes.

The Falcon and the Dove

1

This high-caught hooded Reason broods upon my wrist,
Fetter'd by a so tenuous leash of steel.
We are bound for the myrtle marshes, many leagues away,
And have a fair expectation of quarry.

2

Over the laggard dove, inclining to green boscage
Hovers this intentional doom— till the unsullied sky receives
A precipitation of shed feathers
And the swifter fall of wounded wings.

3

Will the plain aye echo with that loud *hullallo!*
Or retain an impress of our passage?
We have caught Beauty in a wild foray
And now the falcon is hooded and comforted away.

Beata l'Alma

Beata l'alma, ove non corre tempo.
Michelangelo

1

Time ends when vision sees its lapse in
liberty. The seven
sleepers quit their den and wild
lament-
ations fill our voiceless bodies. Echoes only are.

You will never understand the mind's
misanthropy, nor see
that all is foul and fit to
screech in.
It is an eye's anarchy: men are ghoulish stumps

and the air a river of opaque
filth. God! I cannot see
to design these stark reaches, these
bulging
contours pressed against me in the maddening dark.

A blindman's buff and no distilling
of song for the woeful
scenes of agony. Never
will rest
the mind an instant in its birdlike flutterings.

Could I impress my voice on the plas-
　　tic darkness, or lift an
inviolate lanthorn from
　　a ship
in the storm I might have ease. But why? No fellows

would answer my hullallo, and my
　　lanthorn would lurch on the
mast till it dipped under the
　　wet waves
and the hissing darkness healed the wide wound of light.

A cynic race—to bleak ecstasies
　　we are driven by our
sombre destiny. Men's shouts
　　are not
glad enough to echo in our groined hearts. We know

war and its dead, and famine's bleached bones;
　　black rot overreaching
the silent pressure of life
　　in fronds
of green ferns and in the fragile shell of white flesh.

2

New children must be born of gods in
　　a deathless land, where the
uneroded rocks bound clear
　　from cool
glassy tarns, and no flaw is in mind or flesh.

Sense and image they must refashion—
　　they will not recreate
love: love ends in hate; they will
　　not use
words: words lie. The structure of events alone is

comprehensible and to single
    perceptions communic-
ation is not essential.
        Art ends;
the individual world alone is valid

and that gives ease. The water is still;
    the rocks are hard and veined,
metalliferous, yielding
        an ore
of high worth. In the sky the unsullied sun lake.

John Crowe Ransom

Vision by Sweetwater

Go and ask Robin to bring the girls over
To Sweetwater, said my Aunt; and that was why
It was like a dream of ladies sweeping by
The willows, clouds, deep meadowgrass, and the river.

Robin's sisters and my Aunt's lily daughter
Laughed and talked, and tinkled light as wrens
If there were a little colony all hens
To go walking by the steep turn of Sweetwater.

Let them alone, dear Aunt, just for one minute
Till I go fishing in the dark of my mind:
Where have I seen before, against the wind,
These bright virgins, robed and bare of bonnet,

Flowing with music of their strange quick tongue
And adventuring with delicate paces by the stream,—
Myself a child, old suddenly at the scream
From one of the white throats which it hid among?

Captain Carpenter

Captain Carpenter rose up in his prime
Put on his pistols and went riding out
But had got well-nigh nowhere at that time
Till he fell in with ladies in a rout.

It was a pretty lady and all her train
That played with him so sweetly but before
An hour she'd taken a sword with all her main
And twined him of his nose for evermore.

Captain Carpenter mounted up one day
And rode straightway into a stranger rogue
That looked unchristian but be that as may
The Captain did not wait upon prologue.

But drew upon him out of his great heart
The other swung against him with a club
And cracked his two legs at the shinny part
And let him roll and stick like any tub.

Captain Carpenter rode many a time
From male and female took he sundry harms
He met the wife of Satan crying "I'm
The she-wolf bids you shall bear no more arms".

Their strokes and counters whistled in the wind
I wish he had delivered half his blows
But where she should have made off like a hind
The bitch bit off his arms at the elbows.

And Captain Carpenter parted with his ears
To a black devil that used him in this wise
O Jesus ere his threescore and ten years
Another had plucked out his sweet blue eyes.

Captain Carpenter got up on his roan
And sallied from the gate in hell's despite
I heard him asking in the grimmest tone
If any enemy yet there was to fight?

"To any adversary it is fame
If he risk to be wounded by my tongue
Or burnt in two beneath my red heart's flame
Such are the perils he is cast among.

"But if he can he has a pretty choice
From an anatomy with little to lose
Whether he cut my tongue and take my voice
Or whether it be my round red heart he choose."

It was the neatest knave that ever was seen
Stepping in perfume from his lady's bower
Who at this word put in his merry mien
And fell on Captain Carpenter like a tower.

I would not knock old fellows in the dust
But there lay Captain Carpenter on his back
His weapons were the old heart in his bust
And a blade shook between rotten teeth alack.

The rogue in scarlet and gray soon knew his mind
He wished to get his trophy and depart
With gentle apology and touch refined
He pierced him and produced the Captain's heart.

God's mercy rest on Captain Carpenter now
I thought him Sirs an honest gentleman
Citizen husband soldier and scholar enow
Let jangling kites eat of him if they can.

But God's deep curses follow after those
That shore him of his goodly nose and ears
His legs and strong arms at the two elbows
And eyes that had not watered seventy years.

The curse of hell upon the sleek upstart
Who got the Captain finally on his back
And took the red red vitals of his heart
And made the kites to whet their beaks clack clack.

Dead Boy

The little cousin is dead, by foul subtraction,
A green bough from Virginia's aged tree,
And neither the county kin love the transaction
Nor some of the world of outer dark, like me.

He was not a beautiful boy, nor good, nor clever,
A black cloud full of storms too hot for keeping,
A sword beneath his mother's heart, —yet never
Woman bewept her babe as this is weeping.

A pig with a pasty face, I had always said.
Squealing for cookies, kinned by pure pretence
With a noble house. But the little man quite dead,
I can see the forebears' antique lineaments.

The elder men have strode by the box of death
To the wide flag porch, and muttering low send round
The bruit of the day. O friendly waste of breath!
Their hearts are hurt with a deep dynastic wound.

He was pale and little, the foolish neighbors say;
The first-fruits, saith the preacher, the Lord hath taken;
But this was the old tree's late branch wrenched away,
Aggrieving the sapless limbs, the shorn and shaken.

Judith of Bethulia

Beautiful as the flying legend of some leopard,
She had not yet chosen her great captain or prince
Depositary to her flesh, and our defence;
And a wandering beauty is a blade out of its scabbard.
You know how dangerous, gentlemen of three-score?
May you know it yet ten more.

Nor by process of veiling she grew the less fabulous.
Gray or blue veils, we were desperate to study
The invincible emanations of her white body,
And the winds at her ordered raiment were ominous.
Might she walk in the market, sit in the council of soldiers?
Only of the extreme elders.

But a rare chance was the girl's then, when the Invader
Trumpeted from the south, and rumbled from the north,
Beleaguered the city from four quarters of the earth,
Our soldiery too craven and sick to aid her—
Where were the arms could countervail his horde?
Her beauty was the sword.

She sat with the elders, and proved on their 'blear visage
How bright was the weapon unrusted in her keeping,
While he lay surfeiting on their harvest heaping,
Wasting the husbandry of their rarest vintage—
And dreaming of the broad-breasted dames for concubine?
These floated on his wine.

He was lapped with bay-leaves, and grass and fumiter weed,
And from under the wine-film encountered his mortal vision.
For even within his tent she accomplished his derision;
She loosed one veil and another, standing unafraid;
And he perished. Nor brushed her with even so much as a
daisy?
She found his destruction easy.

The heathen are all perished. The victory was furnished,
We smote them hiding in our vineyards, barns, annexes,
And now their white bones clutter the holes of foxes,
And the chieftain's head, with grinning sockets, and
varnished—
Is it hung on the sky with a hideous epitaphy?
No, the woman keeps the trophy.

May God send unto the virtuous lady her prince.
It is stated she went reluctant to that orgy,
Yet a madness fevers our young men, and not the clergy
Nor the elders have turned them unto modesty since.
Inflamed by the thought of her naked beauty with desire?
Yes, and chilled with fear and despair.

David Jones

Two passages from In Parenthesis

1

You can hear the silence of it:
you can hear the rat of no-man's-land
rut-out intricacies,
weasel-out his patient workings,
scrut, scrut, sscrut,
harrow out-earthly, trowel his cunning paw;
redeem the time of our uncharity, to sap his own
amphibious paradise.

You can hear his carrying-parties rustle our corruptions through the night-weeds—contest the choicest morsels in his tiny conduits, bead-eyed feast on us; by a rule of his nature, at night-feast on the broken of us.

Those broad-pinioned;
blue burnished, or brinded-back;
whose proud eyes watched
                    the broken emblems
droop and drag dust,
suffer with us this metamorphosis.

These too have shed their fine feathers; these too have slimed their dark-bright coats; these too have condescended to dig in.

The white-tailed eagle at the battle ebb,
                    where the sea wars against the river
the speckled kite of Maldon
and the crow
have naturally selected to be un-winged;
to go on the belly, to
sap sap sap

with festered spines, arched under the moon; furrit with whiskered snouts the secret parts of us.

When it's all quiet you can hear them:
scrut scrut scrut
when it's as quiet as this is.

It's so very still.

Your body fits the crevice of the bay in the most comfortable fashion imaginable.

It's cushy enough.

2

And the place of their waiting a long burrow,
in the chalk a cutting, and steep clift—
but all but too shallow against his violence.
Like in long-ship, where you flattened face to kelson for the shock-breaking on brittle pavissed free-board, and the gunnel stove, and no care to jettison the dead.

No one to care there for Aneirin Lewis spilled there
who worshipped his ancestors like a Chink
who sleeps in Arthur's lap
who saw Olwen-trefoils some moonlighted night
on precarious slats at Festubert,
on narrow foothold on le Plantin marsh—
more shaved he is to the bare bone than
Yspaddadan Penkawr.

Properly organized chemists can let make more riving power than ever Twrch Trwyth;
more blistered he is than painted Troy Towers
and unwholer, limb from limb, than any of them fallen
at Catraeth
or on the seaboard-down, by Salisbury,
and no maker to contrive his funerary song.

And the little Jew lies next him
cries out for Deborah his bride
and offers for stretcher-bearers
gifts for their pains

and walnut suites in his delirium
                    from Grays Inn Road.
But they already look at their watches and it is zero minus seven minutes.
Seven minutes to go . . . and seventy times seven times to the minute
this drumming of the diaphragm.
  From deeply inward thumping all through you beating
no peace to be still in
and no one is there not anyone to stop
can't anyone—someone turn off the tap
or won't any one before it snaps.
Racked out to another turn of the screw
the acceleration heightens;
the sensibility of these instruments to register,
fails;
needle dithers disorientate.
The responsive mercury plays laggard to such fevers—
you simply can't take any more in.
And the surfeit of fear steadies to dumb incognition, so
that when they give the order to move upward to align
with "A",
hugged already just under the lip of the acclivity inches
below where his traversing machine-guns perforate to
powder
white—
white creature of chalk pounded
and the world crumbled away
and get ready to advance
you have not capacity for added fear only the limbs are
leaden to negotiate the slope and rifles all out of balance,
clumsied with long auxiliary steel
seem five times the regulation weight—
it bitches the aim as well;
                    and we ourselves as those small
cherubs, who trail awkwardly the weapons of the God in
                         Fine Art works.

The returning sun climbed over the hill, to lessen the shadows of small and great things; and registered the minutes to zero hour. Their saucer hats made dial for his passage: long thin line of them, virid domes of them.

cut elliptical with light
as cupola on Byzantine wall,
stout turrets to take the shock
and helmets of salvation.
Long side by side lie like friends lie
on daisy-down on warm days
cuddled close down kindly close with the mole
in down and silky rodent,
and if you look more intimately all manner of small
  creatures,
created-dear things creep about quite comfortably
Yet who travail until now
beneath your tin-hat shade.

He bawls at ear-hole:
Two minutes to go.
Minutes to excuse me to make excuse.
Responde mihi?
for surely I must needs try them
so many, much undone
and lose on roundabouts as well and vari-coloured
polygram
to love and know
and we have a little sister
whose breasts will be as towers
and the gilly flowers will blow next month
below the pound
with Fred Karno billed for *The Holloway*.

He's getting it now more accurately and each salvo brackets more narrowly and a couple right in, just as "D" and "C" are forming for the second wave.

Wastebottom married a wife on his Draft-leave but the
whinnying splinter razored diagonal and mess-tin
fragments drove inward and toxined underwear.

He maintained correct alignment with the others, face down, and you never would have guessed.

Perhaps they'll cancel it.
O blow fall out the officers cantcher, like a wet afternoon or the King's Birthday.
Or you read it again many times to see if it will come different:
you can't believe the Cup won't pass from
or they won't make a better show
in the Garden.
Won't someone forbid the banns
or God himself will stay their hands.
It just can't happen in our family
even though a thousand
and ten thousand at thy right hand.

Talacryn doesn't take it like Wastebottom, he leaps up &
says he's dead, a-slither down the pale face—his limbs
a-girandole at the bottom of the nullah,
but the mechanism slackens, unfed
and he is quite still
which leaves five paces between you and the next live
one to the left.
Sidle over a bit toward where '45 Williams, and use all your lungs:
Get ready me china-plate—but he's got it before he can hear you, but it's a cushy one and he relaxes to the morning sun and smilingly, to wait for the bearers.

Allen Tate

Horatian Epode to the Duchess of Malfi

DUCHESS: "Who am I?"
BOSOLA: "Thou art a box of worm-seed, at best but a salvatory of green mummy."

The stage is about to be swept of corpses.
You have no more chance than an infusorian
Lodged in a hollow molar of an eohippus.
Come, now, no prattle of remergence with the
ὄντως ὄν.

* * *

As (the form requires the myth)
A Greek girl stood once in the prytaneum
Of Carneades, hearing mouthings of Probability,
Then mindful of love dashed her brain on a megalith,

So you, O nameless Duchess who die young,
Meet death somewhat lovingly
And I am filled with a pity of beholding skulls.
There was no pride like yours.

Now considerations of the Void coming after,
Not changed by the strict gesture of your death,
Split the straight line of pessimism
Into two infinities.

It is moot whether there be divinities
As I finish this play by Webster:
The street cars are still running however
And the katharsis fades in the warm water of a yawn.

1922

ALLEN TATE

Idiot

The idiot greens the meadow with his eyes,
The meadow creeps, implacable and still;
A dog barks; the hammock swings; he lies.
One, two, three, the cows bulge on the hill.

Motion, which is not time, erects snowdrifts
While sister's hand sieves waterfalls of lace.
With a palm fan closer than death, he lifts
The Ozarks and tilted seas across his face.

In the long sunset where impatient sound
Strips niggers to a multiple of backs,
Flies yield their heat, magnolias drench the ground
With Appomattox! The shadows lie in stacks.

The julep glass weaves echoes in Jim's kinks
While ashy Jim puts murmurs in the day:
Now in the idiot's heart a chamber stinks
Of dead asters—as the potter's field, of May.

All evening the marsh is a slick pool
Where dream wild hares, witch hazel, pretty girls.
"Up from the important picnic of a fool
Those rotted asters!" Eddy on eddy swirls.

The innocent mansion of a panther's heart!
It crumbles; tick-tick, time drags it in;
And now his arteries lag and now they start
Reverence with the frigid gusts of sin.

The stillness pelts the eye, assaults the hair;
A beech sticks out a branch to warn the stars;
A lightning-bug jerks angles in the air,
Diving. "I am the captain of new wars!"

The dusk runs down the lane, driven like hail;
Far-off a precise whistle is escheat
To the dark; and then the towering weak and pale
Covers his eyes with memory like a sheet.

1926

The Mediterranean

Quem das finem, rex magne, dolorum?

Where we went in the boat was a long bay
A slingshot wide walled in by towering stone,
Peaked margin of antiquity's delay—
And we went there out of time's monotone:

Where we went in the black hull no light moved
But a gull white-winged along the feckless wave;
The breeze, unseen but fierce as a body loved,
That boat drove onward like a willing slave;

Where we went in the small ship the seaweed
Parted and gave to us the murmuring shore
And we made feast and in our secret need
Devoured the very plates Aeneas bore:

Where derelict you see through the low twilight
The green coast that you thunder-tossed would win
Drop sail, and hastening to drink all night
Eat dish and bowl—to take the sweet land in!

Where we feasted and caroused on the sandless
Pebbles, affecting our day of piracy,
What prophecy of eaten plates could landless
Wanderers fulfil by the ancient sea?

We for that time might taste the famous age
Eternal here yet hidden from our eyes
When lust of power undid its stuffless rage;
They, in a wineskin, bore earth's paradise.

—Let us lie down once more by the breathing side
Of ocean, where our live forefathers sleep
As if the Known Sea still were a month wide—
Atlantis howls but is no longer steep!

What country shall we conquer, what fair land
Unman our conquest and locate our blood?
We've cracked the hemispheres with careless hand:
Now, from the Gates of Hercules we flood

Westward, westward till the barbarous brine
Whelms us to the tired world where tasseling corn,
Fat beans, grapes sweeter than muscadine
Rot on the vine: in that land were we born.

1932

The Oath

It was near evening, the room was cold,
Half-dark; Uncle Ben's brass bullet-mould
And powder horn, and Major Bogan's face
Above the fire, in the half-light, plainly said
There's naught to kill but the animated dead;
Horn nor mould nor Major follows the chase.
Being cold I urged Lytle to the fire
In the blank twilight, with not much left untold
By two old friends when neither's a great liar;
We sat down evenly in the smoky chill.
There's precious little to say betwixt day and dark,
Perhaps a few words on the implacable will
Of time sailing like a magic barque
Or something as fine for the amenities,

Till the dusk seals the window, the fire grows bright
And the wind saws the hill with a swarm of bees.
Now mediating a little on the firelight
We heard the darkness grapple with the night
And give an old man's valedictory wheeze
From his westward breast between his polar jaws;
So Lytle asked: Who are the dead?
Who are the living and the dead?...
And nothing more was said;
But I leaving Lytle to that dream
Decided what it is in time that gnaws
The aging fury of a mountain stream,
When suddenly as an ignorant mind will do
I thought I heard the dark pounding its head
On a rock, crying *Who are the dead?*
Lytle turned with an oath—By God, it's true!

1930

Ode to the Confederate Dead

Row after row with strict impunity
The headstones yield their names to the element,
The wind whirrs without recollection;
In the riven troughs the splayed leaves
Pile up, of nature the casual sacrament
To the seasonal eternity of death,
Then driven by the fierce scrutiny
Of heaven to their business in the vast breath,
They sough the rumour of mortality.

Autumn is desolation in the plot
Of a thousand acres, where these memories grow
From the inexhaustible bodies that are not
Dead, but feed the grass row after rich row:
Remember now the autumns that have gone—
Ambitious November with the humors of the year,

With a particular zeal for every slab,
Staining the uncomfortable angels that rot
On the slabs, a wing chipped here, an arm there:
The brute curiosity of an angel's stare
Turns you like them to stone,
Transforms the heaving air,
Till plunged to a heavier world below
You shift your sea-space blindly,
Heaving, turning like the blind crab.

Dazed by the wind, only the wind
The leaves flying, plunge

You know who have waited by the wall
The twilit certainty of an animal;
Those midnight restitutions of the blood
You know—the immitigable pines, the smoky frieze
Of the sky, the sudden call; you know the rage—
The cold pool left by the mounting flood—
The rage of Zeno and Parmenides.
You who have waited for the angry resolution
Of those desires that should be yours tomorrow,
You know the unimportant shrift of death
And praise the vision
And praise the arrogant circumstance
Of those who fall
Rank upon rank, hurried beyond decision—
Here by the sagging gate, stopped by the wall.

Seeing, seeing only the leaves
Flying, plunge and expire

Turn your eyes to the immoderate past
Turn to the inscrutable infantry rising
Demons out of the earth—they will not last.
Stonewall, Stonewall—and the sunken fields of hemp
Shiloh, Antietam, Malvern Hill, Bull Run.
Lost in that orient of the thick and fast
You will curse the setting sun.

Cursing only the leaves crying
Like an old man in a storm

You hear the shout—the crazy hemlocks point
With troubled fingers to the silence which
Smothers you, a mummy, in time. The hound bitch
Toothless and dying, in a musty cellar
Hears the wind only.

Now that the salt of their blood
Stiffens the saltier oblivion of the sea,
Seals the malignant purity of the flood,
What shall we, who count our days and bow
Our heads with a commemorial woe,
In the ribboned coats of grim felicity,
What shall we say of the bones, unclean—
Their verdurous anonymity will grow—
The ragged arms, the ragged heads and eyes
Lost in these acres of the insane green?
The grey lean spiders come; they come and go;
In a tangle of willows without light
The singular screech-owl's bright
Invisible lyric seeds the mind
With the furious murmur of their chivalry.

We shall say only, the leaves
Flying, plunge and expire

We shall say only, the leaves whispering
In the improbable mist of nightfall
That flies on multiple wing:
Night is the beginning and the end,
And in between the ends of distraction
Waits mute speculation, the patient curse
That stones the eyes, or like the jaguar leaps
For his own image in a jungle pool, his victim.

What shall we say who have knowledge
Carried to the heart? Shall we take the act
To the grave? Shall we, more hopeful, set up the grave
In the house? The ravenous grave?

Leave now
The turnstile and the old stone wall:
The gentle serpent, green in the mulberry bush,
Riots with his tongue through the hush—
Sentinel of the grave who counts us all!

1926–30

Hart Crane

North Labrador

A land of leaning ice
Hugged by plaster-grey arches of sky,
Flings itself silently
Into eternity.

"Has no one come here to win you,
Or left you with the faintest blush
Upon your glittering breasts?
Have you no memories, O Darkly Bright?"

Cold-hushed, there is only the shifting of moments
That journey toward no Spring—
No birth, no death, no time nor sun
In answer.

Recitative

Regard the capture here, O Janus-faced,
As double as the hands that twist this glass.
Such eyes at search or rest you cannot see;
Reciting pain or glee, how can you bear!

Twin shadowed halves: the breaking second holds
In each the skin alone, and so it is
I crust a plate of vibrant mercury
Borne cleft to you, and brother in the half.

Inquire this much-exacting fragment smile,
Its drums and darkest blowing leaves ignore,—
Defer though, revocation of the tears
That yield attendance to one crucial sign.

Look steadily—how the wind feasts and spins
The brain's disk shivered against lust. Then watch
While darkness, like an ape's face, falls away,
And gradually white buildings answer day.

Let the same nameless gulf beleaguer us—
Alike suspend us from atrocious sums
Built floor by floor on shafts of steel that grant
The plummet heart, like Absalom, no stream.

The highest tower, —let her ribs palisade
Wrenched gold of Nineveh; —yet leave the tower.
The bridge swings over salvage, beyond wharves;
A wind abides the ensign of your will . . .

In alternating bells have you not heard
All hours clapped dense into a single stride?
Forgive me for an echo of these things,
And let us walk through time with equal pride.

from For the Marriage of Faustus and Helen

III

Capped arbiter of beauty in this street
That narrows darkly into motor dawn,—
You, here beside me, delicate ambassador
Of intricate slain numbers that arise
In whispers, naked of steel;
religious gunman!

Who faithfully, yourself, will fall too soon,
And in other ways than as the wind settles
On the sixteen thrifty bridges of the city:
Let us unbind our throats of fear and pity.

We even,

Who drove speediest destruction
In corymbulous formations of mechanics,—
Who hurried the hill breezes, spouting malice
Plangent over meadows, and looked down
On rifts of torn and empty houses
Like old women with teeth unjubilant
That waited faintly, briefly and in vain:

We know, eternal gunman, our flesh remembers
The tensile boughs, the nimble blue plateaus,
The mounted, yielding cities of the air!
That saddled sky that shook down vertical
Repeated play of fire—no hypogeum
Of wave or rock was good against one hour.
We did not ask for that, but have survived,
And will persist to speak again before
All stubble streets that have not curved
To memory, or known the ominous lifted arm
That lowers down the arc of Helen's brow
To saturate with blessing and dismay.

A goose, tobacco and cologne—
Three winged and gold-shod prophecies of heaven,
The lavish heart shall always have to leaven
And spread with bells and voices, and atone
The abating shadows of our conscript dust.

Anchises' navel, dripping of the sea,—
The hands Erasmus dipped in gleaming tides,
Gathered the voltage of blown blood and vine;
Delve upward for the new and scattered wine,

O brother-thief of time, that we recall.
Laugh out the meagre penance of their days
Who dare not share with us the breath released,
The substance drilled and spent beyond repair
For golden, or the shadow of gold hair.
Distinctly praise the years, whose volatile
Blamed bleeding hands extend and thresh the height
The imagination spans beyond despair,
Outpacing bargain, vocable and prayer.

Cutty Sark

O, the navies old and oaken
O, the Temeraire no more!

Melville

I met a man in South Street, tall—
a nervous shark tooth swung on his chain.
His eyes pressed through green grass
—green glasses, or bar lights made them
so—
shine—
GREEN—
eyes—
stepped out—forgot to look at you
or left you several blocks away—

in the nickel-in-the-slot piano jogged
"Stamboul Nights"—weaving somebody's nickel—
sang—

O Stamboul Rose—dreams weave the rose!

Murmurs of Leviathan he spoke,
and rum was Plato in our heads . . .

"It's S.S. *Ala*—Antwerp—now remember kid
to put me out at three she sails on time.
I'm not much good at time any more keep
weakeyed watches sometimes snooze—" his bony hands
got to beating time . . . "A whaler once—
I ought to keep time and get over it—I'm a
Democrat—I know what time it is—No
I don't want to know what time it is—that
damned white Arctic killed my time . . ."

O Stamboul Rose—drums weave—

"I ran a donkey engine down there on the Canal
in Panama—got tired of that—
then Yucatan selling kitchenware—beads—
have you seen Popocatepetl—birdless mouth
with ashes sifting down—?
and then the coast again . . ."

Rose of Stamboul O coral Queen—
teased remnants of the skeletons of cities—
and galleries, galleries of watergutted lava
snarling stone—green—drums—drown—

Sing!
"—that spiracle!" he shot a finger out the door . . .
"O life's a geyser—beautiful—my lungs—
No—I can't live on land—!"

I saw the frontiers gleaming of his mind;
or are there frontiers—running sands sometimes
running sands—somewhere—sands running . . .
Or they may start some white machine that sings.
Then you may laugh and dance the axletree—
steel—silver—kick the traces—and know—
ATLANTIS ROSE drums wreathe the rose,
the star floats burning in a gulf of tears
and sleep another thousand—
interminably

long since somebody's nickel—stopped—
playing—

A wind worried those wicker-neat lapels, the
swinging summer entrances to cooler hells . . .
Outside a wharf truck nearly ran him down
—he lunged up Bowery way while the dawn
was putting the Statue of Liberty out—that
torch of hers you know—

I started walking home across the Bridge . . .

* * *

Blithe Yankee vanities, turreted sprites, winged
British repartees, skil-
ful savage sea-girls
that bloomed in the spring—Heave, weave
those bright designs the trade winds drive . . .

Sweet opium and tea, Yo-ho!
Pennies for porpoises that bank the keel!
Fins whip the breeze around Japan!

Bright skysails ticketing the Line, wink round the
Horn
to Frisco, Melbourne . . .
Pennants, parabolas—
clipper dreams indelible and ranging,
baronial white on lucky blue!

Perennial-*Cutty*-trophied-*Sark*!

Thermopylæ, Black Prince, Flying Cloud through Sunda
—scarfed of foam, their bellies veered green esplanades,
locked in wind-humors, ran their eastings down;

at Java Head freshened the nip
(sweet opium and tea!)
and turned and left us on the lee . . .

Buntlines tusselling (91 days, 20 hours and anchored!)
Rainbow, Leander
(last trip a tragedy)—where can you be
Nimbus? and you rivals two—

a long tack keeping—

Taeping?
Ariel?

E. E. Cummings

One X

death is more than
certain a hundred these
sounds crowds odours it
is in a hurry
beyond that any this
taxi smile or angle we do

not sell and buy
things so necessary as
is death and unlike shirts
neckties trousers
we cannot wear it out

no sir which is why
granted who discovered
America ether the movies
may claim general importance

to me to you nothing is
what particularly
matters hence in a

little sunlight and less
moonlight ourselves against the worms

hate laugh shimmy

Two X

16 heures
l'Etoile

the communists have fine Eyes
some are young some old none
look alike the flics rush
batter the crowd sprawls collapses
singing knocked down trampled the kicked by
flics rush (the

Flics, tidiyum, are
very tidiyum reassuringly similar,
they all have very tidiyum
mustaches, and very
tidiyum chins, and just above
their very tidiyum ears their
very tidiyum necks begin
                                        let us add

that there are 50 (fifty) flics for every
one (1) communist and
all the flics are very organically
arranged
and their nucleus (composed
of captains in freshly-creased
-uniforms with only-just-
shined buttons
tidiyum
before and behind) has a nucleolus:

the Prefect of Police

(a dapper derbied
creature, swaggers daintily
twiddling
his tiny cane
and mazurkas about tweak-
ing his wing collar pecking at his im

-peccable cravat directing being
shooting his cuffs
saluted everywhere saluting
reviewing processions of minions
tappingpeopleontheback

"allezcirculez")

—my he's brave . . .
the
communists pick
up themselves friends
& their hats legs &

arms brush dirt coats
smile looking hands
spit blood teeth

the Communists have (very) fine eyes
(which stroll hither and thither through the
evening in bruised narrow questioning faces)

Four III

here's a little mouse) and
what does he think about, i
wonder as over this
floor (quietly with

bright eyes) drifts (nobody
can tell because
Nobody knows, or why
jerks Here &, here,
gr(oo)ving the room's Silence) this like
a littlest
poem a
(with wee ears and see?
tail frisks)
        (gonE)
"mouse",
        We are not the same you and

i, since here's a little he
or is
it It
? (or was something we saw in the mirror)?

therefore we'll kiss; for maybe
what was Disappeared
into ourselves
who   (look).   ,startled

72

wild(at our first)beasts uttered human words
—our second coming made stones sing like birds—
but o the starhushed silence which our third's

Basil Bunting

from Briggflatts

IV

Grass caught in willow tells the flood's height that has
  subsided;
overfalls sketch a ledge to be bared tomorrow.
No angler homes with empty creel though mist dims day.
I hear Aneurin number the dead, his nipped voice.
Slight moon limps after the sun. A closing door
stirs smoke's flow above the grate. Jangle
to skald, battle, journey; to priest Latin is bland.
Rats have left no potatoes fit to roast, the gamey tang
recalls ibex guts steaming under a cold ridge,
tomcat stink of a leopard dying while I stood
easing the bolt to dwell on a round's shining rim.
I hear Aneurin number the dead and rejoice,
being adult male of a merciless species.
Today's posts are piles to drive into the quaggy past
on which impermanent palaces balance.
I see Aneurin's pectoral muscle swell under his shirt,
pacing between the game Ida left to rat and raven,
young men, tall yesterday, with cabled thighs.
Red deer move less warily since their bows dropped.
Girls in Teesdale and Wensleydale wake discontent.
Clear Cymric voices carry well this autumn night,
Aneurin and Taliesin, cruel owls
for whom it is never altogether dark, crying
before the rules made poetry a pedant's game.
Columba, Columbanus, as the soil shifts its vest,
Aidan and Cuthbert put on daylight,
wires of sharp western metal entangled in its soft
web, many shuttles as midges darting;
not for bodily welfare nor pauper theorems
but splendour to splendour, excepting nothing that is.

Let the fox have his fill, patient leech and weevil,
cattle refer the rising of Sirius to their hedge horizon,
runts murder the sacred calves of the sea by rule
heedless of herring gull, surf and the text carved by waves
on the skerry. Can you trace shuttles thrown
like drops from a fountain, spray, mist of spiderlines
bearing the rainbow, quoits round the draped moon;
shuttles like random dust desert whirlwinds hoy at their
   tormenting sun?
Follow the clue patiently and you will understand nothing.
Lice in its seams despise the jacket shrunk to the world's core,
crawl with toil to glimpse
from its shoulder walls of flame which could they reach
they'd crackle like popcorn in a skillet.

As the player's breath warms the fipple the tone clears.
It is time to consider how Domenico Scarlatti
condensed so much music into so few bars
with never a crabbed turn or congested cadence,
never a boast or a see-here; and stars and lakes
echo him and the copse drums out his measure,
snow peaks are lifted up in moonlight and twilight
and the sun rises on an acknowledged land.

My love is young but wise. Oak, applewood,
her fire is blanked with ashes till day.
The fells reek of her hearth's scent,
her girdle is greased with lard;
hunger is stayed on her settle, lust in her bed.
Light as spider floss her hair on my cheek which a puff
   scatters,
light as a moth her fingers on my thigh.
We have eaten and loved and the sun is up,
we have only to sing before parting:
Goodbye, dear love.

Her scones are greased with fat of fried bacon,
her blanket comforts my belly like the south.
We have eaten and loved and the sun is up.
Goodbye.

Applewood, hard to rive,
its knots smoulder all day.
Cobweb hair on the morning,
a puff would blow it away.
Rime is crisp on the bent,
ruts stone-hard, frost spangles fleece.
What breeze will fill that sleeve limp on the line?
A boy's jet steams from the wall, time from the year,
care from deed and undoing.
Shamble, cold, content with beer and pickles,
towards a taciturn lodging amongst strangers.

Where rats go go I,
accustomed to penury,
filth, disgust and fury;
evasive to persist,
reject the bait
yet gnaw the best.
My bony feet
sully shelf and dresser,
keeping a beat in the dark,
rap on lath
till dogs bark
and sleep, shed,
slides from the bed.
O valiant when hunters
with stick and terrier bar escape
or wavy ferret leaps,
encroach and cede again,
rat, roommate, unreconciled.

Stars disperse. We too,
further from neighbours
now the year ages.

To Violet, with prewar poems

These tracings from a world that's dead
take for my dust-smothered pyramid.
Count the sharp study and long toil
as pavements laid for worms to soil.
You without knowing it might tread
the grass where my foundation's laid,
your, or another's, house be built
where my weathered stones lie spilt,
and this unread memento be
the only lasting part of me.

1941

Robert Graves

O Love in Me

O love, be fed with apples while you may,
And feel the sun and go in royal array,
A smiling innocent on the heavenly causeway.

Though in what listening horror for the cry
That soars in outer blackness dismally,
The dumb blind beast, the paranoiac fury,

Be warm, enjoy the season, lift your head,
Exquisite in the pulse of tainted blood,
That shivering glory not to be despised.

Take your delight in momentariness,
Walk between dark and dark, a shining space
With the grave's narrowness, though not its peace.

The Bards

Their cheeks are blotched for shame, their running verse
Stumbles, with marrow-bones the drunken diners
Pelt them as they delay:
It is a something fearful in the song
Plagues them, an unknown grief that like a churl
Goes commonplace in cowskin
And bursts unheralded, crowing and coughing,
An unpilled holly-club twirled in his hand,
Into their many-shielded, samite-curtained
Jewel-bright hall where twelve kings sit at chess

Over the white-bronze pieces and the gold,
And by a gross enchantment
Flails down the rafters and leads off the queens—
The wild-swan-breasted, the rose-ruddy-cheeked
Raven-haired daughters of their admiration—
To stir his black pots and to bed on straw.

Flying Crooked

The butterfly, the cabbage-white,
(His honest idiocy of flight)
Will never now, it is too late,
Master the art of flying straight,
Yet has—who knows so well as I?—
A just sense of how not to fly:
He lurches here and here by guess
And God and hope and hopelessness.
Even the aerobatic swift
Has not his flying-crooked gift.

Ogres and Pygmies

Those famous men of old, the Ogres—
They had long beards and stinking arm-pits.
They were wide-mouthed, long-yarded and great-bellied
Yet of not taller stature, Sirs, than you.
They lived on Ogre-Strand, which was no place
But the churl's terror of their proud extent,
Where every foot was three-and-thirty inches
And every penny bought a whole sheep.
Now of their company none survive, not one,
The times being, thank God, unfavourable

To all but nightmare memory of them.
Their images stand howling in the waste,
(The winds enforced against their wide mouths)
Whose granite haunches king and priest must yearly
Buss, and their cold knobbed knees.
So many feats they did to admiration:
With their enormous lips they sang louder
Than ten cathedral choirs, with their grand yards
Stormed the most rare and obstinate maidenheads,
With their strong-gutted and capacious bellies
Digested stones and glass like ostriches.
They dug great pits and heaped great cairns,
Deflected rivers, slew whole armies,
And hammered judgements for posterity—
For the sweet-cupid-lipped and tassel-yarded
Delicate-stomached dwellers
In Pygmy Alley, where with brooding on them
A foot is shrunk to seven inches
And twelve-pence will not buy a spare rib.
And who would choose between Ogres and Pygmies—
The thundering text, the snivelling commentary—
Reading between such covers he will likely
Prove his own disproportion and not laugh.

On Dwelling

Courtesies of good-morning and good-evening
From rustic lips fail as the town encroaches:
Soon nothing passes but the cold quick stare
Of eyes that see ghosts, yet too many for fear.

Here I too walk, silent myself, in wonder
At a town not mine though plainly coextensive
With mine, even in days coincident:
In mine I dwell, in theirs like them I haunt.

And the green country, should I turn again there?
My bumpkin neighbours loom even ghostlier:
Like trees they murmur or like blackbirds sing
Courtesies of good-morning and good-evening.

To Whom Else?

To whom else other than,
To whom else not of man
Yet in human state,
Standing neither in stead
Of self nor idle godhead,
Should I, man in man bounded,
Myself dedicate?

To whom else momently,
To whom else endlessly,
But to you, I?
To you who only,
To you who mercilessly,
To you who lovingly,
Plucked out the lie?

To whom else less acquaint,
To whom else without taint
Of death, death-true?
With great astonishment
Thankfully I consent
To my estrangement
From me in you.

ROBERT GRAVES

On Portents

If strange things happen where she is,
So that men say that graves open
And the dead walk, or that futurity
Becomes a womb and the unborn are shed,
Such portents are not to be wondered at,
Being tourbillions in Time made
By the strong pulling of her bladed mind
Through that ever-reluctant element.

To Juan at the Winter Solstice

There is one story and one story only
That will prove worth your telling,
Whether as learned bard or gifted child;
To it all lines or lesser gauds belong
That startle with their shining
Such common stories as they stray into.

Is it of trees you tell, their months and virtues,
Or strange beasts that beset you,
Of birds that croak at you the Triple will?
Or of the Zodiac and how slow it turns
Below the Boreal Crown,
Prison of all true kings that ever reigned?

Water to water, ark again to ark,
From woman back to woman:
So each new victim treads unfalteringly
The never altered circuit of his fate,
Bringing twelve peers as witness
Both to his starry rise and starry fall.

Or is it of the Virgin's silver beauty,
All fish below the thighs?
She in her left hand bears a leafy quince;
When with her right she crooks a finger, smiling,
How may the King hold back?
Royally then he barters life for love.

Or of the undying snake from chaos hatched,
Whose coils contain the ocean,
Into whose chops with naked sword he springs,
Then in black water, tangled by the reeds,
Battles three days and nights,
To be spewed up beside her scalloped shore?

Much snow is falling, winds roar hollowly,
The owl hoots from the elder,
Fear in your heart cries to the loving-cup:
Sorrow to sorrow as the sparks fly upward.
The log groans and confesses:
There is one story and one story only.

Dwell on her graciousness, dwell on her smiling,
Do not forget what flowers
The great boar trampled down in ivy time.
Her brow was creamy as the crested wave,
Her sea-blue eyes were wild
But nothing promised that is not performed.

The Sea Horse

Since now in every public place
Lurk phantoms who assume your walk and face,
You cannot yet have utterly abjured me
Nor stifled the insistent roar of the sea.

Do as I do: confide your unquiet love
(For one who never owed you less than love)
To this indomitable hippocamp,
Child of your element, coiled a-ramp,
Having ridden out worse tempests than you know of;
Under his horny ribs a blood-red stain
Portends renewal of our pain.
Sweetheart, make much of him and shed
Tears on his taciturn dry head.

Surgical Ward: Men

Something occurred after the operation
To scare the surgeons (though no fault of theirs)
Whose reassurance did not fool me long.
Beyond the shy, concerned faces of nurses
A single white-hot eye, focusing on me,
Forced sweat in rivers down from scalp to belly.
I whistled, gasped or sang, with blanching knuckles
Clutched at my bed-grip almost till it cracked:
Too proud, still, to let loose Bedlamite screeches
And bring the charge-nurse scuttling down the aisle
With morphia-needle levelled. . . .
                                        Lady Morphia—
Her scorpion kiss and dark gyrating dreams—
She in mistrust of whom I dared out-dare,
Two minutes longer than seemed possible,
Pain, that unpurposed, matchless elemental
Stronger than fear or grief, stranger than love.

ROBERT GRAVES

The Narrow Sea

With you for mast and sail and flag,
And anchor never known to drag,
Death's narrow but oppressive sea
Looks not unnavigable to me.

Edith Sitwell

The King of China's Daughter

The King of China's daughter,
She never would love me
Though I hung my cap and bells upon
Her nutmeg tree.
For oranges and lemons,
The stars in bright blue air,
(I stole them long ago, my dear)
Were dangling there.
The Moon did give me silver pence,
The Sun did give me gold,
And both together softly blew
And made my porridge cold;
But the King of China's daughter
Pretended not to see
When I hung my cap and bells upon
Her nutmeg tree.

Hornpipe

Sailors come
To the drum
Out of Babylon;
    Hobby-horses
Foam, the dumb
Sky rhinoceros-glum

Watched the courses of the breakers' rocking-horses and with
Glaucis,
Lady Venus on the settee of the horsehair sea!
Where Lord Tennyson in laurels wrote a gloria free
In a borealic iceberg came Victoria; she
Knew Prince Albert's tall memorial took the colours of the
floreal
And the borealic iceberg; floating on they see
New-arisen Madam Venus for whose sake from far
Came the fat and zebra'd emperor from Zanzibar
Where like golden bouquets lay far Asia, Africa, Cathay,
All laid before that shady lady by the fibroid Shah.
Captain Fracasse stout as any water-butt came, stood
With Sir Bacchus both a-drinking the black tarr'd grapes'
blood
Plucked among the tartan leafage
By the furry wind whose grief age
Could not wither—like a squirrel with a gold star-nut.
Queen Victoria sitting shocked upon the rocking-horse
Of a wave said to the Laureate, "This minx of course
Is as sharp as any lynx and blacker-deeper than the drinks and
quite as
Hot as any hottentot, without remorse!

For the minx,"
Said she,
"And the drinks,
You can see

Are hot as any hottentot and not the goods for me!"

EDITH SITWELL

When Sir Beelzebub

When
Sir
Beelzebub called for his syllabub in the hotel in Hell

Where Prosperine first fell;

Blue as the gendarmerie were the waves of the sea,

(Rocking and shocking the bar-maid).

Nobody comes to give him his rum but the
Rim of the sky hippopotamus-glum
Enhances the chances to bless with a benison
Alfred Lord Tennyson crossing the bar laid
With cold vegetation from pale deputations
Of temperance workers (all signed In Memoriam)
Hoping with glory to trip up the Laureate's feet,

(Moving in classical metres) . . .

Like Balaclava, the lava came down from the
Roof, and the sea's blue wooden gendarmerie
Took them in charge while Beelzebub roared for his
rum.
. . . None of them come!

The Bat

Castellated, tall
From battlements fall
Shades on heroic
Lonely grass,
Where the moonlight's echoes die and pass.
Near the rustic boorish,

Fustian Moorish,
Castle wall of the ultimate Shade,
With his cloak castellated as that wall, afraid,
The mountebank doctor,
The old stage quack,
Where decoy duck dust
Began to clack,
Watched Heliogabalusene the Bat
In his furred cloak hang head down from the flat
Wall, cling to what is convenient,
Lenient.
"If you hang upside down with squeaking shrill,
You will see dust, lust, and the will to kill,
And life is a matter of which way falls
Your tufted turreted Shade near these walls.
For muttering guttering shadow will plan
If you're ruined wall, or pygmy man,"
Said Heliogabalusene, "or a pig,
Or the empty Caesar in tall periwig."
And the mountebank doctor,
The old stage quack,
Spread out a black membraned wing of his cloak
And his shuffling footsteps seem to choke,
Near the Castle wall of the ultimate Shade
Where decoy duck dust
Quacks, clacks, afraid.

Richard Eberhart

The Groundhog

In June, amid the golden fields,
I saw a groundhog lying dead.
Dead lay he; my senses shook,
And mind outshot our naked frailty.
There lowly in the vigorous summer
His form began its senseless change,
And made my senses waver dim
Seeing nature ferocious in him.
Inspecting close his maggot's might
And seething cauldron of his being,
Half with loathing, half with a strange love,
I poked him with an angry stick.
The fever arose, became a frame
And Vigour circumscribed the skies,
Immense energy in the sun,
And through my frame a sunless trembling.
My stick had done nor good nor harm.
Then stood I silent in the day
Watching the object, as before;
And kept my reverence for knowledge
Trying for control, to be still,
To quell the passion of the blood;
Until I had bent down on my knees
Praying for joy in the sight of decay.
And so I left; and I returned
In Autumn strict of eye, to see
The sap gone out of the groundhog,
But the bony sodden hulk remained.
But the year had lost its meaning,
And in intellectual chains
I lost both love and loathing,
Mured up in the wall of wisdom.
Another summer took the fields again

Massive and burning, full of life,
But when I chanced upon the spot
There was only a little hair left,
And bones bleaching in the sunlight
Beautiful as architecture;
I watched them like a geometer,
And cut a walking stick from a birch.
It has been three years, now.
There is no sign of the groundhog.
I stood there in the whirling summer,
My hand capped a withered heart,
And thought of China and of Greece,
Of Alexander in his tent;
Of Montaigne in his tower,
Of Saint Theresa in her wild lament.

The Fury of Aerial Bombardment

You would think the fury of aerial bombardment
Would rouse God to relent; the infinite spaces
Are still silent. He looks on shock-pried faces.
History, even, does not know what is meant.

You would feel that after so many centuries
God would give man to repent; yet he can kill
As Cain could, but with multitudinous will,
No farther advanced than in his ancient furies.

Was man made stupid to see his own stupidity?
Is God by definition indifferent, beyond us all?
Is the eternal truth man's fighting soul
Wherein the Beast ravens in its own avidity?

Of Van Wettering I speak, and Averill,
Names on a list, whose faces I do not recall
But they are gone to early death, who late in school
Distinguished the belt feed lever from the belt holding pawl.

William Empson

The Scales

The proper scale would pat you on the head
But Alice showed her pup Ulysses' bough
Well from behind a thistle, wise with dread;

And though your gulf-sprung mountains I allow
(Snow-puppy curves, rose-solemn dado band)
Charming for nurse, I am not nurse just now.

Why pat or stride them, when the train will land
Me high, through climbing tunnels, at your side,
And careful fingers meet through castle sand.

Claim slyly rather that the tunnels hide
Solomon's gems, white vistas, preserved kings,
By jackal sandhole to your air flung wide.

Say (she suspects) to sea Nile only brings
Delta and indecision, who instead
Far back up country does enormous things.

Invitation to Juno

Lucretius could not credit centaurs;
Such bicycle he deemed asynchronous.
"Man superannuates the horse;
Horse pulses will not gear with ours."

Johnson could see no bicycle would go;
"You bear yourself, and the machine as well."
Gennets for germans sprang not from Othello,
And Ixion rides upon a single wheel.

Courage. Weren't strips of heart culture seen
Of late mating two periodicities?
Could not Professor Charles Darwin
Graft annual upon perennial trees?

Camping Out

And now she cleans her teeth into the lake:
Gives it (God's grace) for her own bounty's sake
What morning's pale and the crisp mist debars:
Its glass of the divine (that Will could break)
Restores, beyond Nature: or lets Heaven take
(Itself being dimmed) her pattern, who half awake
Milks between rocks a straddled sky of stars.

Soap tension the star pattern magnifies.
Smoothly Madonna through-assumes the skies
Whose vaults are opened to achieve the Lord.
No, it is we soaring explore galaxies,
Our bullet boat light's speed by thousands flies.
Who moves so among stars their frame unties;
See where they blur, and die, and are outsoared.

Legal Fiction

Law makes long spokes of the short stakes of men.
Your well fenced out real estate of mind
No high flat of the nomad citizen
Looks over, or train leaves behind.

Your rights extend under and above your claim
Without bound; you own land in Heaven and Hell;
Your part of earth's surface and mass the same,
Of all cosmos' volume, and all stars as well.

Your rights reach down where all owners meet, in Hell's
Pointed exclusive conclave, at earth's centre
(Your spun farm's root still on that axis dwells);
And up, through galaxies, a growing sector.

You are nomad yet; the lighthouse beam you own
Flashes, like Lucifer, through the firmament.
Earth's axis varies; your dark central cone
Wavers, a candle's shadow, at the end.

This Last Pain

This last pain for the damned the Fathers found:
"They knew the bliss with which they were not crowned."
  Such, but on earth, let me foretell,
  Is all, of heaven or of hell.

Man, as the prying housemaid of the soul,
May know her happiness by eye to hole:
  He's safe; the key is lost; he knows
  Door will not open, nor hole close.

"What is conceivable can happen too,"
Said Wittgenstein, who had not dreamt of you;
  But wisely, if we worked it long
  We should forget where it was wrong:

Those thorns are crowns which, woven into knots,
Crackle under and soon boil fools' pots;
  And no man's watching, wise and long,
  Would ever stare them into song.

Thorns burn to a consistent ash, like man;
A splendid cleanser for the frying-pan:
And those who leap from pan to fire
Should this brave opposite admire.

All those large dreams by which men long live well
Are magic-lanterned on the smoke of hell;
This then is real, I have implied,
A painted, small, transparent slide.

These the inventive can hand-paint at leisure,
Or most emporia would stock our measure;
And feasting in their dappled shade
We should forget how they were made.

Feign then what's by a decent tact believed
And act that state is only so conceived,
And build an edifice of form
For house where phantoms may keep warm.

Imagine, then, by miracle, with me,
(Ambiguous gifts, as what gods give must be)
What could not possibly be there,
And learn a style from a despair.

Homage to the British Museum

There is a supreme God in the ethnological section;
A hollow toad shape, faced with a blank shield.
He needs his belly to include the Pantheon,
Which is inserted through a hole behind.
At the navel, at the points formally stressed, at the organs of
sense,
Lice glue themselves, dolls, local deities,
His smooth wood creeps with all the creeds of the world.

Attending there let us absorb the cultures of nations
And dissolve into our judgement all their codes.
Then, being clogged, with a natural hesitation
(People are continually asking one the way out),
Let us stand here and admit that we have no road.
Being everything, let us admit that is to be something,
Or give ourselves the benefit of the doubt;
Let us offer our pinch of dust all to this God,
And grant his reign over the entire building.

Note on Local Flora

There is a tree native in Turkestan,
Or further east towards the Tree of Heaven,
Whose hard cold cones, not being wards to time,
Will leave their mother only for good cause;
Will ripen only in a forest fire;
Wait, to be fathered as was Bacchus once,
Through men's long lives, that image of time's end.
I knew the Phoenix was a vegetable.
So Semele desired her deity
As this in Kew thirsts for the Red Dawn.

Aubade

Hours before dawn we were woken by the quake.
My house was on a cliff. The thing could take
Bookloads off shelves, break bottles in a row.
Then the long pause and then the bigger shake.
It seemed the best thing to be up and go.

And far too large for my feet to step by.
I hoped that various buildings were brought low.
The heart of standing is you cannot fly.

It seemed quite safe till she got up and dressed.
The guarded tourist makes the guide the test.
Then I said The Garden? Laughing she said No.
Taxi for her and for me healthy rest.
It seemed the best thing to be up and go.

The language problem but you have to try.
Some solid ground for lying could she show?
The heart of standing is you cannot fly.

None of these deaths were her point at all.
The thing was that being woken he would bawl
And finding her not in earshot he would know.
I tried saying Half an Hour to pay this call.
It seemed the best thing to be up and go.

I slept, and blank as that I would yet lie.
Till you have seen what a threat holds below,
The heart of standing is you cannot fly.

Tell me again about Europe and her pains,
Who's tortured by the drought, who by the rains.
Glut me with floods where only the swine can row
Who cuts his throat and let him count his gains.
It seemed the best thing to be up and go.

A bedshift flight to a Far Eastern sky.
Only the same war on a stronger toe.
The heart of standing is you cannot fly.

Tell me more quickly what I lost by this,
Or tell me with less drama what they miss
Who call no die a god for a good throw,
Who say after two aliens had one kiss
It seemed the best thing to be up and go.

But as to risings, I can tell you why.
It is on contradiction that they grow.
It seemed the best thing to be up and go.
Up was the heartening and the strong reply.
The heart of standing is we cannot fly.

Let It Go

It is this deep blankness is the real thing strange.
  The more things happen to you the more you can't
    Tell or remember even what they were.

The contradictions cover such a range.
  The talk would talk and go so far aslant.
    You don't want madhouse and the whole thing there.

C. Day Lewis

"As one who wanders into old workings"

As one who wanders into old workings
Dazed by the noonday, desiring coolness,
Has found retreat barred by fall of rockface;
Gropes through galleries where granite bruises
Taut palm and panic patters close at heel;
Must move forward as tide to the moon's nod,
As mouth to breast in blindness is beckoned.
Nightmare nags at his elbow and narrows
Horizon to pinpoint, hope to hand's breadth.
Slow drip the seconds, time is stalactite,
For nothing intrudes here to tell the time,
Sun marches not, nor moon with muffled step.
He wants an opening,—only to break out,
To see the dark glass cut by day's diamond,
To relax again in the lap of light.

But we seek a new world through old workings,
Whose hope lies like seed in the loins of earth,
Whose dawn draws gold from the roots of darkness.
Not shy of light nor shrinking from shadow
Like Jesuits in jungle we journey
Deliberately bearing to brutish tribes
Christ's assurance, arts of agriculture.
As a train that travels underground track
Feels current flashed from far-off dynamos,
Our whirling with impetus elsewhere
Generated we run, are ruled by rails.
Train shall spring from tunnel to terminus,
Out on to plain shall the pioneer plunge,
Earth reveal what veins fed, what hill covered.
Lovely the leap, explosion into light.

"Do not expect again a phoenix hour"

Do not expect again a phoenix hour,
The triple-towered sky, the dove complaining,
Sudden the rain of gold and heart's first ease
Tranced under trees by the eldritch light of sundown.

By a blazed trail our joy will be returning:
One burning hour throws light a thousand ways,
And hot blood stays into familiar gestures.
The best years wait, the body's plenitude.

Consider then, my lover, this is the end
Of the lark's ascending, the hawk's unearthly hover:
Spring season is over soon and first heatwave;
Grave-browed with cloud ponders the huge horizon.

Draw up the dew. Swell with pacific violence.
Take shape in silence. Grow as the clouds grew.
Beautiful brood the cornlands, and you are heavy;
Leafy the boughs—they also hide big fruit.

"You that love England"

You that love England, who have an ear for her music,
The slow movement of clouds in benediction,
Clear arias of light thrilling over her uplands,
Over the chords of summer sustained peacefully;
Ceaseless the leaves' counterpoint in a west wind lively,
Blossom and river rippling loveliest allegro,
And the storms of wood strings brass at year's finale:
Listen. Can you not hear the entrance of a new theme?

You who go out alone, on tandem or on pillion,
Down arterial roads riding in April,
Or sad beside lakes where hill-slopes are reflected
Making fires of leaves, your high hopes fallen:
Cyclists and hikers in company, day excursionists,
Refugees from cursed towns and devastated areas;
Know you seek a new world, a saviour to establish
Long-lost kinship and restore the blood's fulfilment.

You who like peace, good sticks, happy in a small way
Watching birds or playing cricket with schoolboys,
Who pay for drinks all round, whom disaster chose not;
Yet passing derelict mills and barns roof-rent
Where despair has burnt itself out—hearts at a standstill,
Who suffer loss, aware of lowered vitality;
We can tell you a secret, offer a tonic; only
Submit to the visiting angel, the strange new healer.

You above all who have come to the far end, victims
Of a run-down machine, who can bear it no longer;
Whether in easy chairs chafing at impotence
Or against hunger, bullies and spies preserving
The nerve for action, the spark of indignation—
Need fight in the dark no more, you know your enemies.
You shall be leaders when zero hour is signalled,
Wielders of power and welders of a new world.

Maple and Sumach

Maple and sumach down this autumn ride—
Look, in what scarlet character they speak!
For this their russet and rejoicing week
Trees spend a year of sunsets on their pride.
You leaves drenched with the lifeblood of the year—
What flamingo dawns have wavered from the east,

What eves have crimsoned to their toppling crest
To give the fame and transience that you wear!
Leaf-low he shall lie soon: but no such blaze
Briefly can cheer man's ashen, harsh decline;
His fall is short of pride, he bleeds within
And paler creeps to the dead end of his days.
O light's abandon and the fire-crest sky
Speak in me now for all who are to die!

Where are the War Poets?

They who in folly or mere greed
Enslaved religion, markets, laws,
Borrow our language now and bid
Us to speak up in freedom's cause.

It is the logic of our times,
No subject for immortal verse—
That we who lived by honest dreams
Defend the bad against the worse.

W. H. Auden

Prologue

O love, the interest itself in thoughtless Heaven
Make simpler daily the beating of man's heart; within
There in the ring where name and image meet

Inspire them with such a longing as will make his thought
Alive like patterns a murmuration of starlings
Rising in joy over wolds unwittingly weave;

Here too on our little reef display your power,
This fortress perched on the edge of the Atlantic scarp
The mole between All Europe and the exile-crowded sea;

And make us as Newton was who in his garden watching
The apple falling towards England became aware
Between himself and her of an eternal tie.

For now that dream which so long has contented our will,
I mean, of uniting the dead into a splendid empire,
Under whose fertilising flood the Lancashire moss

Sprouted up chimneys and Glamorgan hid a life
Grim as a tidal rock-pool's in its glove-shaped valleys,
Is already retreating into her maternal shadow;

Leaving the furnaces gasping in the impossible air
The flatsam at which Dumbarton gapes and hungers,
While upon wind-loved Rowley no hammer shakes

The cluster of mounds like a midget golf course, graves
Of some who created these intelligible dangerous marvels;
Affectionate people, but crude their sense of glory.

Far-sighted as falcons, they looked down another future.
For the seed in their loins were hostile, though afraid of their
pride,
And tall with a shadow now, inertly wait

In bar, in netted chicken-farm, in lighthouse,
Standing on these impoverished constricting acres,
The ladies and gentlemen apart, too much alone.

Consider the years of the measured world begun,
The barren spiritual marriage of stone and water.
Yet, O, at this very moment of our hopeless sigh

When inland they are thinking their thoughts but are watching
these islands
As children in Chester look to Moel Fammau to decide
On picnics by the clearness or withdrawal of her treeless
crown,

Some dream, say yes, long coiled in the ammonite's slumber
Is uncurling, prepared to lay on our talk and kindness
Its military silence, its surgeon's idea of pain.

And called out of tideless peace by a living sun
As when Merlin, tamer of horses, and his lords to whom
Stonehenge was still a thought, the Pillars passed

And into the undared ocean swung north their prow,
Drives through the night and star-concealing dawn
For the virgin roadsteads of our hearts an unwavering keel.

"Watch any day"

Watch any day his nonchalant pauses, see
His dextrous handling of a wrap as he
Steps after into cars, the beggar's envy.

"There is a free one" many say, but err.
He is not that returning conqueror,
Nor ever the poles' circumnavigator.

But poised between shocking falls on razor-edge
Has taught himself this balancing subterfuge
Of the accosting profile, the erect carriage.

The song, the varied action of the blood
Would drown the warning from the iron wood
Would cancel the inertia of the buried:

Travelling by daylight on from house to house
The longest way to the intrinsic peace,
With love's fidelity and with love's weakness.

"Consider this and in our time"

Consider this and in our time
As the hawk sees it or the helmeted airman:
The clouds rift suddenly—look there
At cigarette-end smouldering on a border
At the first garden party of the year.
Pass on, admire the view of the massif
Through plate-glass windows of the Sport Hotel;
Join there the insufficient units
Dangerous, easy, in furs, in uniform
And constellated at reserved tables
Supplied with feelings by an efficient band
Relayed elsewhere to farmers and their dogs
Sitting in kitchens on the stormy fens.

Long ago, supreme Antagonist,
More powerful than the great northern whale
Ancient and sorry at life's limiting defect,
In Cornwall, Mendip, or the Pennine moor

Your comments on the highborn mining captains,
Found they no answer, made them wish to die
—Lie since in barrows out of harm.
You talk to your admirers every day
But silted harbours, derelict works,
In strangled orchards, and the silent comb
Where dogs have worried or a bird was shot.
Order the ill that they attack at once:
Visit the ports and, interrupting
The leisurely conversation in the bar
Within a stone's throw of the sunlit water,
Beckon your chosen out. Summon
Those handsome and diseased youngsters, those women
Your solitary agents in the country parishes;
And mobilize the powerful forces latent
In soils that make the farmer brutal
In the infected sinus, and the eyes of stoats.
Then, ready, start your rumour, soft
But horrifying in its capacity to disgust
Which, spreading magnified, shall come to be
A polar peril, a prodigious alarm,
Scattering the people, as torn-up paper
Rags and utensils in a sudden gust,
Seized with immeasurable neurotic dread.

Financier, leaving your little room
Where the money is made but not spent,
You'll need your typist and your boy no more;
The game is up for you and for the others,
Who, thinking, pace in slippers on the lawns
Of College Quad or Cathedral Close,
Who are born nurses, who live in shorts
Sleeping with people and playing fives.
Seekers after happiness, all who follow
The convolutions of your simple wish,
It is later than you think; nearer that day
Far other than that distant afternoon
Amid rustle of frocks and stamping feet

They gave the prizes to the ruined boys.
You cannot be away, then, no
Not though you pack to leave within an hour,
Escaping humming down arterial roads:
The date was yours; the prey to fugues,
Irregular breathing and alternate ascendancies
After some haunted migratory years
To disintegrate on an instant in the explosion of mania
Or lapse for ever into a classic fatigue.

"Our hunting fathers"

Our hunting fathers told the story
  Of the sadness of the creatures,
Pitied the limits and the lack
  Set in their finished features;
Saw in the lion's intolerant look,
Behind the quarry's dying glare
Love raging for the personal glory
  That reason's gift would add,
The liberal appetite and power,
  The rightness of a god.

Who nurtured in that fine tradition
  Predicted the result,
Guessed Love by nature suited to
  The intricate ways of guilt;
That human company could so
His southern gestures modify
And make it his mature ambition
  To think no thought but ours,
To hunger, work illegally,
  And be anonymous?

W. H. AUDEN

Law Like Love

Law, say the gardeners, is the sun,
Law is the one
All gardeners obey
To-morrow, yesterday, to-day.

Law is the wisdom of the old,
The important grandfathers feebly scold;
The grandchildren put out a treble tongue,
Law is the senses of the young.

Law, says the priest with a priestly look,
Expounding to an unpriestly people,
Law is the words in my priestly book,
Law is my pulpit and my steeple.

Law, says the judge as he looks down his nose,
Speaking clearly and most severely,
Law is as I've told you before,
Law is as you know I suppose,
Law is but let me explain it once more,
Law is The Law.

Yet law-abiding scholars write:
Law is neither wrong nor right,
Law is only crimes
Punished by places and by times,
Law is the clothes men wear
Anytime, anywhere,
Law is Good morning and Good night.

Others say, Law is our Fate;
Others say, Law is our State;
Others say, others say
Law is no more,
Law has gone away.

And always the loud angry crowd,
Very angry and very loud,
Law is We,
And always the soft idiot softly Me.

If we, dear, know we know no more
Than they about the Law,
If I no more than you
Know what we should and should not do
Except that all agree
Gladly or miserably
That the Law is
And that all know this,
If therefore thinking it absurd
To identify Law with some other word,
Unlike so many men
I cannot say Law is again,
No more than they can we suppress
The universal wish to guess
Or slip out of our own position
Into an unconcerned condition.
Although I can at least confine
Your vanity and mine
To stating timidly
A timid similarity,
We shall boast anyway:
Like love I say.

Like love we don't know where or why,
Like love we can't compel or fly,
Like love we often weep,
Like love we seldom keep.

W. H. AUDEN

Under Sirius

Yes, these are the dog-days, Fortunatus:
The heather lies limp and dead
On the mountain, the baltering torrent
Shrunk to a soodling thread;
Rusty the spears of the legion, unshaven its captain,
Vacant the scholar's brain
Under his great hat,
Drug though She may, the Sybil utters
A gush of table-chat.

And you yourself with a head-cold and upset stomach,
Lying in bed till noon,
Your bills unpaid, your much advertised
Epic not yet begun,
Are a sufferer too. All day, you tell us, you wish
Some earthquake would astonish,
Or the wind of the Comforter's wing
Unlock the prisons and translate
The slipshod gathering.

And last night, you say, you dreamed of that bright blue
morning,
The hawthorn hedges in bloom,
When, serene in their ivory vessels,
The three wise Maries come,
Sossing through seamless waters, piloted in
By sea-horse and fluent dolphin:
Ah! how thc cannons roar,
How jocular the bells as They
Indulge the peccant shore.

It is natural to hope and pious, of course, to believe
That all in the end shall be well,
But first of all, remember,
So the Sacred Books foretell,

The rotten fruit shall be shaken. Would your hope make sense
If today were that moment of silence,
Before it break and drown,
When the insurrected eagre hangs
Over the sleeping town?

How will you look and what will you do when the basalt
Tombs of the sorcerers shatter
And their guardian megalopods
Come after you pitter-patter?
How will you answer when from their qualming spring
The immortal nymphs fly shrieking,
And out of the open sky
The pantocratic riddle breaks—
"Who are you and why?"

For when in a carol under the apple-trees
The reborn featly dance,
There will also, Fortunatus,
Be those who refused their chance,
Now pottering shades, querulous beside the salt-pits,
And mawkish in their wits,
To whom these dull dog-days
Between event seem crowned with olive
And golden with self-praise.

The Shield of Achilles

She looked over his shoulder
For vines and olive trees,
Marble well-governed cities
And ships upon untamed seas,
But there on the shining metal
His hands had put instead
An artificial wilderness
And a sky like lead.

A plain without a feature, bare and brown,
   No blade of grass, no sign of neighbourhood,
Nothing to eat and nowhere to sit down,
   Yet, congregated on its blankness, stood
   An unintelligible multitude,
A million eyes, a million boots in line,
Without expression, waiting for a sign.

Out of the air a voice without a face
   Proved by statistics that some cause was just
In tones as dry and level as the place:
   No one was cheered and nothing was discussed;
   Column by column in a cloud of dust
They marched away enduring a belief
Whose logic brought them, somewhere else, to grief.

She looked over his shoulder
   For ritual pieties,
White flower-garlanded heifers,
   Libation and sacrifice,
But there on the shining metal
   Where the altar should have been,
She saw by his flickering forge-light
   Quite another scene.

Barbed wire enclosed an arbitrary spot
   Where bored officials lounged (one cracked a joke)
And sentries sweated for the day was hot:
   A crowd of ordinary decent folk
   Watched from without and neither moved nor spoke
As three pale figures were led forth and bound
To three posts driven upright in the ground.

The mass and majesty of this world, all
  That carries weight and always weighs the same
Lay in the hands of others; they were small
  And could not hope for help and no help came:
  What their foes liked to do was done, their shame
Was all the worst could wish; they lost their pride
And died as men before their bodies died.

She looked over his shoulder
  For athletes at their games,
Men and women in a dance
  Moving their sweet limbs
Quick, quick, to music,
  But there on the shining shield
His hands had set no dancing-floor
  But a weed-choked field.

A ragged urchin, aimless and alone,
  Loitered about that vacancy; a bird
Flew up to safety from his well-aimed stone:
  That girls are raped, that two boys knife a third,
  Were axioms to him, who'd never heard
Of any world where promises were kept,
Or one could weep because another wept.

The thin-lipped armorer,
  Hephaestos, hobbled away,
Thetis of the shining breasts
  Cried out in dismay
At what the god had wrought
  To please her son, the strong
Iron-hearted man-slaying Achilles
  Who would not live long.

W. H. AUDEN

The History of Truth

In that ago when being was believing.
Truth was the most of many credibles,
More first, more always, than a bat-winged lion,
A fish-tailed dog or eagle-headed fish,
The least like mortals, doubted by their deaths.

Truth was their model as they strove to build
A world of lasting objects to believe in,
Without believing earthenware and legend,
Archway and song, were truthful or untruthful:
The Truth was there already to be true.

This while when, practical like paper-dishes,
Truth is convertible to kilowatts,
Our last to do by is an anti-model,
Some untruth anyone can give the lie to,
A nothing no one need believe is there.

Vespers

If the hill overlooking our city has always been known as Adam's Grave, only at dusk can you see the recumbent giant, his head turned to the west, his right arm resting for ever on Eve's haunch,

can you learn, from the way he looks up at the scandalous pair, what a citizen really thinks of his citizenship,

just as now you can hear in a drunkard's caterwaul his rebel sorrows crying for a parental discipline, in lustful eyes perceive a disconsolate soul, scanning with desperation all passing limbs for some vestige of her faceless angel who in that long ago when wishing was a help mounted her once and vanished:

For Sun and Moon supply their conforming masks, but in this hour of civil twilight all must wear their own faces.

And it is now that our two paths cross.

Both simultaneously recognise his Anti-type: that I am an Arcadian, that he is a Utopian.

He notes, with contempt, my Aquarian belly: I note, with alarm, his Scorpion's mouth.

He would like to see me cleaning latrines: I would like to see him removed to some other planet.

Neither speaks. What experience could we possibly share?

Glancing at a lampshade in a store window, I observe it is too hideous for anyone in their senses to buy: He observes it is too expensive for a peasant to buy.

Passing a slum child with rickets, I look the other way: He looks the other way if he passes a chubby one.

I hope our senators will behave like saints, provided they don't reform me: He hopes they will behave like *baritoni cattivi*, and, when lights burn late in the Citadel,

I (who have never seen the inside of a police station) am shocked and think: "Were the city as free as they say, after sundown all her bureaus would be huge black stones.":

He (who has been beaten up several times) is not shocked at all but thinks: "One fine night our boys will be working up there."

You can see, then, why, between my Eden and his New Jerusalem, no treaty is negotiable.

In my Eden a person who dislikes Bellini has the good manners not to get born: In his New Jerusalem a person who dislikes work will be very sorry he was born.

In my Eden we have a few beam-engines, saddle-tank locomotives, overshot waterwheels and other beautiful pieces of obsolete machinery to play with: In his New Jerusalem even chefs will be cucumber-cool machine minders.

In my Eden our only source of political news is gossip: In his New Jerusalem there will be a special daily in simplified spelling for non-verbal types.

In my Eden each observes his compulsive rituals and superstitious tabus but we have no morals: In his New Jerusalem the temples will be empty but all will practise the rational virtues.

One reason for his contempt is that I have only to close my eyes, cross the iron footbridge to the tow-path, take the barge through the short brick tunnel and

there I stand in Eden again, welcomed back by the krum-horns, doppions, sordumes of jolly miners and a bob major from the Cathedral (romanesque) of St. Sophie (*Die Kalte*):

One reason for my alarm is that, when he closes his eyes, he arrives, not in New Jerusalem, but on some august day of outrage when hellikins cavort through ruined drawing-rooms and fishwives intervene in the Chamber or

some autumn night of delations and noyades, when the unrepentant thieves (including me) are sequestered and those he hates shall hate themselves instead.

So with a passing glance we take the other's posture. Already our steps recede, heading, incorrigible each, towards his kind of meal and evening.

Was it (as it must look to any god of cross-roads) simply a fortuitous intersection of life-paths, loyal to different fibs?

Or also a rendezvous between accomplices who, in spite of themselves, cannot resist meeting.

to remind the other (do both, at bottom, desire truth?) of that half of their secret which he would most like to forget,

forcing us both, for a fraction of a second, to remember our victim (but for him I could forget the blood, but for me he could forget the innocence),

on whose immolation (call him Abel, Remus, whom you will, it is one Sin Offering) arcadias, utopias, our dear old bag of a democracy are alike founded:

For without a cement of blood (it must be human, it must be innocent) no secular wall will safely stand.

A Starling and a Willow-wren

A starling and a willow-wren
   On a may-tree by a weir
Saw them meet and heard him say:
   "Dearest of my dear,
More lively than these waters chortling
   As they leap the dam,
My sweetest duck, my precious goose,
   My white lascivious lamb."

With a smile she listened to him,
  Talking to her there:
What does he want? said the willow-wren;
  Much too much, said the stare.

"Forgive these loves who dwell in me,
  These brats of greed and fear,
The honking bottom-pinching clown,
  The snivelling sonneteer,
That so, between us, even these,
  Who till the grave are mine,
For all they fall so short of may,
  Dear heart, be still a sign."
With a smile she closed her eyes,
  Silent she lay there:
Does he mean what he says? said the willow-wren;
  Some of it, said the stare.

"Hark! Wild Robin winds his horn
  And, as his notes require,
Now our laughter-loving spirits
  Must in awe retire
And let their kinder partners,
  Speechless with desire,
Go in their holy selfishness,
  Unfunny to the fire."
Smiling, silently she threw
  Her arms about him there:
Is it only that? said the willow-wren;
  It's that as well, said the stare.

Waking in her arms he cried,
  Utterly content:
"I have heard the high good noises,
  Promoted for an instant,
Stood upon the shining outskirts
  Of that Joy I thank

For you, my dog and every goody."
There on the grass bank
She laughed, he laughed, they laughed together,
Then they ate and drank:
Did he know what he meant? said the willow-wren—
God only knows, said the stare.

Lullaby

The din of work is subdued,
another day has westered
and mantling darkness arrived.
Peace! Peace! Devoid your portrait
of its vexations and rest.
Your daily round is done with,
you've gotten the garbage out,
answered some tiresome letters
and paid a bill by return,
all *frettolosamente*.
Now you have licence to lie,
naked, curled like a shrimplet,
jacent in bed, and enjoy
its cosy micro-climate:
Sing, Big Baby, sing lullay.

The old Greeks got it all wrong:
Narcissus is an oldie,
tamed by time, released at last
from lust for other bodies,
rational and reconciled.
For many years you envied
the hirsute, the he-man type.
No longer: now you fondle
your almost feminine flesh
with mettled satisfaction,

imagining that you are
sinless and all-sufficient,
snug in the den of yourself,
Madonna and *Bambino:*
Sing, Big Baby, sing lullay.

Let your last thinks all be thanks:
praise your parents who gave you
a Super-Ego of strength
that saves you so much bother,
digit friends and dear them all,
then pay fair attribution
to your age, to having been
born when you were. In boyhood
you were permitted to meet
beautiful old contraptions,
soon to be banished from earth,
saddle-tank loks, beam-engines
and over-shot waterwheels.
Yes, love, you have been lucky:
Sing, Big Baby, sing lullay.

Now for oblivion: let
the belly-mind take over
down below the diaphragm,
the domain of the Mothers,
They who guard the Sacred Gates,
without whose wordless warnings
soon the verbalising I
becomes a vicious despot,
lewd, incapable of love,
disdainful, status-hungry.
Should dreams haunt you, heed them not,
for all, both sweet and horrid,
are jokes in dubious taste,
too jejune to have truck with.
Sleep, Big Baby, sleep your fill.

Louis MacNeice

En Eclogue for Christmas

A. I meet you in an evil time.

B. The evil bells
Put out of our heads, I think, the thought of everything else.

A. The jaded calendar revolves,
Its nuts need oil, carbon chokes the valves,
The excess sugar of a diabetic culture;
Rotting the nerve of life and literature;
Therefore when we bring out the old tinsel and frills
To announce that Christ is born among the barbarous hills
I turn to you whom a morose routine
Saves from the mad vertigo of being what has been.

B. Analogue of me, you are wrong to turn to me,
My country will not yield you any sanctuary,
There is no pinpoint in any of the ordnance maps
To save you when your towns and town-bred thoughts collapse,
It is better to die *in situ* as I shall,
One place is as bad as another. Go back where your instincts call
And listen to the crying of the town-cats and the taxis again,
Or wind your gramophone and eavesdrop on great men.

A. Jazz-weary of years of drums and Hawaiian guitar,
Pivoting on the parquet I seem to have moved far
From bombs and mud and gas, have stuttered on my feet
Clinched to the streamlined and butter-smooth trulls of the élite,

The lights irritating and gyrating and rotating in gauze—
Vomade-dazzle, a slick beauty of gewgaws—
I who was Harlequin in the childhood of the century,
Posed by Picasso beside an endless opaque sea,
Have seen myself sifted and splintered in broken facets,
Tentative pencillings, endless liabilities, no assets,
Abstractions scalpelled with a palette-knife
Without reference to this particular life,
And so it has gone on; I have not been allowed to be
Myself in flesh or face, but abstracting and dissecting me
They have made of me pure form, a symbol or a pastiche,
Stylized profile, anything but soul and flesh:
And that is why I turn this jaded music on
To forswear thought and become an automaton.

B. There are in the country also of whom I am afraid—
Men who put beer into a belly that is dead,
Women in the forties with terrier and setter who whistle
  and swank
Over down and plough and Roman road and daisied bank,
Half-conscious that these barriers over which they stride
Are nothing to the barbed wire that has grown round their
  pride.

A. And two there are, as I drive in the city, who suddenly
  perturb—
The one sirening me to draw up by the kerb
The other, as I lean back, my right leg stretched creating
  speed,
Making me catch and stamp, the brakes shrieking, pull up
  dead:
She wears silk stockings taunting the winter wind,
He carries a white stick to mark that he is blind.

B. In the country they are still hunting, in the heavy shires
Greyness is on the fields and sunset like a line of pyres
Of barbarous heroes smoulders through the ancient air
Hazed with factory dust and, orange opposite, the moon's
  glare,

Goggling yokel-stubborn through the iron trees,
Jeers at the end of us, our bland ancestral ease;
We shall go down like palaeolithic man
Before some new Ice Age or Genghiz Khan.

A. It is time for some new coinage, people have got so old,
Hacked and handled and shiny from pocketing they have made bold
To think that each is himself through these accidents, being blind
To the fact that they are merely the counters of an unknown Mind.

B. A Mind that does not think, if such a thing can be,
Mechanical Reason, capricious Identity.
That I could be able to face this domination nor flinch—

A. The tin boys of the hawker move on the pavement inch by inch
Not knowing that they are wound up; it is better to be so
Than to be, like us, wound up and while running down to know—

B. But everywhere the pretence of individuality recurs—

A. Old faces frosted with powder and choked in furs.

B. The jutlipped farmer gazing over the humpbacked wall.

A. The commercial traveller joking in the urinal.

B. I think things draw to an end, the soil is stale.

A. And over-elaboration will nothing now avail,
The street is up again, gas, electricity or drains,
Ever-changing conveniences, nothing comfortable remains
Un-improved, as flagging Rome improved villa and sewer
(A sound-proof library and a stable temperature).
Our street is up, red lights sullenly mark
The long trench of pipes, iron guts in the dark,

And not till the Goths again come swarming down the hill
Will cease the clangour of the electric drill.
But yet there is beauty narcotic and deciduous
In this vast organism grown out of us:
On all the traffic islands stand white globes like moons,
The city's haze is clouded amber that purrs and croons,
And tilting by the noble curve bus after tall bus comes
With an osculation of yellow light, with a glory like
chrysanthemums.

B. The country gentry cannot change, they will die in their
shoes
From angry circumstance and moral self-abuse,
Dying with a paltry fizzle they will prove their lives to be
An ever-diluted drug, a spiritual tautology.
They cannot live once their idols are turned out,
None of them can endure, for how could they, possibly,
without
The flotsam of private property, pekingese and polyanthus,
The good things which in the end turn to poison and pus,
Without the bandy chairs and the sugar in the silver tongs
And the inter-ripple and resonance of years of
dinner-gongs?
Or if they could find no more that cumulative proof
In the rain dripping off the conservatory roof

What will happen when the only sanction the
country-dweller has—

A. What will happen to us, planked and panelled with jazz?
Who go to the theatre where a black man dances like an eel,
Where pink thighs flash like the spokes of a wheel, where
we feel
That we know in advance all the jogtrot and the cake-walk
jokes,
All the bumfun and the gags of the comedians in boaters
and toques,
All the tricks of the virtuosos who invert the usual—

B. What will happen to us when the State takes down the
 manor wall,
 When there is no more private shooting or fishing, when
 the trees are all cut down,
 When faces are all dials and cannot smile or frown—

A. What will happen when the sniggering machine-guns in the
 hands of the young men
 Are trained on every flat and club and beauty parlour and
 Father's den

 What will happen when our civilisation like a long pent
 balloon—

B. What will happen will happen; the whore and the buffoon
 Will come off best; no dreamers, they cannot lose their
 dream
 And are at least likely to be reinstated in the new régime.
 But one thing is not likely—

A. Do not gloat over yourself
 Do not be your own vulture, high on some mountain shelf
 Huddle the pitiless abstractions bald about the neck
 Who will descend when you crumple in the plains a wreck.
 Over the randy of the theatre and cinema I hear songs
 Unlike anything—

B. The lady of the house poises the silver tongs
 And picks a lump of sugar, "ne plus ultra" she says
 "I cannot do otherwise, even to prolong my days"—

A. I cannot do otherwise either, tonight I will book my seat—

B. I will walk about the farm-yard which is replete
 As with the smell of dung so with memories—

A. I will gorge myself to satiety with the oddities
 Of every artiste, official or amateur,
 Who has pleased me in my rôle of hero-worshipper
 Who has pleased me in my rôle of individual man—

B. Let us lie once more, say "What we think, we can"
The old idealist lie—

A. And for me before I die
Let me go the round of the garish glare—

B. And on the bare and high
Places of England, the Wiltshire Downs and the Long Mynd
Let the balls of my feet bounce on the turf, my face burn in the wind
My eyelashes stinging in the wind, and the sheep like grey stones
Humble my human pretensions—

A. Let the saxophones and the xylophones
And the cult of every technical excellence, the miles of canvas in the galleries
And the canvas of the rich man's yacht snapping and tacking on the seas
And the perfection of a grilled steak—

B. Let all these so ephemeral things
Be somehow permanent like the swallow's tangent wings:
Goodbye to you, this day remember is Christmas, this morn
They say, interpret it your own way, Christ is born.

Sunday Morning

Down the road someone is practising scales,
The notes like little fishes vanish with a wink of tails,
Man's heart expands to tinker with his car
For this is Sunday morning, Fate's great bazaar;
Regard these means as ends, concentrate on this Now,
And you may grow to music or drive beyond Hindhead anyhow,

Take corners on two wheels until you go so fast
That you can clutch a fringe or two of the windy past,
That you can abstract this day and make it to the week of time
A small eternity, a sonnet self-contained in rhyme.

But listen, up the road, something gulps, the church spire
Opens its eight bells out, skulls' mouths which will not tire
To tell how there is no music or movement which secures
Escape from the weekday time. Which deadens and endures.

Snow

The room was suddenly rich and the great bay-window was
Spawning snow and pink roses against it
Soundlessly collateral and incompatible:
World is suddener than we fancy it.

World is crazier and more of it than we think,
Incorrigibly plural. I peel and portion
A tangerine and spit the pips and feel
The drunkenness of things being various.

And the fire flames with a bubbling sound for world
Is more spiteful and gay than one supposes—
On the tongue on the eyes on the ears in the palms of one's
hands—
There is more than glass between the snow and the huge roses.

LOUIS MACNEICE

Soap Suds

This brand of soap has the same smell as once in the big
House he visited when he was eight: the walls of the bathroom
open
To reveal a lawn where a great yellow ball rolls back through a
hoop
To rest at the head of a mallet held in the hands of a child.

And these were the joys of that house: a tower with a telescope;
Two great faded globes, one of the earth, one of the stars;
A stuffed black dog in the hall; a walled garden with bees;
A rabbit warren; a rockery; a vine under glass; the sea.

To which he has now returned. The day of course is fine
And a grown-up voice cries Play! The mallet slowly swings,
Then crack, a great gong booms from the dog-dark hall and the
ball
Skims forward through the hoop and then through the next
and then

Through hoops where no hoops were and each dissolves in turn
And the grass has grown head-high and an angry voice cries
Play!
But the ball is lost and the mallet slipped long since from the
hands
Under the running tap that are not the hands of a child.

Thalassa

Run out the boat, my broken comrades;
Let the old seaweed crack, the surge
Burgeon oblivious of the last
Embarkation of feckless men,
Let every adverse force converge—
Here we must needs embark again.

Run up the sail, my heartsick comrades;
Let each horizon tilt and lurch—
You know the worst: your wills are fickle,
Your values blurred, your hearts impure
And your past life a ruined church—
But let your poison be your cure.

Put out to sea, ignoble comrades,
Whose record shall be noble yet;
Butting through scarps of moving marble
The narwhal dares us to be free;
By a high star our course is set,
Our end is Life. Put out to sea.

Stephen Spender

The Prisoners

Far far the least of all, in want,
Are these,
The prisoners
Turned massive with their vaults and dark with dark.

They raise no hands, which rest upon their knees,
But lean their solid eyes against the night,
Dimly they feel
Only the furniture they use in cells.

Their Time is almost Death. The silted flow
Of years on years
Is marked by dawns
As faint as cracks on mud-flats of despair.

My pity moves amongst them like a breeze
On walls of stone
Fretting for summer leaves, or like a tune
On ears of stone.

Then, when I raise my hands to strike,
It is too late,
There are no chains that fall
Nor visionary liquid door
Melted with anger.

When have their lives been free from walls and dark
And airs that choke?
And where less prisoner to let my anger
Like a sun strike?

If I could follow them from room to womb
To plant some hope
Through the black silk of the big-bellied gown
There would I win.

No, no, no,
It is too late for anger,
Nothing prevails
But pity for the grief they cannot feel.

"In railway halls"

In railway halls, on pavements near the traffic,
They beg, their eyes made big by empty staring
And only measuring Time, like the blank clock.

No, I shall weave no tracery of pen-ornament
To make them birds upon my singing-tree:
Time merely drives these lives which do not live
As tides push rotten stuff along the shore.

—There is no consolation, no, none
In the curving beauty of that line
Traces on our graphs through history, where the
 oppressor
Starves and deprives the poor.

Paint here no draped despairs, no saddening clouds
Where the soul rests, proclaims eternity.
But let the wrong cry out as raw as wounds
This Time forgets and never heals, far less transcends.

STEPHEN SPENDER

"Not palaces, an era's crown"

Not palaces, an era's crown
Where the mind dwells, intrigues, rests;
The architectural gold-leaved flower
From people ordered like a single mind,
I build. This only what I tell:
It is too late for rare accumulation
For family pride, for beauty's filtered dusts;
I say, stamping the words with emphasis,
Drink from here energy and only energy,
As from the electric charge of a battery,
To will this Time's change.
Eye, gazelle, delicate wanderer,
Drinker of horizon's fluid line;
Ear that suspends on a chord
The spirit drinking timelessness;
Touch, love, all senses;
Leave your gardens, your singing feasts,
Your dreams of suns circling before our sun,
Of heaven after our world.
Instead, watch images of flashing brass
That strike the outward sense, the polished will
Flag of our purpose which the wind engraves.
No spirit seek here rest. But this: No man
Shall hunger: Man shall spend equally.
Our goal which we compel: Man shall be man.

That programme of the antique Satan
Bristling with guns on the indented page
With battleship towering from hilly waves:
For what? Drive of a ruining purpose
Destroying all but its age-long exploiters.
Our programme like this, yet opposite,
Death to the killers, bringing light to life.

"After they have tired"

After they have tired of the brilliance of cities
And of striving for office where at last they may languish
Hung round with easy chains until
Death and Jerusalem glorify also the crossing-sweeper:
Then those streets the rich built and their easy love
Fade like old cloths, and it is death stalks through life
Grinning white through all faces
Clean and equal like the shine from snow.

In this time when grief pours freezing over us,
When the hard light of pain gleams at every street corner,
When those who were pillars of that day's gold roof
Shrink in their clothes; surely from hunger
We may strike fire, like fire from flint?
And our strength is now the strength of our bones
Clean and equal like the shine from snow
And the strength of famine and of our enforced idleness,
And it is the strength of our love for each other.

Readers of this strange language,
We have come at last to a country
Where light equal, like the shine from snow, strikes all faces,
Here you may wonder
How it was that works, money, interest, building, could ever
hide
The palpable and obvious love of man for man.

Oh comrades, let not those who follow after
—The beautiful generation that shall spring from our sides—
Let not them wonder how after the failure of banks
The failure of cathedrals and the declared insanity of our
rulers,

We lacked the Spring-like resources of the tiger
Or of plants who strike out new roots to gushing waters.
But through torn-down portions of old fabric let their eyes
Watch the admiring dawn explode like a shell
Around us, dazing us with light like snow.

The North

Our single purpose was to walk through snow
With faces swung to their prodigious North
Like compass iron. As clerks in whited Banks
With bird-claw pens column virgin paper
To snow we added footprints.
Extensive whiteness drowned
All sense of space. We tramped through
Static, glaring days, Time's suspended blank.
That was in Spring and Autumn. Then Summer stuck
Water over rocks, and half the world
Became a ship with a deep keel, the booming floes
And icebergs with their little birds.
Twittering Snow Bunting, Greenland Wheatear
Red throated Divers; imagine butterflies
Sulphurous cloudy yellow; glory of bees
That suck from saxifrage; crowberry,
Bilberry, cranberry, *Pyrola uniflora*.
There followed winter in a frozen hut
Warm enough at the kernel, but dare to sleep
With head against the wall—ice gummed my hair.
Hate Culver's loud breathing, despite Freeman's
Fidget for washing; love only the dogs
That whine for scraps and scratch. Notice
How they run better (on short journeys) with a bitch.
In that, different from us.

Return, return, you warn. We do. There is
A network of railways, money, words, words, words.
Meals, papers, exchanges, debates,
Cinema, wireless; the worst is Marriage.
We cannot sleep. At night we watch
A speaking clearness through cloudy paranoia.
These questions are white rifts. Was
Ice our anger transformed? The raw, the motionless
Skies, were these the spirit's hunger?
The continual and hypnotized march through snow
The dropping nights of precious extinction, were these
Only the wide invention of the will,
The frozen will's evasion? If this exists
In us as madness here, as coldness
In these summer, civilized sheets: is the North
Over there, a tangible real madness
A glittering simpleton, one without towns
Only with bears and fish, a staring eye,
A new and singular sex?

An Elementary School Classroom

Far far from gusty waves, these children's faces
Like rootless weeds the torn hair round their paleness;
The tall girl with her weighed-down head; the paper-
seeming boy with rat's eyes; the stunted unlucky heir
Of twisted bones, reciting a father's gnarled disease,
His lesson from his desk. At back of the dim class
One unnoted, mild and young: his eyes live in a dream
Of squirrel's game, in tree room, other than this.

On sour cream walls, donations; Shakespeare's head
Cloudless at dawn, civilized dome riding all cities;
Belled, flowery, Tyrolese valley; open-handed map
Awarding the explicit world, of every name but here.

To few, too few, these are real windows: world and words and
  waving
Leaves, to heal. For those young lives, guilty and dangerous
Is fantasy of travel. Surely, Shakespeare is wicked

To lives that wryly turn, under the structural Lie,
Toward smiles or hate? Amongst their heap, these children
Wear skins peeped through by bones, and spectacles of steel
With mended glass, like bottle bits in slag.
Tyrol is wicked; map's promising a fable:
All of their time and space are foggy slum,
So blot their maps with slums as big as doom.

Unless, dowager, governor, these pictures, in a room
Columned above childishness, like our day's future drift
Of smoke concealing war, are voices shouting
O that beauty has words and works which break
Through coloured walls and towers. The children stand
As in a climbing mountain train. This lesson illustrates
The world green in their many valleys beneath:
The total summer heavy with their flowers.

Ice

To M——

She came in from the snowing air
Where icicle-hung architecture
Strung white fleece round the Baroque square.
I saw her face freeze in her fur,
Then my lips ran to her with fire
From the chimney corner of the room,
Where I had waited in my chair.
I kissed their heat against her skin
And watched the red make the white bloom,
While, at my care, her smiling eyes

Shone with the brilliance of the ice
Outside, whose dazzling they brought in.
  That day, until this, I forgot.
How is it now I so remember
Who, when she came indoors, saw not
The passion of her white December?

Elizabeth Bishop

Faustina, or Rock Roses

Tended by Faustina
yes in a crazy house
upon a crazy bed,
frail, of chipped enamel,
blooming above her head
into four vaguely roselike
  flower-formations,

the white woman whispers to
herself. The floorboards sag
this way and that. The crooked
towel-covered table
bears a can of talcum
and five pasteboard boxes
  of little pills,

most half-crystallized.
The visitor sits and watches
the dew glint on the screen
and in it two glow-worms
burning a drowned green.
Meanwhile the eighty-watt bulb
  betrays us all,

discovering the concern
within our stupefaction;
lighting as well on heads
of tacks in the wallpaper,
on a paper wall-pocket,
violet-embossed, glistening
  with mica flakes.

It exposes the fine white hair,
the gown with the undershirt
showing at the neck,
the pallid palm-leaf fan
she holds but cannot wield,
her white disordered sheets
like wilted roses.

Clutter of trophies,
chamber of bleached flags!
—Rags or ragged garments
hung on the chairs and hooks
each contributing its
shade of white, confusing
as undazzling.

The visitor is embarrassed
not by pain nor age
nor even nakedness,
though perhaps by its reverse.
By and by the whisper
says, "*Faustina, Faustina . . .*"
"*¡Vengo, señora!*" . . .

On bare scraping feet
Faustina nears the bed.
She exhibits the talcum powder,
the pills, the cans of "cream",
the white bowl of farina,
requesting for herself
a little *coñac;*

complaining of, explaining,
the terms of her employment.
She bends above the other.
Her sinister kind face
presents a cruel black
coincident conundrum.
Oh, is it

freedom at last, a lifelong
dream of time and silence,
dream of protection and rest?
Or is it the very worst,
the unimaginable nightmare
that never before dared last
  more than a second?

The acuteness of the question
forks instantly and starts
a snake-tongue flickering;
blurs further, blunts, softens,
separates, falls, our problems
becoming helplessly
  proliferative.

There is no way of telling.
The eyes say only either.
At last the visitor rises,
awkwardly proffers her bunch
of rust-perforated roses
and wonders oh, whence come
  all the petals.

Filling Station

Oh, but it is dirty!
—this little filling station,
oil-soaked, oil-permeated
to a disturbing, over-all
black translucency.
Be careful with that match!

Father wears a dirty,
oil-soaked monkey suit
that cuts him under the arms,
and several quick and saucy
and greasy sons assist him
(it's a family filling station),
all quite thoroughly dirty.

Do they live in the station?
It has a cement porch
behind the pumps, and on it
a set of crushed and grease-
impregnated wickerwork;
on the wicker sofa
a dirty dog, quite comfy.

Some comic books provide
the only note of color—
of certain color. They lie
upon a big dim doily
draping a taboret
(part of the set), beside
a big hirsute begonia.

Why the extraneous plant?
Why the taboret?
Why, oh why, the doily?
(Embroidered in daisy stitch
with marguerites, I think,
and heavy with gray crochet.)

Somebody embroidered the doily.
Somebody waters the plant,
or oils it, maybe. Somebody
arranges the rows of cans
so that they softly say:
ESSO—SO—SO—SO
to high-strung automobiles.
Somebody loves us all.

Charles Madge

Blocking the Pass

With an effort Grant swung the great block,
The swivel operated and five or six men
Crouched under the lee of the straight rock.

They waited in silence, or counting ten,
They thrust their fingers in their wet hair,
The steel sweated in their hands. And then

The clouds hurried across a sky quite bare,
The sounds of the station, three miles off, ceased,
The dusty birds hopped keeping watch. And there

Arose to what seemed as high as the sky at least,
Arose a giant and began to die,
Arose such a shape as the night in the East.

The stones sobbed, the trees gave a cry,
A tremulous wonder shook animal and plant,
And a decapitating anger stirred the sky

And alone, on a tall stone, stood Grant.

Fortune

The natural silence of a tree,
The motion of a mast upon the fresh-tossing sea,
Now foam-inclined, now to the sun with dignity,

Or the stone brow of a mountain
Regarded from a town, or the curvet-fountain,
Or one street-stopped in wonder at the fountain,

Or a great cloud entering the room of the sky,
Napoleon of his century,
Heard come to knowing music consciously,

Such, not us, reflect and have their day,
We are but vapour of today
Unless love's chance fall on us and call us away

As the wind takes what it can
And blowing on the fortunate face, reveals the man.

Loss

Like the dark germs across the filter clean
So in the clear day of a thousand years
This dusty cloud is creeping to our eyes,

Here, as we grow, and are as we have been
Or living give for life some morning tears
The flowering hour bent and unconscious lies.

As in Vienna now, the wounded walls
Silently speak, as deep in Austria
The battered shape of man is without shade

So, time in metaphor, tomorrow falls
On Europe, Asia and America,
And houses vanish, even as they were made,

For yesterday is always sad, its nature
Darker than love would wish in every feature.

CHARLES MADGE

Solar Creation

The sun, of whose terrain we creatures are,
Is the director of all human love,
Unit of time, and circle round the earth,

And we are the commotion born of love
And slanted rays of that illustrious star,
Peregrine of the crowded fields of birth,

The crowded lane, the market and the tower.
Like sight in pictures, real at remove,
Such is our motion on dimensional earth.

Down by the river, where the ragged are,
Continuous the cries and noise of birth,
While to the muddy edge dark fishes move,

And over all, like death, or sloping hill,
Is nature, which is larger and more still.

At War

Fire rides calmly in the air
That blows across the fields of water
That laps the papped curve of the outspread earth.

Earth is bone and builds the house
Water the blood that softly runs inside
Air is the breath by which the fire is fed.

Earth's mouth is open and will suck you down
Water climbs over earth to reach you
The assassin air is at your throat
And fire will presently split the air.

Lusty Juventus

The sea is an acre of dull glass, the land is a table
My eyes jump down from the table and go running down as far
as they are able
While one is still young and still able to employ
Nerves muscles sinews eyes mouth teeth head
A giant that threw a stone at Cærodunum
Transforming England into a salty pancake
Lichen-alive governed in gametosporous colonies
Crescented with calciform corollæ, a great stone marsh
With the dragons of dead Hercules debating
There is no end there is no end to the labours of Hercules
While one is still young and still able to employ
Feet fist eyes in the head a spade a spanner
Down down we go down the emblematic abyss
Adorned with the kisses of the gentry, come out on primrose
day
To greet the Young Bolshevik Bolus rolling up with banners
Across the passes of snake and ladder country
Idly I flung down pieces, but the fit is ended
When one was very young and able to employ
The empty salads of English advent and the formulæ of seajoy.

A Monument

All moves within the visual frame
All walks upon the ground or stands
Casting a shadow,

All grass, day's eye, the folded man
Suffer or wither up in stone
And stare there.

CHARLES MADGE

They call upon the end of the world
And the last waters overwhelming
To wash the unborn things

Bedded on time's distracted coast
Bald stones and smiling silences,
Severed, they shrink.

The hovering certainty of death
Unites the water and the sky,
Their small choice

Of evils on the watching shore.

Roy Fuller

Those of Pure Origin

After a throbbing night, the house still dark, pull
Back the curtains, see the cherry standing there—
Grain of the paper under wash of rain-clouds.

No, our disguises are not intended to
Deceive. On the contrary. And could you name
Us we shouldn't be compelled to appear so
Confusingly—smothered in white stars, whistling
Hymn tunes, putting out scaly paws to attract
Attention. Under comic aliases—
Even the specific for insomnia:
Peppermint, lime blossom, betony, scullcap—
We entice you into our dissident realms.
The staggering plots you invent in hours
Abbreviated by anxiety are
Hatched by our logic. Just as when you try to
Talk with the girl of fifteen we tilt her shoe
Inward to imply her different order.

For it's *your* world we're expounding. Don't mistake
Our endeavours. We can't tell you where you're from.
Indeed, despite our immanence we're the last
Who could reveal more than is there already.

Let alone where you're going! Darwin's infant
Enquired about his friend's father: "Where does
He do his barnacles?"—assumption of a
Universal preoccupation no more
Naive than yours, whether of indifference or
Concern. It's quite plausible that the concept
Of outside disappears outside—in that place
Where nebulae no longer have to awake
And pretend to be happy.

Our advice is:
Prefer the less likely explanation.
Different evenings, the evening star appearing
In different corners of the pane—conceive
No senseless revolution in the heavens
But a lucky change of erotic fortune;
A goddess steeped not in urine but in love.
And then so often you've been wrong why shouldn't
You be wrong about the extinction of man?

It's true we tend to avoid you, fatal as
You are in general to our fragility.
But sometimes one of us, whom you knew in flight
And particularly admired for his looks,
Lies down and allows the wind to blow the wrong way
His once glossy pinions. Look into his eye.
It regards you still, though fixed as well on worlds
More real than at that moment you can bear.
Of course, you'll soon take your spade and among
Pebbles, lapis worms, inter the eye from sight.

"Considering my present condition,
I can neither concentrate on poetry
Nor enjoy poetry." That final letter
May seem a defeat after a lifetime of
Assuming the reality of the art.
Not to us, though it's we are the defeated.
For we boast of our patience—coral *croissants*
Anchored at last to just too-heavy hill-tops;
Laboratories of finches; Galapagos
Of revelation awaiting an observer.
And you, even in the children's puzzle, are
You certain you've seen all the hidden objects?

Yes, there's the extrusion of the wall in
A clawed hump, and a grey frayed rope-end blown round
And round a bough. But what are the abstract shapes
As enigmatic in significance as
Those painters find incised from oceans by arcs
Of a parasol or enclosed from a beach
By the severe bay of a young throat and jaw?

That countenance whose eyes are as pale as if
The flesh had been clipped out to show the ash sky
Behind it . . . The voice that unavailingly
Says: "Do you remember taking your laundry
To the woman with elephant legs?" . . . The past
As ambiguous as hailstones in the gales
Of Spring: the future certain—the instant when
You stop being convinced of our existence,
And meaningless that blackbirds masquerade as owls,
That also in the dusk, making free of it
For assignations, jealousies (those affairs
Of energy and waiting unwearying,
Of obsession with menstrual blood), occur
The strange pre-marital flights of humans.

What does it matter that the baptistry proves
As dusty and void as bad nuts when its doors
Provide a progression of style, the basher
Of bronze breaking out from pious platitudes
Into arcades of applied geometry,
Thronged with our perfect but realistic forms?

The mad poet called us, untranslatably:
"Those of pure origin"—left you to divine
Whether we rise from phenomena or,
Perhaps more likely, also require your presence,
As the cathedral the plague, pity thc war.

But how can we pretend our hemisphere-wide
Lament, the random trickling and joining of tears
On acres of glass, is entirely for your
Predicament—as your lives, borne upon the
More and more dubiously physical, move
To regions of abnegation and concern
Whose angels we are; though, under cruel casques,
Our curls, our thick, parted lips ever youthful,
Complexions marked with still unmalignant moles
Of the actual, scabs on unfolding leaves?

Lawrence Durrell

from The Death of General Uncebunke: A Biography in Little

1938

To Kay in Tahiti: now dead.

"Not satire but an exercise in ironic compassion."

I

My uncle sleeps in the image of death.
In the greenhouse and in the potting-shed
The wrens junket: the old girl with the trowel
Is a pillar of salt, insufferably brittle.
His not to reason why, though a thinking man.
Beside his mesmeric incomprehension
The little mouse mopping and mowing,
The giraffe and the spin-turtle, these can
On my picture-book look insufferably little
But knowing, incredibly Knowing.

II

My uncle has gone beyond astronomy.
He sleeps in the music-room of the Host.
Voyage was always his entertainment
Who followed a crooked needle under Orion,
Saw the griffin, left notes on the baobab,
Charted the Yellow Coast.

He like a faultless liner, finer never took air,
But snow on the wings altered the altitude,
She paused in a hollow pocket, faltered:
The enormous lighted bird is dashed in snow.
Now in the labyrinth God will put him wise,
Correct the instruments, will alter even
The impetuous stance, the focus of the eyes.

III

Aunt Prudence, she was the eye of the needle.
Sleeping, a shepherdess of ghostly sheep.
"Thy will be done in Baden Baden.
In Ouchy, Lord, and in Vichy."
In the garden of the vicarage sorting stamps
Was given merit of the poor in spirit
For dusting a cinquefoil, tuning the little lamps.

Well, God sends weather, the English apple,
The weeping willow.
Grum lies the consort of Prudence quite:
Mum as a long fiddle in regimentals:
This sudden IT between two tropical thumbs.
Unwrinkle him, Lord, unriddle this strange gorgon,
For tall Prudence who softens the small lamps,
Gives humble air to the organ that it hums.

VIII

My uncle has gone beyond astronomy.
Three, six, nine of the dead languages
Are folded under his lip
He has crossed over into Tartary,
Burnt his boats, dragged the black ice for bodies,
Seen trees in the water, skippered God's little ship.

He is now luggage, excess baggage,
Not wanted on voyage, scaling a pass,
Or swinging a cutlass in the Caribbean,
Under Barbados chewing the frantic marsh-rice,
Seven dead men, a crooked foot, a cracked jaw,
Ten teeth like hollow dice.

My uncle is sleeping in economy.
No word is wasted for the common ghost
Speaks inwards: he lies in the status
Of death's dumb music, the dumb dead king
On an ivory coast.

IX

Prudence had no dog and but one cat,
Black of bonnet the Lord's plain precept saw
At the at-home, on Calvary, in the darkest nook
He was there; He leaned on a window smiling,
The God Shepherd crooking his ghostly crook.
Prudence did dip and delve in the Holy Book,
Alpha to omega angels told her the tale,
Feeding the parrot, pensive over a croquet-hoop:

"Once upon a time was boy and girl,
Living on cherry, berry, fisherman's silver catch.
Now the crass cock crows in the coop,
Prudence, the door dangles, lacking a latch."

XIII

My uncle sleeps in the image of death.
The shadow of other worlds, deep-water penumbra
Covers his marble: he is past sighing,
Body a great slug there, a fine white
Pike in a green pond lying.
My uncle was a red man. The dead man
Knew to shoe horses: the habits of the owl,
Time of tillage, foison, cutting of lumber,
Like Saint Columba,
Could coax the squirrels into his cowl.

Heu! for the tombeau, the sombre flambeau,
Immanent with God he lies in Limbo.
Break punic rock. Weather-man of the tomb,
We are left among little mice and insects,
Time's clock-work womb.

XIV

Prudence sweetly sang both crotchet and quaver,
Death riped an eyeball, the dog-days
Proffered salt without savour, the cards were cut.
She heard a primordial music, the Host's tune
For the guest's swoon—God going the gamut.
Honour a toast for the regimental mascot,
The thin girl the boys of the blue fourteenth,
Driving to Ascot: a wedding under the sabres,
Tinker and tailorman, soldier or sailor,
Lads of the village entering harbour,
O respect also those windowless features,
The stainless face of the provincial barber.

Prudence plays monumental patience by candles:
The puffins sit in a book: the muffins are molten:
The crass clock chimes,
Timely the hour and deserved.
Presently will come the two welcome angels
Noise in the hall, the last supper be served.

On First Looking into Loeb's Horace

I found your Horace with the writing in it;
Out of time and context came upon
This lover of vines and slave to quietness,
Walking like a figure of smoke here, musing
Among his high and lovely Tuscan pines.

All the small-holder's ambitions, the yield
Of wine-bearing grape, pruning and drainage
Laid out by laws, almost like the austere
Shell of his verses—a pattern of Latin thrift;
Waiting so patiently in a library for
Autumn and the drying of the apples;
The betraying hour-glass and its deathward drift.

Surely the hard blue winterset
Must have conveyed a message to him—
The premonitions that the garden heard
Shrunk in its shirt of hair beneath the stars,
How rude and feeble a tenant was the self,
An Empire, the body with its members dying—
And unwhistling now the vanished Roman bird?

The fruit-trees dropping apples; he counted them;
The soft bounding fruit on leafy terraces,
And turned to the consoling winter rooms
Where, facing south, began the great prayer,
With his reed laid upon the margins
Of the dead, his stainless authors,
Upright, severe on an uncomfortable chair.

Here, where your clear hand marked up
"The hated cypress" I added "Because it grew
On tombs, revealed his fear of autumn and the urns",
Depicting a solitary at an upper window
Revising metaphors for the winter sea: "O
Dark head of storm-tossed curls"; or silently
Watching the North Star which like a fever burns

Away the envy and neglect of the common,
Shining on this terrace, lifting up in recreation
The sad heart of Horace who must have seen it only
As a metaphor for the self and its perfection—
A burning heart quite constant in its station.

Easy to be patient in the summer,
The light running like fishes among the leaves,
Easy in August with its cones of blue
Sky uninvaded from the north; but winter
With its bareness pared his words to points
Like stars, leaving them pure but very few.

He will not know how we discerned him, disregarding
The post of sufficiency, the landed man,
Found a suffering limb on the great Latin tree
Whose roots live in the barbarian grammar we
Use, yet based in him, his mason's tongue;
Describing clearly a bachelor, sedentary,
With a fond weakness for bronze-age conversation,
Disguising a sense of failure in a hatred for the young,

Who built in the Sabine hills this forgery
Of completeness, an orchard with a view of Rome;
Who studiously developed his sense of death
Till it was all around him, walking at the circus,
At the baths, playing dominoes in a shop—
The escape from self-knowledge with its tragic
Imperatives: *Seek, suffer, endure*. The Roman
In him feared the Law and told him where to stop.

So perfect a disguise for one who had
Exhausted death in art—yet who could guess
You would discern the liar by a line,
The suffering hidden under gentleness
And add upon the flyleaf in your tall
Clear hand: "Fat, human and unloved,
And held from loving by a sort of wall,
Laid down his books and lovers one by one,
Indifference and success had crowned them all."

George Barker

Summer Idyll

Sometimes in summer months, the gestate earth
Loaded to gold, the boughs arching downward
Burdened, the shallow and glucose streams
Teeming, flowers out, all gold camouflage
Of the collusive summer; but under the streams
Winter lies coldly, and coldly embedded in
The corn hunger lies germinally, want under
The abundance, poverty pulling down
The tautened boughs, and need is the seed.

Robe them in superb summer, at angles
Their bones penetrate, or with a principality
Of Spring possess them, under the breast
Space of a vacancy spreads like a foul
Ghost flower, want; and the pressure upon
The eyeballs of their spirits, upon the organs
Of their spare bodies, the pressure upon
Their movement and their merriment, loving and
Living, the pressure upon their lives like deep
Seas, becomes insufferable, to be suffered.

Sometimes the summer lessens a moment the pressure.
Large as the summer rose some rise
Bathing in rivers or at evening harrying rabbits,
Indulging in games in meadows—and some are idle, strewn
Over the parks like soiled paper like summer
Insects, bathed in sweat or at evening harried
By watchmen, park-keepers, policemen—indulge in games
Dreaming as I dream of rest and cleanliness and cash.

And the gardens exhibit the regalia of the season
Like debutante queans, between which they wander
Blown with vague odours, seduced by the pure
Beauty, like drowned men floating in bright coral.
Summer, denuding young women, also denudes
Them, removes jackets, exposing backs—
Summer moves many up the river in boats

Trailing their fingers in the shadowed water; they
Too move by the river, and in the water shadows
Trail a hand, which need not find a bank,
Face downward like bad fruit. Cathedrals and Building
Societies, as they appear, disappear; and Beethoven
Is played more loudly to deafen the Welsh echoes,
And Summer, blowing over the Mediterranean
Like swans, like perfect swans.

To My Mother

Most near, most dear, most loved and most far,
Under the window where I often found her
Sitting as huge as Asia, seismic with laughter,
Gin and chicken helpless in her Irish hand,
Irresistible as Rabelais, but most tender for
The lame dogs and hurt birds that surround her,—
She is a procession no one can follow after
But bc like a little dog following a brass band.

She will not glance up at the bomber, or condescend
To drop her gin and scuttle to a cellar,
But lean on the mahogany table like a mountain
Whom only faith can move, and so I send
O all my faith, and all my love to tell her
That she will move from mourning into morning.

Sonnet of Fishes

Bright drips the morning from its trophied nets
Looped along a sky flickering fish and wing,
Cobbles like salmon crowd up waterfalling
Streets where life dies thrashing as the sea forgets,
True widow what she has lost; and ravished, lets
The knuckledustered sun shake bullying
A fist of glory over her. Every thing,
Even the sly night, gives up its lunar secrets.

And I with pilchards cold in my pocket make
Red-eyed a way to bed. But in my blood
Crying I hear, still, the leap of the silver diver
Caught in four cords after his fatal strake:
And then, the immense imminence not understood,
Death, in a dark, in a deep, in a dream, for ever.

from In Memory of David Archer

XIV

Images! Venerable as Druidical trees,
pockmarked, meaningless, daubed with woad
And spit and sperm like mistletoe, they sit,
the old gods of the imagination
presiding over the woods of the intellect
with a power drawn from sources far too deep
for the axe to reach. Like wounds they provide
an egress through which the lifeblood can escape
and the atavistic memories return. All images
transcend their own specifications simply
because they involve all other images, just as
the nexus of individual existence involves
all of us in a sort of infinitely

complex and singular law of effects. Thus it is that
the Yarmouth windmill seen by a dirty pond
from which the skeleton of an old bicycle points
up at the sky, this may call up from the memory
a day when we dreamed of death by exhaustion in
the illusions of Hither Arabia. What law operates here?
It is the law of Medusa's antitheses, so
that every image carries all other images
on its small back in an ascending order
until, at the top, there sits the opposite
and contradiction. St George gives birth to The Dragon.

The Oak and the Olive

Seven years lived in Italy leave me convinced
that the angel guarding us knows only too well
what she is doing. There is a curious sense
in which that place whose floral sophistication
—whose moral sophistication—we all happily acknowledge,
resembles in fact a delicious garden inhabited
by seven-year-old children. I can perceive
this innocence of spirit even in the most cynical
of Italians I have loved, and I think that
this innocence ensues simply from the sun. There
it is perfectly possible to assassinate one's best friend
with a kind of histrionic guiltlessness, because
the sun would continue to shine after the crime,
the gardens to dream in the afternoon, and later
the evening cast a benevolent shadowing over
the corpse of one's cold friend. Furthermore years
of white and gold sunlight tend to deprive one of
the pessimistic faculty. It is harder to indulge there
the natural Anglosaxon melancholy
because I, for instance, found a bough of oranges
growing through the skylight of my lavatory.

And all these mother of pearl evenings and these
serene Venus green skies and Lucullan landscapes
have in the end the effect of depriving one
of precisely that consciousness of shame out
of which the adult Nordic monster
of evil is generated. There are no Grendls here.
And so it is possible often in the Borghese
Gardens to act as though one was, of course,
a criminal cynic but a criminal cynic whom
the sun does not decline to befriend, to whom small
birds still confide, and whom the sylvan
evening landscape is still prepared to sleep with.
Then it seems likely that Providence or Italy or
even the conscience has forgiven us the enormities
that brought us here. When the chilling
rain falls upon me in the North I know
only too well that it does so as
a moral punitive. I write this in
a Norfolk August and the rains pour down
daily upon a landscape which derives
its masculine nobility from the simple
fact that it has survived. It has survived
the flood, the winter, the fall and the Black
nor'-easter. The old oak tree hangs out
that great twisted bough from which the corpse
of the criminal cynic has just dropped in decay.
The clouds do not decorate the sky, they entomb it,
and the streams have swollen to cataracts. Weeds
flourish and the summer corn is crushed flat.
What could even come from all this hopeless
melancholy save a knowledge, as by allegory,
of our culpability? Why, then, should I find
a child's face bright with tears haunting my mind?

R. S. Thomas

Welsh Landscape

To live in Wales is to be conscious
At dusk of the spilled blood
That went to the making of the wild sky,
Dyeing the immaculate rivers
In all their courses.
It is to be aware,
Above the noisy tractor
And hum of the machine
Of strife in the strung woods,
Vibrant with sped arrows.
You cannot live in the present,
At least not in Wales.
There is the language for instance,
The soft consonants
Strange to the ear.
There are cries in the dark at night
As owls answer the moon,
And thick ambush of shadows,
Hushed at the fields' corners.
There is no present in Wales,
And no future;
There is only the past,
Brittle with relics,
Wind-bitten towers and castles
With sham ghosts;
Mouldering quarries and mines;
And an impotent people,
Sick with inbreeding,
Worrying the carcase of an old song.

In a Country Church

To one kneeling down no word came,
Only the wind's song, saddening the lips
Of the grave saints, rigid in glass;
Or the dry whisper of unseen wings,
Bats not angels, in the high roof.

Was he balked by silence? He kneeled long,
And saw love in a dark crown
Of thorns blazing, and a winter tree
Golden with fruit of a man's body.

Postscript

As life improved, their poems
Grew sadder and sadder. Was there oil
For the machine? It was
The vinegar in the poet's cup.

The tins marched to the music
Of the conveyor belt. A billion
Mouths opened. Production,
Production, the wheels

Whistled. Among the forests
Of metal the one human
Sound was the lament of
The poets for deciduous language.

R. S. THOMAS

Petition

And I standing in the shade
Have seen it a thousand times
Happen: first theft, then murder;
Rape; the rueful acts
Of the blind hand. I have said
New prayers, or said the old
In a new way. Seeking the poem
In the pain, I have learned
Silence is best, paying for it
With my conscience. I am eyes
Merely, witnessing virtue's
Defeat; seeing the young born
Fair, knowing the cancer
Awaits them. One thing I have asked
Of the disposer of the issues
Of life: that truth should defer
To beauty. It was not granted.

Selah

A procession of honest men
going to their doom, wind-broken
their hands, their dreams withering
behind them like the afterbirth
of a machine. To a hero a
harbour is that which he sets out
from. Is it history that is the salt
in his spittle? We demand our reason
from skies that have the emptiness
of our affirmations. In Israel once
the chastity of the unthinking
body was violated by

the spirit, but the earth had
its revenge; kings opened
their veins over the aridity
of the treaties. The nations proceeded
to the manufacture of the angels
with steel wings, hurrying
to and fro with their unnecessary
message. Beyond the horizons
of our knowledge, in deserts
not of its own making, the self
sought for the purpose that had brought it there.

Dylan Thomas

"The force that through the green fuse drives the flower"

The force that through the green fuse drives the flower
Drives my green age; that blasts the roots of trees
Is my destroyer.
And I am dumb to tell the crooked rose
My youth is bent by the same wintry fever.

The force that drives the water through the rocks
Drives my red blood; that dries the mouthing streams
Turns mine to wax.
And I am dumb to mouth unto my veins
How at the mountain spring the same mouth sucks.

The hand that whirls the water in the pool
Stirs the quicksand; that ropes the blowing wind
Hauls my shroud sail.
And I am dumb to tell the hanging man
How of my clay is made the hangman's lime.

The lips of time leech to the fountain head;
Love drips and gathers, but the fallen blood
Shall calm her sores.
And I am dumb to tell a weather's wind
How time has ticked a heaven round the stars.

And I am dumb to tell the lover's tomb
How at my sheet goes the same crooked worm.

"Light breaks where no sun shines"

Light breaks where no sun shines;
Where no sea runs, the waters of the heart
Push in their tides;
And, broken ghosts with glowworms in their heads,
The things of light
File through the flesh where no flesh decks the bones.

A candle in the thighs
Warms youth and seed and burns the seeds of age;
Where no seed stirs,
The fruit of man unwrinkles in the stars,
Bright as a fig;
Where no wax is, the candle shows its hairs.

Dawn breaks behind the eyes;
From poles of skull and toe the windy blood
Slides like a sea;
Nor fenced, nor staked, the gushers of the sky
Spout to the rod
Divining in a smile the oil of tears.

Night in the sockets rounds,
Like some pitch moon, the limit of the globes;
Day lights the bone;
Where no cold is, the skinning gales unpin
The winter's robes;
The film of spring is hanging from the lids.

Light breaks on secret lots,
On tips of thought where thoughts smell in the rain;
When logics die,
The secret of the soil grows through the eye,
And blood jumps in the sun;
Above the waste allotments the dawn halts.

DYLAN THOMAS

After the Funeral

In memory of Ann Jones

After the funeral, mule praises, brays,
Windshake of sailshaped ears, muffle-toed tap
Tap happily of one peg in the thick
Grave's foot, blinds down the lids, the teeth in black,
The spittled eyes, the salt ponds in the sleeves,
Morning smack of the spade that wakes up sleep,
Shakes a desolate boy who slits his throat
In the dark of the coffin and sheds dry leaves,
That breaks one bone to light with a judgment clout,
After the feast of tear-stuffed time and thistles
In a room with a stuffed fox and a stale fern,
I stand, for this memorial's sake, alone
In the snivelling hours with dead, humped Ann
Whose hooded, fountain heart once fell in puddles
Round the parched worlds of Wales and drowned each sun
(Though this for her is a monstrous image blindly
Magnified out of praise; her death was a still drop;
She would not have me sinking in the holy
Flood of her heart's fame; she would lie dumb and deep
And need no druid of her broken body).
But I, Ann's bard on a raised hearth, call all
The seas to service that her wood-tongued virtue
Babble like a bellbuoy over the hymning heads,
Bow down the walls of the ferned and foxy woods
That her love sing and swing through a brown chapel,
Bless her bent spirit with four, crossing birds.
Her flesh was meek as milk, but this skyward statue
With the wild breast and blessed and giant skull
Is carved from her in a room with a wet window
In a fiercely mourning house in a crooked year.
I know her scrubbed and sour humble hands
Lie with religion in their cramp, her threadbare
Whisper in a damp word, her wits drilled hollow,
Her fist of a face died clenched on a round pain;
And sculptured Ann is seventy years of stone.

These cloud-sopped, marble hands, this monumental
Argument of the hewn voice, gesture and psalm,
Storm me forever over her grave until
The stuffed lung of the fox twitch and cry Love
And the strutting fern lay seeds on the black sill.

from Altarwise by Owl-light

I

Altarwise by owl-light in the half-way house
The gentleman lay graveward with his furies;
Abaddon in the hangnail cracked from Adam,
And, from his fork, a dog among the fairies,
The atlas-eater with a jaw for news,
Bit out the mandrake with to-morrow's scream.
Then, penny-eyed, that gentleman of wounds,
Old cock from nowheres and the heaven's egg,
With bones unbuttoned to the half-way winds,
Hatched from the windy salvage on one leg,
Scraped at my cradle in a walking word
That night of time under the Christward shelter:
I am the long world's gentleman, he said,
And share my bed with Capricorn and Cancer.

IV

What is the metre of the dictionary?
The size of genesis? the short spark's gender?
Shade without shape? the shape of Pharaoh's echo?
(My shape of age nagging the wounded whisper).
Which sixth of wind blew out the burning gentry?
(Questions are hunchbacks to the poker marrow).
What of a bamboo man among your acres?
Corset the boneyards for a crooked boy?
Button your bodice on a hump of splinters,

My camel's eyes will needle through the shroud.
Love's reflection of the mushroom features,
Stills snapped by night in the bread-sided field,
Once close-up smiling in the wall of pictures,
Arc-lamped thrown back upon the cutting flood.

VII

Now stamp the Lord's Prayer on a grain of rice,
A Bible-leaved of all the written woods
Strip to this tree: a rocking alphabet,
Genesis in the root, the scarecrow word,
And one light's language in the book of trees.
Doom on deniers at the wind-turned statement.
Time's tune my ladies with the teats of music,
The scaled sea-sawers, fix in a naked sponge
Who sucks the bell-voiced Adam out of magic,
Time, milk, and magic, from the world beginning.
Time is the tune my ladies lend their heartbreak,
From bald pavilions and the house of bread
Time tracks the sound of shape on man and cloud,
On rose and icicle the ringing handprint.

X

Let the tale's sailor from a Christian voyage
Atlaswise hold half-way off the dummy bay
Time's ship-racked gospel on the globe I balance:
So shall winged harbours through the rockbirds' eyes
Spot the blown word, and on the seas I image
December's thorn screwed in a brow of holly.
Let the first Peter from a rainbow's quayrail
Ask the tall fish swept from the bible east,
What rhubarb man peeled in her foam-blue channel
Has sown a flying garden round that sea-ghost?
Green as beginning, let the garden diving
Soar, with its two bark towers, to that Day
When the worm builds with the gold straws of venom
My nest of mercies in the rude, red tree.

A Refusal to Mourn the Death, by Fire, of a Child in London

Never until the mankind making
Bird beast and flower
Fathering and all humbling darkness
Tells with silence the last light breaking
And the still hour
Is come of the sea tumbling in harness

And I must enter again the round
Zion of the water bead
And the synagogue of the ear of corn
Shall I let pray the shadow of a sound
Or sow my salt seed
In the least valley of sackcloth to mourn

The majesty and burning of the child's death.
I shall not murder
The mankind of her going with a grave truth
Nor blaspheme down the stations of the breath
With any further
Elegy of innocence and youth.

Deep with the first dead lies London's daughter,
Robed in the long friends,
The grains beyond age, the dark veins of her mother,
Secret by the unmourning water
Of the riding Thames.
After the first death, there is no other.

David Gascoyne

Landscape

Across the correct perspective to the painted sky
Scores of reflected bridges merging
One into the other pass, and crowds with flags
Rush over them, and clouds like acrobats
Swing on an invisible trapeze.

The light like a sharpened pencil
Writes histories of darkness on the wall,
While walls fall inwards, septic wounds
Burst open like sewn mouths, and rain
Eternally descends through planetary space.

We ask: Whence comes this light?
Whence comes the rain, the planetary
Silences, these aqueous monograms
Of our unique and isolated selves?
Only a dusty statue lifts and drops its hand.

In Defence of Humanism

To M. Salvador Dali

The face of the precipice is black with lovers;
The sun above them is a bag of nails; the spring's
First rivers hide among their hair.
Goliath plunges his hand into the poisoned well
And bows his head and feels my feet walk through his brain.
The children chasing butterflies turn round and see him there,
With his hand in the well and my body growing from his head,
And are afraid. They drop their nets and walk into the wall like
smoke.

The smooth plain with its rivers listens to the cliff
Like a basilisk eating flowers.
And the children, lost in the shadows of the catacombs,
Call to the mirrors for help:
"Strong-bow of salt, cutlass of memory,
Write on my map the name of every river."

A flock of banners fight their way through the telescoped forest
And fly away like birds towards the sound of roasting meat.
Sand falls into the boiling rivers through the telescopes' mouths
And forms clear drops of acid with petals of whirling flame.
Heraldic animals wade through the asphyxia of planets,
Butterflies burst from their skins and grow long tongues like
plants,
The plants play games with a suit of mail like a cloud.

Mirrors write Goliath's name upon my forehead,
While the children are killed in the smoke of the catacombs
And lovers float down from the cliff like rain.

John Berryman

Dream Song No. 69

Love her he doesn't but the thought he puts
into that young woman
would launch a national product
complete with TV spots & skywriting
outlets in Bonn & Tokyo
I mean it

Let it be known that nine words have not passed
between herself and Henry;
looks, smiles.
God help Henry, who deserves it all
every least part of that infernal & unconscious
woman, and the pain.

I feel as if, unique, she . . . Biddable?
Fates, conspire.
—Mr Bones, *please*.
—Vouchsafe me, Sleepless One,
a personal experience of the body of Mrs Boogry
before I pass from lust!

from His Toy, His Dream, His Rest

147

Henry's mind grew blacker the more he thought.
He looked onto the world like the act of an aged whore.
Delmore, Delmore.
He flung to pieces and they hit the floor.
Nothing was true but what Marcus Aurelius taught,
"All that is foul smell & blood in a bag."

He lookt on the world like the leavings of a hag.
Almost his love died from him, any more.
His mother & William
were vivid in the same mail Delmore died.
The world is lunatic. This is the last ride.
Delmore, Delmore.

High in the summer branches the poet sang.
His throat ached, and he could sing no more.
All ears closed
across the heights where Delmore & Gertrude sprang
so long ago, in the goodness of which it was composed.
Delmore, Delmore!

153

I'm cross with god who has wrecked this generation.
First he seized Ted, then Richard, Randall, and now Delmore.
In between he gorged on Sylvia Plath.
That was a first rate haul. He left alive
fools I could number like a kitchen knife
but Lowell he did not touch.

Somewhere the enterprise continues, not—
yellow the sun lies on the baby's blouse—
in Henry's staggered thought.
I suppose the word would be, we must submit.
Later.
I hang, and I will not be part of it.

A friend of Henry's contrasted God's career
with Mozart's, leaving Henry with nothing to say
but praise for a word so apt.
We suffer on, a day, a day, a day.
And never again can come, like a man slapped,
news like this

366

Chilled in this Irish pub I wish my loves
well, well to strangers, well to all his friends,
seven or so in number,
I forgive my enemies, especially two,
races his heart, at so much magnanimity,
can it all be true?

—Mr Bones, you on a trip outside yourself.
Has you seen a medicine man? You sound will-like,
a testament & such.
Is you going?—Oh, I suffer from a strike
& a strike & three balls: I stand up for much,
Wordsworth & that sort of thing.

The pitcher dreamed. He threw a hazy curve,
I took it in my stride & out I struck,
lonesome Henry.
These Songs are not meant to be understood, you understand.
They are only meant to terrify & comfort.
Lilac was found in his hand.

Sonnet: 115

All we were going strong last night this time,
the *mots* were flying & the frozen daiquiris
were downing, supine on the floor lay Lise
listening to Schubert grievous & sublime,
my head was frantic with a following rime:
it was a good evening, an evening to please,
I kissed her in the kitchen—ecstasies—
among so much good we tamped down the crime.

The weather's changing. This morning was cold,
as I made for the grove, without expectation,
some hundred Sonnets in my pocket, old,
to read her if she came. Presently the sun
yellowed the pines & my lady came not
in blue jeans & a sweater. I sat down & wrote.

Gavin Ewart

A Christmas Message

In the few warm weeks
   before Christmas and the cold
the Toy Department is organized like a factory floor.
They're using epitaxial planar techniques
   in the labs. The toys are sold
and there's rationalized packaging and at the hot core

of the moving mass
   sweats a frost-powdered Father Christmas
in a red dressing-gown and an off-white beard.
What he wants most is a draught Bass.
   On a dry Hellenic isthmus
Zeus was a god who was equally hated and feared;

England is a Peloponnese
   and Father Christmas a poor old sod
like any other, autochthonous. Who believes
in the beard and the benevolence? Even in Greece
   or Rome there is only a bogus God
for children under five. Those he loves, he deceives.

The Deceptive Grin of the Gravel Porters

Through the rain forests, up a long river,
over greensand and clay and red earth,
they toil like ants in their long procession,
hacking at difficulties that grow and close again,
covering once more the path behind them.

Following these unimportant carriers of the unimportant,
we seldom see them. When we do, they grin.
After the bad patches they turn with a kind of smirk
and beckon us. There are large animals too
that rustle through the hemispheres.

Travelling over chalk to a familiar sea
is all we dream of where the trees are strangled
by the great sneering creepers. Sunlit birds
yakkety yak above our own deep gloom,
hundreds of feet over our inadequate heads.

How did they do it? We see the marks on trees
but made by what? teeth, weapons, little axes.
They don't communicate except to grin.
We know they're there but jungles grow so fast
and all we have are bruised and bleeding hands.

Robert Lowell

Mr Edwards and the Spider

I saw the spiders marching through the air,
Swimming from tree to tree that mildewed day
In late August when the hay
Came creaking to the barn. But where
The wind is westerly,
Where gnarled November makes the spiders fly
Into the apparitions of the sky,
They purpose nothing but their ease and die
Urgently beating east to sunrise and the sea;

What are we in the hands of the great God?
It was in vain you set up thorn and briar
In battle array against the fire
And treason crackling in your blood;
For the wild thorns grow tame
And will do nothing to oppose the flame;
Your lacerations tell the losing game
You play against a sickness past your cure.
How will the hands be strong? How will the heart endure?

A very little thing, a little worm,
Or hourglass-blazoned spider, it is said,
Can kill a tiger. Will the dead
Hold up his mirror and affirm
To the four winds the smell
And flash of his authority? It's well
If God who holds you to the pit of hell,
Much as one holds a spider, will destroy,
Baffle and dissipate your soul. As a small boy

On Windsor Marsh, I saw the spider die
When thrown into the bowels of fierce fire:
There's no long struggle, no desire
To get up on its feet and fly—
It stretches out its feet
And dies. This is the sinner's last retreat;
Yes, and no strength exerted on the heat
Then sinews the abolished will, when sick
And full of burning, it will whistle on a brick.

But who can plumb the sinking of that soul?
Josiah Hawley, picture yourself cast
Into a brick-kiln where the blast
Fans your quick vitals to a coal—
If measured by a glass,
How long would it seem burning! Let there pass
A minute, ten, ten trillion; but the blaze
Is infinite, eternal: this is death,
To die and know it. This is the Black Widow, death.

A Mad Negro Soldier Confined at Munich

"We're all Americans, except the Doc,
a Kraut DP, who kneels and bathes my eye.
The boys who floored me, two black maniacs, try
to pat my hands. Rounds, rounds! Why punch the clock?

In Munich the zoo's rubble fumes with cats;
hoydens with air-guns prowl the Koenigsplatz,
and pink the pigeons on the mustard spire.
Who but my girl-friend set the town on fire?

Cat-houses talk cold turkey to my guards;
I found my *fraulein* stitching outing shirts
in the black forest of the coloured wards—
lieutenants squawked like chickens in her skirts.

Her German language made my arteries harden—
I've no annuity from the pay we blew.
I chartered an aluminium canoe,
I had her six times in the English Garden.

Oh mama, mama, like a trolley-pole
sparking at contact, her electric shock—
the power-house! . . . The doctor calls our roll—
no knives, nor forks. We file before the clock,

and fancy minnows, slaves of habit, shoot
like starlight through their air-conditioned bowl.
It's time for feeding. Each subnormal boot-
black heart is pulsing to its ant-egg dole."

Skunk Hour

For Elizabeth Bishop

Nautilus Island's hermit
heiress still lives through winter in her Spartan cottage;
her sheep still graze above the sea.
Her son's a bishop. Her farmer
is first selectman in our village;
she's in her dotage.

Thirsting for
the hierarchic privacy
of Queen Victoria's century,
she buys up all
the eyesores facing her shore,
and lets them fall.

The season's ill—
we've lost our summer millionaire,
who seemed to leap from an L.L. Bean
catalogue. His nine-knot yawl
was auctioned off to lobstermen:
A red fox stain covers Blue Hill.

And now our fairy
decorator brightens his shot for fall;
his fishnet's filled with orange cork,
orange, his cobbler's bench and awl;
there is no money in his work,
he'd rather marry.

One dark night,
my Tudor Ford climbed the hill's skull;
I watched for love-cars. Lights turned down,
they lay together, hull to hull,
where the graveyard shelves on the town. . . .
My mind's not right.

A car radio bleats,
"Love, O careless Love. . . ." I hear
my ill-spirit sob in each blood cell,
as if my hand were at its throat. . . .
I myself am hell;
nobody's here—

only skunks, that search
in the moonlight for a bite to eat.
They march on their soles up Main Street:
white stripes, moonstruck eyes' red fire
under the chalk-dry and spar spire
of the Trinitarian Church.

I stand on top
of our back steps and breathe the rich air—
a mother skunk with her column of kittens swills the garbage
  pail.
She jabs her wedge-head in a cup
of sour cream, drops her ostrich tail,
and will not scare.

ROBERT LOWELL

Waking Early Sunday Morning

O to break loose, like the chinook
salmon jumping and falling back,
nosing up to the impossible
stone and bone-crushing waterfall—
raw-jawed, weak-fleshed there, stopped by ten
steps of the roaring ladder, and then
to clear the top on the last try,
alive enough to spawn and die.

Stop, back off. The salmon breaks
water, and now my body wakes
to feel the unpolluted joy
and criminal leisure of a boy—
no rainbow smashing a dry fly
in the white run is free as I,
here squatting like a dragon on
time's hoard before the day's begun!

Vermin run for their unstopped holes;
in some dark nook a fieldmouse rolls
a marble, hours on end, then stops;
the termite in the woodwork sleeps—
listen, the creatures of the night
obsessive, casual, sure of foot,
go on grinding, while the sun's
daily remorseful blackout dawns.

Fierce, fireless mind, running downhill.
Look up and see the harbor fill:
business as usual in eclipse
goes down to the sea in ships—
wake of refuse, dacron rope,
bound for Bermuda or Good Hope,
all bright before the morning watch
the wine-dark hulls of yawl and ketch.

I watch a glass of water wet
with a fine fuzz of icy sweat,
silvery colors touched with sky,
serene in their neutrality—
yet if I shift, or change my mood,
I see some object made of wood,
background behind it of brown grain,
to darken it, but not to stain.

O that the spirit could remain
tinged but untarnished by its strain!
Better dressed and stacking birch,
or lost with the Faithful at Church—
anywhere, but somewhere else!
And now the new electric bells,
clearly chiming, "Faith of our fathers",
and now the congregation gathers.

O Bible chopped and crucified
in hymns we hear but do not read,
none of the milder subtleties
of grace or art will sweeten these
stiff quatrains shovelled out four-square—
they sing of peace, and preach despair;
yet they gave darkness some control,
and left a loophole for the soul.

No, put old clothes on, and explore
the corners of the woodshed for
its dregs and dreck: tools with no handle,
ten candle-ends not worth a candle,
old lumber banished from the Temple,
damned by Paul's precept and example,
cast from the kingdom, banned in Israel,
the wordless sign, the tinkling cymbal.

When will we see Him face to face?
Each day, He shines through darker glass.
In this small town where everything
is known, I see His vanishing
emblems, His white spire and flag-
pole sticking out above the fog,
like old white china doorknobs, sad,
slight, useless things to calm the mad.

Hammering military splendor,
top-heavy Goliath in full armor—
little redemption in the mass
liquidations of their brass,
elephant and phalanx moving
with the times and still improving,
when that kingdom hit the crash:
a million foreskins stacked like trash . . .

Sing softer! But what if a new
diminuendo brings no true
tenderness, only restlessness,
excess, the hunger for success,
sanity of self-deception
fixed and kicked by reckless caution,
while we listen to the bells—
anywhere, but somewhere else!

O to break loose, All life's grandeur
is something with a girl in summer . . .
elated as the President
girdled by his establishment
this Sunday morning, free to chaff
his own thoughts with his bear-cuffed staff,
swimming nude, unbuttoned, sick
of his ghost-written rhetoric!

No weekends for the gods now. Wars
flicker, earth licks its open sores,
fresh breakage, fresh promotions, chance
assassinations, no advance.
Only man thinning out his kind
sounds through the Sabbath noon, the blind
swipe of the pruner and his knife
busy about the tree of life . . .

Pity the planet, all joy gone
from this sweet volcanic cone;
peace to our children when they fall
in small war on the heels of small
war—until the end of time
to police the earth, a ghost
orbiting forever lost
in our monotonous sublime.

Robespierre and Mozart as Stage

Robespierre could live with himself: "The republic
of Virtue without *la terreur* is a disaster.
Loot the chateaux, dole bread to Saint Antoine."
He found the guillotine was not an idler
hearing *mort à Robespierre* from the Convention floor,
the high harsh laughter of the innocents,
the Revolution returning to grand tragedy—
to life the place where we find happiness,
or not at all. . . . Ask the voyeur
what blue movie is worth a look through the keyhole. . . .
Even the prompted Louis Seize was living theater,
sternly and lovingly judged by his critics, who knew
Mozart's barber *Figaro* could never
cut the gold thread of the suffocating curtain.

ROBERT LOWELL

Saint-Just 1767–93

Saint-Just: his name seems stolen from the Missal. . . .
His chamois coat, the dandy's vast cravat
knotted with pretentious negligence;
he carried his head like the Holy Sacrament.
He thought only the laconic fit to rule
the austerity of his hideous cardboard Sparta.
"I must move with the stone footsteps of the sun—
faction plagues the course of revolution,
as reptiles follow the dry bed of a torrent.
I am young and therefore close to nature.
Happiness is a new idea in Europe;
we bronzed liberty with the guillotine.
I'm still twenty, I've done badly, I'll do better."
He did, the scaffold, "Je sais où je vais."

Martin Bell

Winter Coming On

A caricature from Laforgue

Fine feelings under blockade! Cargoes just in from
  Kamschatka!
Rain falling and falling and night falling
And how the wind howls . . .
Halloween, Christmas, New Year's Day
Sodden in drizzle—all my tall chimneys—
Industrial smoke through the rain!

No sitting down, all the park-benches are wet.
It's finished, I tell you, till next season.
Park-benches wet and all the leaves rust-eaten,
Horns and their echoes—dying, dying . . .

Rally of rain-clouds! Procession from the Channel—
You certainly spoiled our last free Sunday.

Drizzles:
And in wet woods the spider's webs
Weigh down with rain-drops: and that's their lot.
O golden delegates from harvest festivals,
Broad suns from cattle-shows,
Where have they buried you?
This evening a sun lies, shagged, on top of the hill,
On a tramp's mattress, rags in the gorse—
A sun as white as a blob of spittle
On tap-room saw-dust, on a litter of yellow gorse,
Of yellow October gorse.
And the horns echo and call to him—
Come back! Won't you come back?

View halloo, Tally-ho . . . Gone away.
O oratorio chorus, when will you be done?
Carrying on like mad things . . .
And there he lies, like a torn-out gland on a neck,
Shivering, with no one by.
Tally-ho, then, and get on with it.
It's good old Winter coming, we know that.
By-passes empty, turning on main roads
With no Red Riding Hood to be picked up.
Ruts from the wheels of last month's traffic—
Quixotic tram-lines to the rescue of
Cloud-patrols scurrying
Bullied by winds to transatlantic sheep-folds.
Get a move on, it's the well-known season coming, now.
And the wind last night, on top of its form,
Smashing suburban front-gardens—what a mess!
Disturbing my night's sleep with dreams of axes.

These branches, yesterday, had all their dead leaves—
Nothing but compost now, just lying about.
Dead leaves of various shapes and sizes
May a good breeze whirlpool you away
To lie on ponds, decorative,
To glow in the park-keeper's fire,
To stuff ambulance mattresses, comforts
For our soldiers overseas.

Time of year, time of year: the rust is eating,
The rust is gnawing long miles of ennui,
Telegraph-wires along main roads, deserted.

Horns, again horns . . . the echoes dying,
Dying . . .
Now changing key, going north
With the North Wind, Wagnerian,
Up to all those bloody skalds and Vikings . . .

Myself, I can't change key; too many echoes!
What beastly weather! Good-bye autumn, good-bye
ripeness . . .
And here comes the rain with the diligence of an angel.
Good-bye harvest, good-bye baskets for nutting,
And Watteau picnics under the chestnut trees.
It's barrack-room coughing again,
The landlady's horrible herbal tea—
It's TB in the garden suburb,
All the sheer misery of satellite towns.

Wellingtons, long underwear, cash chemists, dreams,
Undrawn curtains over verandas, shores
Of the red-brick sea of roofs and chimney-pots,
Lamp-shades, tea and biscuits, all the picture papers—
You'll have to be my only loves!
(And known them, have you? ritual more portentous
Than the sad pianos tinkling through the dusk,
The registrar's returns of births and deaths,
In small type weekly in the press.)

No! It's the time of year, and this clown of a planet!
O please let the wind, let the high wind
Unknit the bed-socks Time is knitting herself!
Time of year, things tearing, time of year!
O let me every year, every year, just at this time
Join in the chorus, sound the right sour note.

Footnote to Enright's "Apocalypse"

Cultivated Signals types
During the campaign in Italy

Used to tune sets in
To German stations:

"The Nazis do Beethoven beautifully."
And one American boasted

He'd caught "Freischutz" complete—
Thus diminishing his boredom.

(Our chief culture-martyr
Was Glenn Miller.)

The Tedeschi certainly bought
Their magic bullets.

What have we bought?
What have we paid for?

W. S. Graham

Letter VI

A day the wind was hardly
Shaking the youngest frond
Of April I went on
The high moor we know.
I put my childhood out
Into a cocked hat
And you moving the myrtle
Walked slowly over.
A sweet clearness became.
The Clyde sleeved in its firth
Reached and dazzled me.
I moved and caught the sweet
Courtesy of your mouth.
My breath to your breath.
And as you lay fondly
In the crushed smell of the moor
The courageous and just sun
Opened its door.
And there we lay halfway
Your body and my body
On the high moor. Without
A word then we went
Our ways. I heard the moor
Curling its cries far
Across the still loch.
The great verbs of the sea
Come down on us in a roar.
What shall I answer for?

W. S. GRAHAM

Johann Joachim Quantz's Five Lessons

The First Lesson

So that each person may quickly find that
Which particularly concerns him, certain metaphors
Convenient to us within the compass of this
Lesson are to be allowed. It is best I sit
Here where I am to speak on the other side
Of language. You, of course, in your own time
And incident (I speak in the small hours.)
Will listen from your side. I am very pleased
We have sought us out. No doubt you have read
My Flute Book. Come. The Guild clock's iron men
Are striking out their few deserted hours
And here from my high window Brueghel's winter
Locks the canal below. I blow my fingers.

The Second Lesson

Good morning, Karl. Sit down. I have been thinking
About your progress and my progress as one
Who teaches you, a young man with talent
And the rarer gift of application. I think
You must now be becoming a musician
Of a certain calibre. It is right maybe
That in our lessons now I should expect
Slight and very polite impatiences
To show in you. Karl, I think it is true,
You are now nearly able to play the flute.

Now we must try higher, aware of the terrible
Shapes of silence sitting outside your ear
Anxious to define you and really love you.
Remember silence is curious about its opposite
Element which you shall learn to represent.

Enough of that. Now stand in the correct position
So that the wood of the floor will come up through you.
Stand, but not too stiff. Keep your elbows down.
Now take a simple breath and make me a shape
Of clear unchained started and finished tones.
Karl, as well as you are able, stop
Your fingers into the breathing apertures
And speak and make the cylinder delight us.

The Third Lesson

Karl, you are late. The traverse flute is not
A study to take lightly. I am cold waiting.
Put one piece of coal in the stove. This lesson
Shall not be prolonged. Right. Stand in your place.

Ready? Blow me a little ladder of sound
From a good stance so that you feel the heavy
Press of the floor coming up through you and
Keeping your pitch and tone in character.

Now that is something, Karl. You are getting on.
Unswell your head. One more piece of coal.
Go on now but remember it must be always
Easy and flowing. Light and shadow must
Be varied but be varied in your mind
Before you hear the eventual return sound.

Play me the dance you made for the barge-master.
Stop stop Karl. Play it as you first thought
Of it in the hot boat-kitchen. That is a pleasure
For me. I can see I am making you good.
Keep the stove red. Hand me the matches. Now
We can see better. Give me a shot at the pipe.
Karl, I can still put on a good flute-mouth
And show you in this high cold room something
You will be famous to have said you heard.

W. S. GRAHAM

The Fourth Lesson

You are early this morning. What we have to do
Today is think of you as a little creator
After the big creator. And it can be argued
You are as necessary, even a composer
Composing in the flesh an attitude
To slay the ears of the gentry. Karl,
I know you find great joy in the great
Composers. But now you can put your lips to
The messages and blow them into sound
And enter and be there as well. You must
Be faithful to who you are speaking from
And yet it is all right. You will be there.

Take your coat off. Sit down. A glass of Bols
Will help us both. I think you are good enough
To not need me anymore. I think you know
You are not only an interpreter.
What you will do is always something else
And they will hear you simultaneously with
The Art you have been given to read. Karl,

I think the Spring is really coming at last.
I see the canal boys working. I realise
I have not asked you to play the flute today.
Come and look. Are the barges not moving?
You must forgive me. I am not myself today.
Be here on Thursday. When you come, bring
Me five herrings. Watch your fingers. Spring
Is apparent but it is still chilblain weather.

The Last Lesson

Dear Karl, this morning is our last lesson.
I have been given the opportunity to
Live in a certain person's house and tutor
Him and his daughters on the traverse flute.
Karl, you will be all right. In those recent
Lessons my heart lifted to your playing.

I know. I see you doing well, invited
In a great chamber in front of the gentry. I
Can see them with their dresses settling in
And bored mouths beneath moustaches sizing
You up as you are, a lout from the canal
With big ears but an angel's tread on the flute.

But you will be all right. Stand in your place
Before them. Remember Johann. Begin with good
Nerve and decision. Do not intrude too much
Into the message you carry and put out.

One last thing, Karl, remember when you enter
The joy of those quick high archipelagoes,
To make to keep your finger-stops as light
As feathers but definite. What can I say more?
Do not be sentimental or in your Art.
I will miss you. Do not expect applause.

The Thermal Stair

For the painter Peter Lanyon killed in a gliding accident 1964

I called today, Peter, and you were away.
I look out over Botallack and over Ding
Dong and Levant and over the jasper sea.

Find me a thermal to speak and soar to you from
Over Lanyon Quoit and the circling stones standing
High on the moor over Gurnard's Head where some

Time three foxglove summers ago, you came.
The days are shortening over Little Parc Owles.
The poet or painter steers his life to maim

Himself somehow for the job. His job is Love
Imagined into words or paint to make
An object that will stand and will not move.

Peter, I called and you were away, speaking
Only through what you made and at your best.
Look, there above Botallack, the buzzard riding

The salt updraught slides off the broken air
And out of sight to quarter a new place.
The Celtic sea, the Methodist sea is there.

You said once in the Engine
House below Morvah
That words make their world
In the same way as the painter's
Mark surprises him
Into seeing new.
Sit here on the sparstone
In this ruin where
Once the early beam
Engine pounded and broke
The air with industry.

Now the chuck of daws
And the listening sea.

"Shall we go down" you said
"Before the light goes
And stand under the old
Tinworkings around
Morvah and St Just?"
You said "Here is the sea
Made by alfred wallis
Or any poet or painter's
Eye it encountered.
Or is it better made
By all those vesselled men
Sometime it maintained?
We all make it again."

Give me your hand, Peter,
To steady me on the word.

Seventy-two by sixty,
Italy hangs on the wall.
A woman stands with a drink
In some polite place
And looks at SARACINESCO
And turns to mention space.
That one if she could
Would ride Artistically
The thermals you once rode.
Peter, the phallic boys
Begin to wink their lights.
Godrevy and the Wolf
Are calling Opening Time.
We'll take the quickest way
The tin singers made.
Climb here where the hand
Will not grasp on air.
And that dark-suited man
Has set the dominoes out
On the Queen's table.
Peter, we'll sit and drink
And go in the sea's roar
To Labrador with wallis
Or rise on Lanyon's stair.

Uneasy, lovable man, give me your painting
Hand to steady me taking the word-road home.
Lanyon, why is it you're earlier away?
Remember me wherever you listen from.
Lanyon, dingdong dingdong from carn to carn.
It seems tonight all Closing bells are tolling
Across the Duchy shire wherever I turn.

Philip Larkin

The Whitsun Weddings

That Whitsun, I was late getting away:
  Not till about
One-twenty on the sunlit Saturday
Did my three-quarters-empty train pull out,
All windows down, all cushions hot, all sense
Of being in a hurry gone. We ran
Behind the backs of houses, crossed a street
Of blinding windscreens, smelt the fish-dock; thence
The river's level drifting breadth began,
Where sky and Lincolnshire and water meet.

All afternoon, through the tall heat that slept
  For miles inland,
A slow and stopping curve southwards we kept.
Wide farms went by, short-shadowed cattle, and
Canals with floatings of industrial froth;
A hothouse flashed uniquely: hedges dipped
And rose: and now and then a smell of grass
Displaced the reek of buttoned carriage-cloth
Until the next town, new and nondescript,
Approached with acres of dismantled cars.

At first, I didn't notice what a noise
  The weddings made
Each station that we stopped at: sun destroys
The interest of what's happening in the shade,
And down the long cool platforms whoops and skirls
I took for porters larking with the mails,
And went on reading. Once we started, though,
We passed them, grinning and pomaded, girls
In parodies of fashion, heels and veils,
All posed irresolutely, watching us go,

As if out on the end of an event
  Waving goodbye
To something that survived it. Struck, I leant
More promptly out next time, more curiously,
And saw it all again in different terms:
The fathers with broad belts under their suits
And seamy foreheads; mothers loud and fat;
An uncle shouting smut; and then the perms,
The nylon gloves and jewellery-substitutes,
The lemons, mauves, and olive-ochres that

Marked off the girls unreally from the rest.
  Yes, from cafés
And banquet-halls up yards, and bunting-dressed
Coach-party annexes, the wedding-days
Were coming to an end. All down the line
Fresh couples climbed aboard: the rest stood round;
The last confetti and advice were thrown,
And, as we moved, each face seemed to define
Just what it saw departing: children frowned
At something dull; fathers had never known

Success so huge and wholly farcical;
  The women shared
The secret like a happy funeral;
While girls, gripping their handbags tighter, stared
At a religious wounding. Free at last,
And loaded with the sum of all they saw,
We hurried towards London, shuffling gouts of steam.
Now fields were building-plots, and poplars cast
Long shadows over major roads, and for
Some fifty minutes, that in time would seem

Just long enough to settle hats and say
  I nearly died,
A dozen marriages got under way.
They watched the landscape, sitting side by side
—An Odeon went past, a cooling tower,

And someone running up to bowl—and none
Thought of the others they would never meet
Or how their lives would all contain this hour.
I thought of London spread out in the sun,
Its postal districts packed like squares of wheat:

There we were aimed. And as we raced across
  Bright knots of rail
Past standing Pullmans, walls of blackened moss
Came close, and it was nearly done, this frail
Travelling coincidence; and what it held
Stood ready to be loosed with all the power
That being changed can give. We slowed again,
And as the tightened brakes took hold, there swelled
A sense of falling, like an arrow-shower
Sent out of sight, somewhere becoming rain.

Water

If I were called in
To construct a religion
I should make use of water.

Going to church
Would entail a fording
To dry, different clothes;

My litany would employ
Images of sousing,
A furious devout drench,

And I should raise in the east
A glass of water
Where any-angled light
Would congregate endlessly.

Days

What are days for?
Days are where we live.
They come, they wake us
Time and time over.

They are to be happy in:
Where can we live but days?

Ah, solving that question
Brings the priest and the doctor
In their long coats
Running over the fields.

High Windows

When I see a couple of kids
And guess he's fucking her and she's
Taking pills or wearing a diaphragm,
I know this is paradise

Everyone old has dreamed of all their lives—
Bonds and gestures pushed to one side
Like an outdated combine harvester,
And everyone young going down the long slide

To happiness, endlessly. I wonder if
Anyone looked at me, forty years back,
And thought, *That'll be the life;*
No God any more, or sweating in the dark

About hell and that, or having to hide
What you think of the priest. He
And his lot will all go down the long slide
Like free bloody birds. And immediately

Rather than words comes the thought of high windows:
The sun-comprehending glass,
And beyond it, the deep blue air, that shows
Nothing, and is nowhere, and is endless.

The Explosion

On the day of the explosion
Shadows pointed towards the pithead:
In the sun the slagheap slept.

Down the lane came men in pitboots
Coughing oath-edged talk and pipe-smoke,
Shouldering off the freshened silence.

One chased after rabbits; lost them;
Came back with a nest of lark's eggs;
Showed them; lodged them in the grasses.

So they passed in beards and moleskins,
Fathers, brothers, nicknames, laughter,
Through the tall gates standing open.

At noon, there came a tremor; cows
Stopped chewing for a second; sun,
Scarfed as in a heat-haze, dimmed.

The dead go on before us, they
Are sitting in God's house in comfort,
We shall see them face to face—

Plain as lettering in the chapels
It was said, and for a second
Wives saw men of the explosion

Larger than in life they managed—
Gold as on a coin, or walking
Somehow from the sun towards them,

One showing the eggs unbroken.

Keith Douglas

Behaviour of Fish in an Egyptian Tea Garden

As a white stone draws down the fish
she on the seafloor of the afternoon
draws down men's glances and their cruel wish
for love. Her red lip on the spoon

slips-in a morsel of ice-cream. Her hands
white as a shell, are submarine
fronds, sink with spread fingers, lean
along the table, carmined at the ends.

A cotton magnate, an important fish
with great eyepouches and a golden mouth
through the frail reefs of furniture swims out
and idling, suspended, stays to watch.

A crustacean old man clamped to his chair
sits near her and might coldly see
her charms through fissures where the eyes should be;
or else his teeth are parted in a stare.

Captain on leave, a lean dark mackerel,
lies in the offing, turns himself and looks
through currents of sound. The flat-eyed flatfish sucks
on a straw, staring from its repose, laxly.

And gallants in shoals swim up and lag,
circling and passing near the white attraction—
sometimes pausing, opening a conversation—
fish pause so to nibble or tug.

But now the ice-cream is finished, is
paid for. The fish swim off on business
and she sits alone at the table, a white stone
useless except to a collector, a rich man.

Vergissmeinicht

Three weeks gone and the combatants gone,
returning over the nightmare ground
we found the place again, and found
the soldier sprawling in the sun.

The frowning barrel of his gun
overshadowing. As we came on
that day, he hit my tank with one
like the entry of a demon.

Look. Here in the gunpit spoil
the dishonoured picture of his girl
who has put: *Steffi. Vergissmeinicht*
in a copybook gothic script.

We see him almost with content
abased, and seeming to have paid
and mocked at by his own equipment
that's hard and good when he's decayed.

But she would weep to see to-day
how on his skin the swart flies move;
the dust upon the paper eye
And the burst stomach like a cave.

For here the lover and killer are mingled
who had one body and one heart.
And death who had the soldier singled
has done the lover mortal hurt.

KEITH DOUGLAS

How to Kill

Under the parabola of a ball,
a child turning into a man,
I looked into the air too long.
The ball fell in my hand, it sang
in the closed fist: *Open Open*
Behold a gift designed to kill.

Now in my dial of glass appears
the soldier who is going to die.
He smiles, and moves about in ways
his mother knows, habits of his.
The wires touch his face: I cry
NOW. Death, like a familiar, hears

and look, has made a man of dust
of a man of flesh. This sorcery
I do. Being damned, I am amused
to see the centre of love diffused
and the waves of love travel into vacancy.
How easy it is to make a ghost.

The weightless mosquito touches
her tiny shadow on the stone,
and with how like, how infinite
a lightness, man and shadow meet.
They fuse. A shadow is a man
when the mosquito death approaches.

Aristocrats

"I think I am becoming a God"

The noble horse with courage in his eye
clean in the bone, looks up at a shellburst:
away fly the images of the shires
but he puts the pipe back in his mouth.

Peter was unfortunately killed by an 88:
it took his leg away, he died in the ambulance.
I saw him crawling on the sand; he said
It's most unfair, they've shot my foot off.

How can I live among this gentle
obsolescent breed of heroes, and not weep?
Unicorns, almost,
for they are falling into two legends
in which their stupidity and chivalry
are celebrated. Each, fool and hero, will be an immortal.

The plains were their cricket pitch
and in the mountains the tremendous drop fences
brought down some of the runners. Here then
under the stones and earth they dispose themselves,
I think with their famous unconcern.
It is not gunfire I hear but a hunting horn.

Richard Wilbur

Museum Piece

The good grey guardians of art
Patrol the halls on spongy shoes,
Impartially protective, though
Perhaps suspicious of Toulouse.

Here dozes one against the wall,
Disposed upon a funeral chair.
A Degas dancer pirouettes
Upon the parting of his hair.

See how she spins! The grace is there,
But strain as well is plain to see.
Degas loved the two together:
Beauty joined to energy.

Edgar Degas purchased once
A fine El Greco, which he kept
Against the wall beside his bed
To hang his pants on while he slept.

Shame

It is a cramped little state with no foreign policy,
Save to be thought inoffensive. The grammar of the language
Has never been fathomed, owing to the national habit
Of allowing each sentence to trail off in confusion.
Those who have visited Scusi, the capital city,
Report that the railway-route from Schuldig passes
Through country best described as unrelieved.

Sheep are the national product. The faint inscription
Over the city gates may perhaps be rendered,
"I'm afraid you won't find much of interest here."
Census-reports which give the population
As zero are, of course, not to be trusted,
Save as reflecting the natives' flustered insistence
That they do not count, as well as their modest horror
Of letting one's sex be known in so many words.
The uniform grey of the nondescript buildings, the absence
Of churches or comfort-stations, have given observers
An odd impression of ostentatious meanness,
And it must be said of the citizens (muttering by
In their ratty sheepskins, shying at cracks in the sidewalk)
That they lack the peace of mind of the truly humble.
The tenor of life is careful, even in the stiff
Unsmiling carelessness of the border-guards
And *douaniers*, who admit, whenever they can,
Not merely the usual carloads of deodorant
But gypsies, g-strings, hasheesh, and contraband pigments.
Their complete negligence is reserved, however,
For the hoped-for invasion, at which time the happy people
(Sniggering, ruddily naked, and shamelessly drunk)
Will stun the foe by their overwhelming submission,
Corrupt the generals, infiltrate the staff,
Usurp the throne, proclaim themselves to be sun-gods,
And bring about the collapse of the whole empire.

A Summer Morning

Her young employers, having got in late
From seeing friends in town
And scraped the right front fender on the gate,
Will not, the cook expects, be coming down.

She makes a quiet breakfast for herself.
The coffee-pot is bright,
The jelly where it should be on the shelf.
She breaks an egg into the morning light,

Then, with the bread-knife lifted, stands and hears
The sweet efficient sounds
Of thrush and catbird, and the snip of shears
Where, in the terraced backward of the grounds,

A gardener works before the heat of day.
He straightens for a view
Of the big house ascending stony-gray
Out of his beds mosaic with the dew.

His young employers having got in late,
He and the cook alone
Receive the morning on their old estate,
Possessing what the owners can but own.

Cottage Street, 1953

Framed in her phoenix fire-screen, Edna Ward
Bends to the tray of Canton, pouring tea
For frightened Mrs Plath; then, turning toward
The pale, slumped daughter, and my wife, and me,

Asks if we would prefer it weak or strong.
Will we have milk or lemon, she enquires?
The visit seems already strained and long.
Each in his turn, we tell her our desires.

It is my office to exemplify
The published poet in his happiness,
Thus cheering Sylvia, who has wished to die;
But half-ashamed, and impotent to bless,

I am a stupid life-guard who has found,
Swept to his shallows by the tide, a girl
Who, far from shore, has been immensely drowned,
And stares through water now with eyes of pearl.

How large is her refusal; and how slight
The genteel chat whereby we recommend
Life, of a summer afternoon, despite
The brewing dusk which hints that it may end.

And Edna Ward shall die in fifteen years,
After her eight-and-eighty summers of
Such grace and courage as permit no tears,
The thin hand reaching out, the last word *love*,

Outliving Sylvia who, condemned to live,
Shall study for a decade, as she must,
To state at last her brilliant negative
In poems free and helpless and unjust.

Anthony Hecht

The End of the Weekend

A dying firelight slides along the quirt
Of the cast-iron cowboy where he leans
Against my father's books. The lariat
Whirls into darkness. My girl, in skin-tight jeans,
Fingers a page of Captain Marryat,
Inviting insolent shadows to her shirt.

We rise together to the second floor.
Outside, across the lake, an endless wind
Whips at the headstones of the dead and wails
In the trees for all who have and have not sinned.
She rubs against me and I feel her nails.
Although we are alone, I lock the door.

The eventual shapes of all our formless prayers,
This dark, this cabin of loose imaginings,
Wind, lake, lip, everything awaits
The slow unloosening of her underthings.
And then the noise. Something is dropped. It grates
Against the attic beams.
                                        I climb the stairs,

Armed with a belt.
                                A long magnesium strip
Of moonlight from the dormer cuts a path
Among the shattered skeletons of mice.
A great black presence beats its wings in wrath.
Above the boneyard burn its golden eyes.
Some small grey fur is pulsing in its grip.

Lizards and Snakes

On the summer road that ran by our front porch
        Lizards and snakes came out to sun.
It was hot as a stove out there, enough to scorch
        A buzzard's foot. Still, it was fun
To lie in the dust and spy on them. Near but remote,
        They snoozed in the carriage ruts, a smile
In the set of the jaw, a fierce pulse in the throat
Working away like Jack Doyle's after he'd run the mile.

Aunt Martha had an unfair prejudice
        Against them (as well as being cold
Towards bats.) She was pretty inflexible in this,
        Being a spinster and all, and old.
So we used to slip them into her knitting box.
        In the evening she'd bring in things to mend
And a nice surprise would slide out from under the socks.
It broadened her life, as Joe said. Joe was my friend.

But we never did it again after the day
        Of the big wind when you could hear the trees
Creak like rockingchairs. She was looking away
        Off, and kept saying, "Sweet Jesus, please
Don't let him near me. He's as like as twins.
        He can crack us like lice with his fingernail.
I can see him plain as a pikestaff. Look how he grins
And swinges the scaly horror of his folded tail."

Christopher Middleton

News from Norwood

Professor Palamedes darts down Westow Street.
Nothing explains how he avoids
Colliding with mutton, plastics, pianos.
Professor Palamedes, darting down Westow Street,
Tunnels through petrol fumes and tundra;
Rhomboid oysterbeds under his rubbers,
Sparrows and sandwiches scatter before him.

Where is he going, Professor Palamedes?
It's well past three. What has he forgotten?
What can he have forgotten, Professor Palamedes,
Who stood with Agur by Solomon's elbow,
Who flogged the sea, full of nymphs and sheep,
Whom meat moods or helpful harmonies do not perplex?

Let us say he is going toward the stranger.
Again: he is going toward the stranger.
No matter who. The stranger. Who showed his face.
Who showed his face over Solomon's shoulder;
Who saw at Salamis, as planks buckled and the nymphs
Cheered, how sheep just went on cropping grass,
Side by side, to a tinkling of bells.

In the Secret House

for Ann

Why lean over the fire, and who is this
Being
Vaguely human, who
Watches the steam float from wet boots
And regards the rose interiors

Various woods keep
Recomposing themselves; nothing holds
In the fire, the fire is always
Less than it was, the fire—

Expulsion
Of old smells, new intangible horizons
Does not hear through its decay,
Calling in the cold
Rain, the little owl, one note
Over and over

Nor, under its breath, does the fire give
A thought to the petrified
Print of a snail, its broken wheel—
Rays on a rock at the hearth's edge. Who
Is this, and who thinks

Through the fire, sees the rayed shell,
Solid axis, the whirling death
Of some incorrigible small thing
Before the ice came

Before the ice came carving out the mountain
And the fire took
Or took care of someone
And the house was constructed
In a cloud of goats, coming, going,
Before the cockerels

Put down their tracks, cry and claw,
Through generations, this fly
Settled on the breadloaf—

So stare, into the fire, and what for
The important
Citadel, towers of light, crepuscular
Tunnels, simply face
The black rain, blue wave
Of mountain birdsong

Mud on my hands, little owl, it is
No grief to share with you,
Little owl,
The one note, not lost, for nothing

Charles Tomlinson

Descartes and the Stove

Thrusting its armoury of hot delight,
  Its negroid belly at him, how the whole
Contraption threatened to melt him
  Into recognition. Outside, the snow
Starkened all that snow was not—
  The boughs' nerve-net, angles and gables
Denting the brilliant hoods of it. The foot-print
  He had left on entering, had turned
To a firm dull gloss, and the chill
  Lined it with a fur of frost. Now
The last blaze of day was changing
  All white to yellow, filling
With bluish shade the slots and spoors
  Where, once again, badger and fox would wind
Through the phosphorescence. All leaned
  Into that frigid burning, corded tight
By the lightlines as the slow sun drew
  Away and down. The shadow, now,
Defined no longer: it filled, then overflowed
  Each fault in snow, dragged everything
Into its own anonymity of blue
  Becoming black. The great mind
Sat with his back to the unreasoning wind
  And doubted, doubted at his ear
The patter of ash and, beyond, the snow-bound farms,
  Flora of flame and iron contingency
And the moist reciprocation of his palms.

CHARLES TOMLINSON

The Chances of Rhyme

The chances of rhyme are like the chances of meeting—
In the finding fortuitous, but once found, binding:
They say, they signify and they succeed, where to succeed
Means not success, but a way forward
If unmapped, a literal, not a royal succession;
Though royal (it may be) is the adjective or region
That we, nature's royalty, are led into.
Yes. We are led, though we seem to lead
Through a fair forest, an Arden (a rhyme
For Eden)—breeding ground for beasts
Not bestial, but loyal and legendary, which is more
Than nature's are. Yet why should we speak
Of art, of life, as if the one were all form
And the other all Sturm-und-Drang? And I think
Too, we should confine to Crewe or to Mow
Cop, all those who confuse the fortuitousness
Of art with something to be met with only
At extremity's brink, reducing thus
Rhyme to a kind of rope's end, a glimpsed grass
To be snatched at as we plunge past it—
Nostalgic, after all, for a hope deferred.
To take chances, as to make rhymes
Is human, but between chance and impenitence
(A half-rhyme) come dance, vigilance
And circumstance (meaning all that is there
Besides you, when you are there). And between
Rest-in-peace and precipice,
Inertia and perversion, come the varieties
Increase, lease, re-lease (in both
Senses); and immersion, conversion—of inert
Mass, that is, into energies to combat confusion.
Let rhyme be my conclusion.

Swimming Chenango Lake

Winter will bar the swimmer soon.
  He reads the water's autumnal hesitations
A wealth of ways: it is jarred,
  It is astir already despite its steadiness,
Where the first leaves at the first
  Tremor of the morning air have dropped
Anticipating him, launching their imprints
  Outwards in eccentric, overlapping circles.
There is a geometry of water, for this
  Squares off the clouds' redundances
And sets them floating in a nether atmosphere
  All angles and elongations: every tree
Appears a cypress as it stretches there
  And every bush that shows the season,
A shaft of fire. It is a geometry and not
  A fantasia of distorting forms, but each
Liquid variation answerable to the theme
  It makes away from, plays before:
It is a consistency, the grain of the pulsating flow.
  But he has looked long enough, and now
Body must recall the eye to its dependence
  As he scissors the waterscape apart
And sways it to tatters. Its coldness
  Holding him to itself, he grants the grasp,
For to swim is also to take hold
  On water's meaning, to move in its embrace
And to be, between grasp and grasping, free.
  He reaches in-and-through to that space
The body is heir to, making a where
  In water, a possession to be relinquished
Willingly at each stroke. The image he has torn
  Flows-to behind him, healing itself,
Lifting and lengthening, splayed like the feathers
  Down an immense wing whose darkening spread

Shadows his solitariness: alone, he is unnamed
  By this baptism, where only Chenango bears a name
In a lost language he begins to construe—
  A speech of densities and derisions, of half-
Replies to the questions his body must frame
  Frogwise across the all but penetrable element.
Human, he fronts it and, human, he draws back
  From the interior cold, the mercilessness
That yet shows a kind of mercy sustaining him.
  The last sun of the year is drying his skin
Above a surface a mere mosaic of tiny shatterings,
  Where a wind is unscaping all images in the flowing
    obsidian,
The going-elsewhere of ripples incessantly shaping.

John Ashbery

An Additional Poem

Where then shall hope and fear their objects find?
The harbor cold to the mating ships,
And you have lost as you stand by the balcony
With the forest of the sea calm and gray beneath.
A strong impression torn from the descending light
But night is guilty. You knew the shadow
In the trunk was raving
But as you keep growing hungry you forget.
The distant box is open. A sound of grain
Poured over the floor in some eagerness—we
Rise with the night let out of the box of wind.

De Imagine Mundi

The many as noticed by the one:
The noticed one, confusing itself with the many
Yet perceives itself as an individual
Traveling between two fixed points.
Such glance as dares dart out
To pin you in your afternoon lair is only a reflex,
A speech in a play consisting entirely of stage directions
Because there happened to be a hole for it there.
Unfortunately, fewer than one half of one per cent
Recognized the divined gesture as currency
(Which it is, albeit inflated)
And the glance comes to rest on top of a steeple
With about as much interest as a bird's.

They had moved out here from Boston
Those two. (The one, a fair sample
Of the fair-sheaved many,
The other boggling into single oddness
Plays at it when he must
Not getting better or younger.)

The weather kept them at their small tasks:
Sorting out the news, mending this and that.
The great poker face impinged on them. And rejoiced
To be a living reproach to
Something new they've got.
Skeeter collecting info: "Did you know
About the Mugwump of the Final Hour?"
Their even flesh tone
A sign of "Day off",
The buses moving along quite quickly on the nearby island
Also registered, as per his plan.

Taking a path you never saw before
Thought you knew the area
(The many perceive they fight off sleep).
"A few gaffers stay on
To the end of the line
Tho that is between bookends."
The note is struck finally
With just sufficient force but like a thunderbolt
As only the loudest can be imagined.
And they stay on to talk it over.

Fear of Death

What is it now with me
And is it as I have become?
Is there no state free from the boundary lines
Of before and after? The window is open today

And the air pours in with piano notes
In its skirts, as though to say, "Look, John,
I've brought these and these"—that is,
A few Beethovens, some Brahmses,

A few choice Poulenc notes. . . . Yes,
It is being free again, the air, it has to keep coming back
Because that's all it's good for.
I want to stay with it out of fear

That keeps me from walking up certain steps,
Knocking at certain doors, fear of growing old
Alone, and of finding no one at the evening end
Of the path except another myself

Nodding a curt greeting: "Well, you've been awhile
But now we're back together, which is what counts."
Air in my path, you could shorten this,
But the breeze has dropped, and silence is the last word.

Thom Gunn

Autumn Chapter in a Novel

Through woods, Mme Une Telle, a trifle ill
With idleness, but no less beautiful,
Walks with the young tutor, round their feet
Mob syllables slurred to a fine complaint,
Which in their time held off the natural heat.

The sun is distant, and they fill out space
Sweatless as watercolour under glass.
He kicks abruptly. But we may suppose
The leaves he scatters thus will settle back
In much the same position as they rose.

A tutor's indignation works on air,
Altering nothing; action bustles where,
Towards the pool by which they lately stood,
The husband comes discussing with his bailiff
Poachers, the broken fences round the wood.

Pighead! The poacher is at large, and lingers,
A dead mouse gripped between his sensitive fingers:
Fences already keep the live game out:
See how your property twists her parasol,
Hesitates in the tender trap of doubt.

Here they repair, here daily handle lightly
The brief excitements that disturb them nightly;
Sap draws back inch by inch, and to the ground
The words they uttered rustle constantly:
Silent, they watch the growing, weightless mound.

They leave at last a chosen element,
Resume the motions of their discontent;
She takes her sewing up, and he again
Names to her son the deserts on the globe,
And leaves thrust violently upon the pane.

In Santa Maria del Popolo

Waiting for when the sun an hour or less
Conveniently oblique makes visible
The painting on one wall of this recess
By Caravaggio, of the Roman School,
I see how shadow in the painting brims
With a real shadow, drowning all shapes out
But a dim horse's haunch and various limbs,
Until the very subject is in doubt.

But evening gives the act, beneath the horse
And one indifferent groom, I see him sprawl,
Foreshortened from the head, with hidden face,
Where he has fallen, Saul becoming Paul.
O wily painter, limiting the scene
From a cacophony of dusty forms
To the one convulsion, what is it you mean
In that wide gesture of the lifting arms?

No Ananias croons a mystery yet,
Casting the pain out under name of sin.
The painter saw what was, an alternate
Candour and secrecy inside the skin.
He painted, elsewhere, that firm insolent
Young whore in Venus' clothes, those pudgy cheats,
Those sharpers; and was strangled, as things went,
For money, by one such picked off the streets.

I turn, hardly enlightened, from the chapel
To the dim interior of the church instead,
In which there kneel already several people,
Mostly old women: each head closeted
In tiny fists holds comfort as it can.
Their poor arms are too tired for more than this
—For the large gesture of solitary man,
Resisting, by embracing, nothingness.

My Sad Captains

One by one they appear in
the darkness: a few friends, and
a few with historical
names. How late they start to shine!
but before they fade they stand
perfectly embodied, all

the past lapping them like a
cloak of chaos. They were men
who, I thought, lived only to
renew the wasteful force they
spent with each hot convulsion.
They remind me, distant now.

True, they are not at rest yet,
but now that they are indeed
apart, winnowed from failures,
they withdraw to an orbit
and turn with disinterested
hard energy, like the stars.

Faustus Triumphant

The dazzled blood
submits, carries the
flame through me to every
organ till blood itself
is flamy
            flame animates me
with delight in time's things
so intense that I am
almost lost to time

Already vining the
arbours of my body, flame
starts from my fingers!
now my flame-limbs wrap round
marble   ebony   fur   flesh
without combusting what
they embrace. I
lick everything.
                        What
tracks led

                There.
and there and there
where I pricked the
arm where I
got the blood to sign

I remember there was
a bargain made but I
think I'm safe. For
vein and artery are not
store keepers, nor is
Nature a lawyer.

THOM GUNN

My joy so great
that if hell threatens, the
memory alone of flame
protects me. There is
no terror in combustion.
I shall rejoice to
enter into him
                    Father-
Nature, the Great Flame

Ted Hughes

The Thought-Fox

I imagine this midnight moment's forest:
Something else is alive
Beside the clock's loneliness
And this blank page where my fingers move.

Through the window I see no star:
Something more near
Though deeper within darkness
Is entering the loneliness:

Cold, delicately as the dark snow,
A fox's nose touches twig, leaf;
Two eyes serve a movement, that now
And again now, and now, and now

Sets neat prints into the snow
Between trees, and warily a lame
Shadow lags by stump and in hollow
Of a body that is bold to come

Across clearings, an eye,
A widening deepening greenness,
Brilliantly, concentratedly,
Coming about its own business

Till, with a sudden sharp hot stink of fox
It enters the dark hole of the head.
The window is starless still; the clock ticks,
The page is printed.

TED HUGHES

Thrushes

Terrifying are the attent sleek thrushes on the lawn,
More coiled steel than living—a poised
Dark deadly eye, those delicate legs
Triggered to stirrings beyond sense—with a start, a bounce, a stab
Overtake the instant and drag out some writhing thing.
No indolent procrastinations and no yawning states,
No sighs or head-scratchings. Nothing but bounce and stab
And a ravening second.

Is it their single-mind-sized skulls, or a trained
Body, or genius, or a nestful of brats
Gives their days this bullet and automatic
Purpose? Mozart's brain had it, and the shark's mouth
That hungers down the blood-smell even to a leak of its own
Side and devouring of itself; efficiency which
Strikes too streamlined for any doubt to pluck at it
Or obstruction deflect.

With a man it is otherwise. Heroisms on horseback,
Outstripping his desk-diary at a broad desk,
Carving at a tiny ivory ornament
For years: his act worships itself—while for him,
Though he bends to be blent in the prayer, how loud and above what
Furious spaces of fire do the distracting devils
Orgy and hosannah, under what wilderness
Of black silent waters weep.

Pike

Pike, three inches long, perfect
Pike in all parts, green tigering the gold.
Killers from the egg: the malevolent aged grin.
They dance on the surface among the flies.

Or move, stunned by their own grandeur,
Over a bed of emerald, silhouette
Of submarine delicacy and horror.
A hundred feet long in their world.

In ponds, under the heat-struck lily pads—
Gloom of their stillness:
Logged on last year's black leaves, watching upwards.
Or hung in an amber cavern of weeds

The jaws' hooked clamp and fangs
Not to be changed at this date;
A life subdued to its instrument;
The gills kneading quietly, and the pectorals.

Three we kept behind glass,
Jungled in weed: three inches, four,
And four and a half: fed fry to them—
Suddenly there were two. Finally one

With a sag belly and the grin it was born with.
And indeed they spare nobody.
Two, six pounds each, over two feet long,
High and dry and dead in the willow-herb—

One jammed past its gills down the other's gullet:
The outside eye stared: as a vice locks—
The same iron in this eye
Though its film shrank in death.

A pond I fished, fifty yards across,
Whose lilies and muscular tench
Had outlasted every visible stone
Of the monastery that planted them—

Stilled legendary depth:
It was as deep as England. It held
Pike too immense to stir, so immense and old
That past nightfall I dared not cast

But silently cast and fished
With the hair frozen on my head
For what might move, for what eye might move.
The still splashes on the dark pond,

Owls hushing the floating woods
Frail on my ear against the dream
Darkness beneath night's darkness had freed,
That rose slowly towards me, watching.

Snowdrop

Now is the globe shrunk tight
Round the mouse's dulled wintering heart.
Weasel and crow, as if moulded in brass,
Move through an outer darkness
Not in their right minds,
With the other deaths. She, too, pursues her ends,
Brutal as the stars of this month,
Her pale head heavy as metal.

The Bear

In the huge, wide-open, sleeping eye of the mountain
The bear is the gleam in the pupil
Ready to awake
And instantly focus.

The bear is glueing
Beginning to end
With glue from people's bones
In his sleep.

The bear is digging
In his sleep
Through the wall of the Universe
With a man's femur.

The bear is a well
Too deep to glitter
Where your shout
Is being digested.

The bear is a river
Where people bending to drink
See their dead selves.

The bear sleeps
In a kingdom of walls
In a web of rivers.

He is the ferryman
To dead land.

His price is everything.

TED HUGHES

Theology

No, the serpent did not
Seduce Eve to the apple.
All that's simply
Corruption of the facts.

Adam ate the apple.
Eve ate Adam.
The serpent ate Eve.
This is the dark intestine.

The serpent, meanwhile,
Sleeps his meal off in Paradise—
Smiling to hear
God's querulous calling.

Kreutzer Sonata

Now you have stabbed her good
A flower of unknown colour appallingly
Blackened by your surplus of bile
Blooms wetly on her dress.

"Your mystery! Your mystery! . . ."
All facts, with all absence of facts,
Exhale as the wound there
Drinks its roots and breathes them to nothing.

Vile copulation! Vile!——etcetera.
But now your dagger has outdone everybody's.
Say goodbye, for your wife's sweet flesh goes off,
Booty of the envious spirit's assault.

A sacrifice, not a murder.
One hundred and forty pounds
Of excellent devil, for God.
She tormented Ah demented you

With that fat lizard Trukachevsky,
That fiddling, leering penis.
Yet why should you castrate yourself
To be rid of them both?

Now you have stabbed her good
Trukachevsky is cut off
From any further operation on you,
And she can find nobody else.

Rest in peace, Tolstoy!
It must have taken supernatural greed
To need to corner all the meat in the world,
Even from your own hunger.

Pibroch

The sea cries with its meaningless voice,
Treating alike its dead and its living,
Probably bored with the appearance of heaven
After so many millions of nights without sleep,
Without purpose, without self-deception.

Stone likewise. A pebble is imprisoned
Like nothing in the Universe.
Created for black sleep. Or growing
Conscious of the sun's red spot occasionally,
Then dreaming it is the foetus of God.

Over the stone rushes the wind,
Able to mingle with nothing,
Like the hearing of the blind stone itself.
Or turns, as if the stone's mind came feeling
A fantasy of directions.

Drinking the sea and eating the rock
A tree struggles to make leaves—
An old woman fallen from space
Unprepared for these conditions.
She hangs on, because her mind's gone completely.

Minute after minute, aeon after aeon,
Nothing lets up or develops.
And this is neither a bad variant nor a tryout.
This is where the staring angels go through.
This is where all the stars bow down.

Roy Fisher

The Entertainment of War

I saw the garden where my aunt had died
And her two children and a woman from next door;
It was like a burst pod filled with clay.

A mile away in the night I had heard the bombs
Sing and then burst themselves between cramped houses
With bright soft flashes and sounds like banging doors;

The last of them crushed the four bodies into the ground,
Scattered the shelter, and blasted my uncle's corpse
Over the housetop and into the street beyond.

Now the garden lay stripped and stale; the iron shelter
Spread out its separate petals around a smooth clay saucer,
Small, and so tidy it seemed nobody had ever been there.

When I saw it, the house was blown clean by blast and care:
Relations had already torn out the new fireplaces;
My cousin's pencils lasted me several years.

And in his office notepad that was given me
I found solemn drawings in crayon of blondes without dresses.
In his lifetime I had not known him well.

These were the things I noticed at ten years of age;
Those, and the four hearses outside our house,
The chocolate cakes, and my classmates' half-shocked envy.

But my grandfather went home from the mortuary
And for five years tried to share the noises in his skull,
Then he walked out and lay under a furze-bush to die.

When my father came back from identifying the daughter
He asked us to remind him of her mouth.
We tried. He said "I think it was the one".

These were marginal people I had met only rarely
And the end of the whole household meant that no grief was seen;
Never have people seemed so absent from their own deaths.

This bloody episode of four whom I could understand better dead
Gave me something I needed to keep a long story moving;
I had no pain of it; can find no scar even now.

But had my belief in the fiction not been thus buoyed up
I might, in the sigh and strike of the next night's bombs
Have realized a little what they meant, and for the first time been afraid.

As He Came Near Death

As he came near death things grew shallower for us:
We'd lost sleep and now sat muffled in the scent of tulips, the medical odours, and the street sounds going past, going away;
And he, too, slept little, the morphine and the pink light the curtains let through floating him with us,
So that he lay and was worked out on to the skin of his life and left there,
And we had to reach only a little way into the warm bed to scoop him up.

A few days, slow tumbling escalators of visitors and cheques, and something like popularity;

During this time somebody washed him in a soap called
Narcissus and mounted him, frilled with satin, in a
polished case.

Then the hole: this was a slot punched in a square of plastic
grass rug, a slot lined with white polythene, floored
with dyed green gravel.
The box lay in it; we rode in the black cars round a corner, got
out into our coloured cars and dispersed in easy
stages.

After a time the grave got up and went away.

Alan Brownjohn

Of Dancing

My dancing is, in my opinion, good,
In the right, cramped circumstances, and provided
Other people are too preoccupied with
Their own to notice mine. I am happy
To have lived into an informal age when
Standing and shaking in approximate rhythm, not
Bowing and guiding, is the idea. Because to
Have to know regulated steps and be skilful was what
I could never manage at all when it was the thing.

So I do dance. But I'm never entirely sure.
It's a kind of movement you would never make
In the normal course, and how much it always seems
To obtrude on the natural in an embarrassing
Way wherever people get it started!
Set it apart, on a stage, with a large
Orchestra, it's all right, it's undoubtedly clever,
And the costumes are glorious to gawp at, but
It still looks a little bit foolish, moving like *that?*

To speak of how all its origins are so
Utterly primal—the planets, the seasons,
The rhythms of mating, and so on, and so on,
Is to list a lot of fundamental things,
Explain them, and exorcise dancing:
Because simply why dance if you've come to understand
What dancing mimes so roughly, or makes such
A repetitive pantomime of? Sleights of courtship,
Postures of delight, grief, vanity, idolatry I see

All around me more sharp and subtle for not being
Done in a style. Dancing has social uses,
I know, but so did elemental spears and punches before
They invented tables for eating and conducting
Verbal negotiation (and does hands
Gripping slyly under a table ever happen
In the middle of a fandango?)
Moreover, if the elemental stuff
Of dancing is banal, the ancient, ritual and customary

Panoply of "the dance" is incredibly peculiar;
Fellows in feathers, or kilts, or puma-skins,
Guys trinkling little bells down there in Hampshire,
Or folding arms over black boots flicking in the
Urals . . . one surely turns away to find somewhere quieter,
Where one needn't be part of a silly circle
Of grins, clapping hands in moronic unison (I once
Took a pocket torch in, to go on reading—*The Listener*,
I believe—all the way through a Gene Kelly musical).

For ostensible moralist reasons, the
Puritans disliked dancing: but they also
Opposed all giving and wearing of jewellery,
In which they may well have been right; so with dancing,
They may also have come at the truth
From a wrong, religious direction. But, down Oxford Street
These days, whatever the mortgage rate, there jogs
In shine or rain an irrelevant group of chanters
Shuffling to the rhythm of tiny cymbals, opposing

Shaven sublimity to the big, crude, selling
Metropolis around; and *dancing*, in sandals, for converts.
They'd like to see everyone join them . . . how unlikely,
I think; and how such unlikelihood shows
That most of us only don or discard our
Finery, to dance, in a fit of social desperation.
I recall that outside the Hammersmith Palais,
There once was an illuminated sign announcing
A group of performers known as THE SANDS OF TIME.

For months, the words, I surmised, were a motto
Of that establishment: a thousand grains shaken
Nightly in that vast box, a thousand softies
Sifting for life-partners as the hours and days
Ticked on in tawdry, implacable rhythms. Yet the
Dancing prospers—telling how many the world leaves
Despoiled of words, of gestures diverse and specific,
Of shades of forehead, or hintings of finger-tips,
Or any more delicate tremor that speaks the whole thing;

And this is the crux. Tides vary, exact shelvings
Of pebbles on shores don't repeat, while patterns of clouds
Are never the same, are never *patterns*. Raindrops,
At unforeseen moments run, and weigh, down, minutely,
A million particular grass-blades: movement, movement,
Everlastingly novel shifts of a universe not
Gracelessly ordered, not presided by a setter of
Regulations. Vanity is so sad pretending to represent
Nature with humans dancing. Those who can move need not
dance.

Peter Redgrove

Intimate Supper

He switched on the electric light and laughed,
He let light shine in the firmament of his ceiling,
He saw the great light shine around and it was good,
The great light that rilled through its crystalline pendentives,
And marvelled at its round collection in a cheval glass,
And twirled the scattered crystal rays in his champagne glass.
He spun the great winds through his new hoover
And let light be in the kitchen and that was good too
For he raised up the lid of the stock-pot
And dipped a deep spoon in the savours that were rich
And swarming, and felt the flavours live in his mouth
Astream with waters. He danced to the fire and raked it and
  created red heat
And skipped to the bathroom and spun the shining taps
Dividing air from the deep, and the water, good creature,
Gave clouds to his firmament for he had raked the bowels
Of the seamy coal that came from the deep earth.
And he created him Leviathan and wallowed there,
Rose, and made his own image in the steamy mirrors
Having brooded over them, wiping them free
Again from steamy chaos and the mist that rose from the deep,
But the good sight faded
For there was no help, no help meet for him at all,
And he set his table with two stars pointed on wax
And with many stars in the cutlery and clear crystal
And he set thereon fruits of the earth, and thin clean bowls
For the clear waters of the creatures of earth that love to be
  cooked,
And until the time came that he had appointed
Walked in his garden in the cool of the evening, waited.

PETER REDGROVE

The Idea of Entropy at Maenporth Beach

"C'est elle! Noire et pourtant lumineuse."

A boggy wood as full of springs as trees.
Slowly she slipped into the muck.
It was a white dress, she said, and that was not right.
Leathery polished mud, that stank as it split.
It is a smooth white body, she said, and that is not right,
Not quite right; I'll have a smoother,
Slicker body, and my golden hair
Will sprinkle rich goodness everywhere.
So slowly she backed into the mud.

If it were a white dress, she said, with some little black,
Dressed with a little flaw, a smut, some swart
Twinge of ancestry, or if it were all black
Since I am white, but—it's my mistake.
So slowly she slunk, all pleated, into the muck.

The mud spatters with rich seed and ranging pollens.
Black darts up the pleats, black pleats
Lance along the white ones, and she stops
Swaying, cut in half. Is it right, she sobs
As the fat, juicy, incredibly tart muck rises
Round her throat and dims the diamond there?
It is right, so she stretches her white neck back
And takes a deep breath once and a one step back.
Some golden strands afloat pull after her.

The mud recoils, lies heavy, queasy, swart.
But then this soft blubber stirs, and quickly she comes up
Dressed like a mound of lickerish earth,
Swiftly ascending in a streaming pat
That grows tall, smooths brimming hips, and steps out
On flowing pillars, darkly draped.
And then the blackness breaks open with blue eyes
Of this black Venus rising helmeted in night
Who as she glides grins brilliantly, and drops
Swatches superb as molasses on her path.

Who is that negress running on the beach
Laughing excitedly with teeth as white
As the white waves kneeling, dazzled, to the sands?
Clapping excitedly the black rooks rise,
Running delightedly in slapping rags
She sprinkles substance, and the small life flies!

She laughs aloud, and bares her teeth again, and cries:
Now that I am all black, and running in my richness
And knowing it a little, I have learnt
It is quite wrong to be all white always;
And knowing it a little, I shall take great care
To keep a little black about me somewhere.
A snotty nostril, a mourning nail will do.
Mud is a good dress, but not the best.
Ah, watch, she runs into the sea. She walks
In streaky white on dazzling sands that stretch
Like the whole world's pursy mud quite purged.
The black rooks coo like doves, new suns beam
From every droplet of the shattering waves,
From every crystal of the shattered rock.
Drenched in the mud, pure white rejoiced,
From this collision were new colours born,
And in their slithering passage to the sea
The shrugged-up riches of deep darkness sang.

Minerals of Cornwall, Stones of Cornwall

A case of samples

Splinters of information, stones of information,
Drab stones in a drab box, specimens of a distant place,
Granite, galena, talc, lava, kaolin, quartz,
Landscape in a box, under the dull sky of Leeds—

One morning was awake, in Cornwall, by the estuary,
In the tangy pearl-light, tangy tin-light,
And the stones were awake, these ounce-chips,
Had begun to think, in the place they came out of.

Tissues of the earth, in their proper place,
Quartz tinged with the rose, the deep quick,
Scrap of tissue of the slow heart of the earth,
Throbbing the light I look at it with,
Pumps slowly, most slowly, the deep organ of the earth;
And galena too, snow-silvery, its chipped sample
Shines like sun on peaks, it plays and thinks with the mineral
  light,
It sends back its good conclusions, it is exposed,
It sends back the light silked and silvered,
And talc, and kaolin, why they are purged, laundered,
As I see the white sand of some seamless beaches here
Is laundered and purged like the whole world's mud
Quite cleansed to its very crystal; talc a white matt,
Kaolin, the white wife of Cornwall
Glistening with inclusions, clearly its conclusions
Considered and laid down, the stone-look
Of its thoughts and opinions of flowers
And turf riding and seeding above it in the wind,
Thoughts gathered for millennia as they blossomed in millions
Above its then kaolin-station within the moor,
The place of foaming white streams and smoking blanched
  mountains.
Asbestos had found this bright morning
Its linear plan of fibres, its simple style,
Lay there, declaring, like the others;
Granite, the great rock, the rock of rocks,
At home now, flecked green, heavily contented in its box,
Riding with me high above its general body,
The great massif, while its fellows, the hills of it
Rise high around us; nor was lava silent
Now it remembered by glistening in this light
Boiling, and was swart with great content

Having seen God walking over the burning marl, having seen
A Someone thrusting his finger into the mountainside
To make it boil—here is the issue of this divine intrusion,
I am the issue of this divine intrusion,
My heart beats deep and fast, my teeth
Glisten over the swiftness of my breath,
My thoughts hurry like lightning, my voice
Is a squeak buried among the rending of mountains,
I am a mist passing through the crevices of these great seniors
Enclosed by me in a box, now free of the light, conversing
Of all the issue this homecoming has awakened in the stone
  mind
The mines like frozen bolts of black lightning deep in the land
Saying, and the edge of their imaginings cuts across my mind:
We are where we were taken from, and so we show ourselves
Ringing with changes and calls of fellowship
That call to us ton to ounce across Cornish valleys.

The valleys throng with the ghosts of stone so I may scarcely
  pass,
Their loving might crush, they cry out at their clumsiness,
Move away, death-dealing hardnesses, in love.
The house is full of a sound of running water,
The night is a black honey, crystals wink at the brim,
A wind blows through the clock, the black mud outside
Lies curled up in haunches like a sleeping cat.

George MacBeth

Scissor-Man

I am dangerous
   in a crisis
with sharp legs and a screw

   in my genitals. I slice
bacon-rind for a living. At nights I
   lie dried

under the draining-board, dreaming
   of Nutcrackers
and the Carrot-grater. If I should

   catch him rubbing
those tin nipples of hers
   in the bread-bin

(God rust his pivot!) so much for
   secrecy. I'd have his
washer off. And

   then what? It scarcely pays
to be "Made In Hamburg". Even
   our little salt-spoon

can sound snooty
   with an E.P.N.S. under
his armpit. Even the pie-server

   who needs re-dipping. In sixteen
stainless years dividing
   chippolata-links I

am still denied
 a place in the sink unit. And
you can imagine

 what pairing-off is possible
with a wriggle of cork-screws
 in an open knife-box. So I

keep my legs
 crossed. I never cut up
rough. I lie with care

 in a world where a squint leg
could be fatal. I sleep like a weapon
 with a yen for a pierced ear.

The Killing

In a wooden room, surrounded by lights and
  Faces, the place where death had
Come to its sharpest point was exposed. In a
  Clear shell they examined the
  Needle of death. How many
 Million deaths were concentrated in

A single centre! The compass of death was
  Lifted, detached and broken,
Taken and burned. The seed of death lay in the
  Hold. Without disturbance or
  Ceremony they sealed it
 In foil. The ship stirred at the quay. The

Pilot was ready. A long shadow slanted
  On the harbour water. The
Fin bearing the ignorant crew on their brief
  Journey cut through the air. Three
  Furlongs out at sea the
 Strike of the engine fell. The screws turned

At ease on the rim of the world. The hour had
Come. The action was taken.
The doors opened. And the ash went out to sea
Borne with the moon on the tide
Away from the shore towards the
Open water. The shell rocked on the

Livid waves. The captain washed his hands in the
Salt to cleanse the illusion
Of blood. The light casket lay on the soaked planks
Emptied of all it held. And
A pale fish that used to leap
For a fly or a grub to the bare

Trees and then sink back to the living water
Forgot the way: and died in
The dry branches. The baked island was crusted
With the blue eggs of terns from
Which no soft wings would ever
Break to fly in the sun. And the raw

Turtle crawled inland instead of towards the
Sea, believing the parched soil
Would change to sand again. They thought the killing
Was over: but the needle
Had run wild in the shell. The
Poison was in the salt current of

The world. Let no Jew or Gentile believe that
The fly in the brain of the
Bald man adjusting his earphones annuls his
Own nature; nor pity the
Man imprisoned for stealing
Fire from heaven. He, too, is guilty.

Geoffrey Hill

Ovid in the Third Reich

non peccat, quaecumque potest peccasse negare,
solaque famosam culpa professa facit.

Amores, III, xiv

I love my work and my children. God
Is distant, difficult. Things happen.
Too near the ancient troughs of blood
Innocence is no earthly weapon.

I have learned one thing: not to look down
So much upon the damned. They, in their sphere,
Harmonize strangely with the divine
Love. I, in mine, celebrate the love-choir.

A Song from Armenia

Roughly-silvered leaves that are the snow
On Ararat seen through those leaves.
The sun lays down a foliage of shade.

A drinking-fountain pulses its head
Two or three inches from the troughed stone.
An old woman sucks there, gripping the rim.

Why do I have to relive, even now,
Your mouth, and your hand running over me
Deft as a lizard, like a sinew of water?

GEOFFREY HILL

from Mercian Hymns

I

King of the perennial holly-groves, the riven sandstone: overlord of the M5: architect of the historic rampart and ditch, the citadel at Tamworth, the summer hermitage in Holy Cross: guardian of the Welsh Bridge and the Iron Bridge: contractor to the desirable new estates: saltmaster: money-changer: commissioner for oaths: martyrologist: the friend of Charlemagne.

"I liked that," said Offa, "sing it again."

XI

Coins handsome as Nero's; of good substance and weight. *Offa Rex* resonant in silver, and the names of his moneyers. They struck with accountable tact. They could alter the king's face.

Exactness of design was to deter imitation; mutilation if that failed. Exemplary metal, ripe for commerce. Value from a sparse people, scrapers of salt-pans and byres.

Swathed bodies in the long ditch; one eye upstaring. It is safe to presume, here, the king's anger. He reigned forty years. Seasons touched and retouched the soil.

Heathland, new-made watermeadow. Charlock, marsh-marigold. Crepitant oak forest where the boar furrowed black mould, his snout intimate with worms and leaves.

XIII

Trim the lamp; polish the lens; draw, one by one, rare coins to the light. Ringed by its own lustre, the masterful head emerges, kempt and jutting, out of England's well. Far from his underkingdom of crinoid and crayfish, the rune-stone's province, *Rex Totius Anglorum Patriae,* coiffured and ageless, portrays the self-possession of his possession, cushioned on a legend.

XVIII

At Pavia, a visitation of some sorrow. Boethius' dungeon. He shut his eyes, gave rise to a tower out of the earth. He willed the instruments of violence to break upon meditation. Iron buckles gagged; flesh leaked rennet over them; the men stooped, disentangled the body.

He wiped his lips and hands. He strolled back to the car, with discreet souvenirs for consolation and philosophy. He set in motion the furtherance of his journey. To watch the Tiber foaming out much blood.

XXIX

"Not strangeness, but strange likeness. Obstinate, outclassed forefathers, I too concede, I am your staggeringly-gifted child."

So, murmurous, he withdrew from them. Gran lit the gas, his dice whirred in the ludo-cup, he entered into the last dream of Offa the King.

Sylvia Plath

Flute Notes from a Reedy Pond

Now coldness comes sifting down, layer after layer,
To our bower at the lily root.
Overhead the old umbrellas of summer
Wither like pithless hands. There is little shelter.

Hourly the eye of the sky enlarges its blank
Dominion. The stars are no nearer.
Already frog-mouth and fish-mouth drink
The liquor of indolence, and all things sink

Into a soft caul of forgetfulness.
The fugitive colors die.
Caddis worms drowse in their silk cases,
The lamp-headed nymphs are nodding to sleep like statues.

Puppets, loosed from the strings of the puppet-master,
Wear masks of horn to bed.
This is not death, it is something safer.
The wingy myths won't tug at us any more:

The molts are tongueless that sang from above the water
Of golgotha at the tip of a reed,
And how a god flimsy as a baby's finger
Shall unhusk himself and steer into the air.

The Arrival of the Bee Box

I ordered this, this clean wood box
Square as a chair and almost too heavy to lift.
I would say it was the coffin of a midget
Or a square baby
Were there not such a din in it.

The box is locked, it is dangerous.
I have to live with it overnight
And I can't keep away from it.
There are no windows, so I can't see what is in there.
There is only a little grid, no exit.

I put my eye to the grid.
It is dark, dark,
With the swarmy feeling of African hands
Minute and shrunk for export,
Black on black, angrily clambering.

How can I let them out?
It is the noise that appals me most of all,
The unintelligible syllables.
It is like a Roman mob,
Small, taken one by one, but my god, together!

I lay my ear to furious Latin.
I am not a Caesar.
I have simply ordered a box of maniacs.
They can be sent back.
They can die, I need feed them nothing, I am the owner.

I wonder how hungry they are.
I wonder if they would forget me
If I just undid the locks and stood back and turned into a tree.
There is the laburnum, its blond colonnades,
And the petticoats of the cherry.

They might ignore me immediately
In my moon suit and funeral veil.
I am no source of honey
So why should they turn on me?
Tomorrow I will be sweet God, I will set them free.

The box is only temporary.

The Moon and the Yew Tree

This is the light of the mind, cold and planetary.
The trees of the mind are black. The light is blue.
The grasses unload their griefs on my feet as if I were God,
Prickling my ankles and murmuring of their humility.
Fumey, spiritous mists inhabit this place
Separated from my house by a row of headstones.
I simply cannot see where there is to get to.

The moon is no door. It is a face in its own right,
White as a knuckle and terribly upset.
It drags the sea after it like a dark crime; it is quiet
With the O-gape of complete despair. I live here.
Twice on Sunday, the bells startle the sky——
Eight great tongues affirming the Resurrection.
At the end, they soberly bong out their names.

The yew tree points up. It has a Gothic shape.
The eyes lift after it and find the moon.
The moon is my mother. She is not sweet like Mary.
Her blue garments unloose small bats and owls.
How I would like to believe in tenderness——
The face of the effigy, gentled by candles,
Bending, on me in particular, its mild eyes.

I have fallen a long way. Clouds are flowering
Blue and mystical over the face of the stars.
Inside the church, the saints will be all blue,
Floating on their delicate feet over the cold pews,
Their hands and faces stiff with holiness.
The moon sees nothing of this. She is bald and wild.
And the message of the yew tree is blackness—blackness and silence.

Among the Narcissi

Spry, wry, and grey as these March sticks,
Percy bows, in his blue peajacket, among the narcissi.
He is recuperating from something on the lung.

The narcissi, too, are bowing to some big thing:
It rattles their stars on the green hill where Percy
Nurses the hardship of his stitches, and walks and walks.

There is a dignity to this; there is a formality—
The flowers vivid as bandages, and the man mending.
They bow and stand: they suffer such attacks!

And the octogenarian loves the little flocks.
He is quite blue; the terrible wind tries his breathing.
The narcissi look up like children, quickly and whitely.

Mary's Song

The Sunday lamb cracks in its fat.
The fat
Sacrifices its opacity. . . .

A window, holy gold.
The fire makes it precious,
The same fire

Melting the tallow heretics,
Ousting the Jews.
Their thick palls float

Over the cicatrix of Poland, burnt-out
Germany.
They do not die.

Grey birds obsess my heart,
Mouth-ash, ash of eye.
They settle. On the high

Precipice
That emptied one man into space
The ovens glowed like heavens, incandescent.

It is a heart,
This holocaust I walk in,
O golden child the world will kill and eat.

Seamus Heaney

Requiem for the Croppies

The pockets of our great coats full of barley—
No kitchens on the run, no striking camp—
We moved quick and sudden in our own country.
The priest lay behind ditches with the tramp.
A people, hardly marching—on the hike—
We found new tactics happening each day:
We'd cut through reins and rider with the pike
And stampede cattle into infantry,
Then retreat through hedges where cavalry must be thrown.
Until, on Vinegar Hill, the fatal conclave.
Terraced thousands died, shaking scythes at cannon.
The hillside blushed, soaked in our broken wave.
They buried us without shroud or coffin
And in August the barley grew up out of the grave.

Cana Revisited

No round-shouldered pitchers here, no stewards
To supervise consumption or supplies
And water locked behind the taps implies
No expectation of miraculous words.

But in the bone-hooped womb, rising like yeast,
Virtue intact is waiting to be shown,
The consecration wondrous (being their own)
As when the water reddened at the feast.

SEAMUS HEANEY

Traditions

For Tom Flanagan

I

Our guttural muse
was bulled long ago
by the alliterative tradition,
her uvula grows

vestigial, forgotten
like the coccyx
or a Brigid's Cross
yellowing in some outhouse

while custom, that "most
sovereign mistress",
beds us down into
the British isles.

II

We are to be proud
of our Elizabethan English:
"varsity", for example,
is grass-roots stuff with us;

we "deem" or we "allow"
when we suppose
and some cherished archaisms
are correct Shakespearean.

Not to speak of the furled
consonants of lowlanders
shuttling obstinately
between bawn and mossland.

III

MacMorris, gallivanting
round the Globe, whinged
to courtier and groundling
who had heard tell of us

as going very bare
of learning, as wild hares,
as anatomies of death:
"What ish my nation?"

And sensibly, though so much
later, the wandering Bloom
replied, "Ireland," said Bloom,
"I was born here. Ireland."

The Tollund Man

I

Some day I will go to Aarhus
To see his peat-brown head,
The mild pods of his eye-lids,
His pointed skin cap.

In the flat country nearby
Where they dug him out,
His last gruel of winter seeds
Caked in his stomach,

Naked except for
The cap, noose and girdle,
I will stand a long time.
Bridegroom to the goddess,

She tightened her torc on him
And opened her fen,
Those dark juices working
Him to a saint's kept body,

Trove of the turfcutters'
Honeycombed workings.
Now his stained face
Reposes at Aarhus.

II

I could risk blasphemy,
Consecrate the cauldron bog
Our holy ground and pray
Him to make germinate

The scattered, ambushed
Flesh of labourers,
Stockinged corpses
Laid out in the farmyards,

Tell-tale skin and teeth
Flecking the sleepers
Of four young brothers, trailed
For miles along the lines.

III

Something of his sad freedom
As he rode the tumbril
Should come to me, driving,
Saying the names

Tollund, Grabulle, Nebelgard,
Watching the pointing hands
Of country people,
Not knowing their tongue.

Out there in Jutland
In the old man-killing parishes
I will feel lost,
Unhappy and at home.

Douglas Dunn

A Removal from Terry Street

On a squeaking cart, they push the usual stuff,
A mattress, bed ends, cups, carpets, chairs,
Four paperback westerns. Two whistling youths
In surplus U.S. Army battle-jackets
Remove their sister's goods. Her husband
Follows, carrying on his shoulders the son
Whose mischief we are glad to see removed,
And pushing, of all things, a lawnmower.
There is no grass in Terry Street. The worms
Come up cracks in concrete yards in moonlight.
That man, I wish him well. I wish him grass.

The Musical Orchard

Girls on mopeds rode to Fécamp parties,
And as they passed the ripened orchard
Cheered an old man's music,
Not knowing it was sad.
Those French tunes on the saxophone,
The music inside fruit!

Supreme Death

Fishing on a wide river from a boat
A corpse was caught, her black hair like a huge weed,
The hook stuck in a black shroud strangely marked.

There were others. Hundreds gathered round the boat,
Some turning, their white faces like pillows.
I lost my oars, and the river quickened.

On the towpath, men in their hundreds
Ran with the tide, singing, and pushing,
When they felt like it, some poor fool into the river.

Death, the best of all mysteries, layer
After layer is peeled off your secrecy
Until all that is left is an inexplicable ooze.

Too late, it is myself.
Too late, my heart is a beautiful top.
Too late, all the dead in the river are my friends.

Emblems

Rich nights in another climate—
White tables and the best Moselle,
A garden that slopes to a clear river;
Style I cannot make and was not born to claim.

And the factory is humming at full production
Just over the hill, making money,
Whispering, a big fish without eyes,
The most profound unhappiness.

The Estuarial Republic

The saltmarsh on the horizon
Signals with vertical smoke.
The ferry is brilliant
With ultimate parties,
A revelry of pistons,
Flushing lavatories, glasses
In hands and at shouting mouths.

The dark bed opens its mouth and howls.

"Here is a ticket
To the other side of the river,
It is very lazy but will get you there.
Here are some coins; here is the hat
You wear on deck, by the life-rafts.
Here are the gumboots
For the saltmarsh with the hulks,
It is stupid to get your feet wet.
Here are silver bullets and a gun
To defend yourself with,
It is every man's right to carry one there.
Here is the notepaper,
And the birthday pen. Come when you can
But first drop us a line.
You won't like all of it,
But the danger is fun,
And everyone visits, at least once.
You will get a chance to shoot someone,
For the horsemen raid us,
And *that* is fun. They are so stupid and reckless,
They love to die in battle,
It's a pity they are so handsome.
Their code is such it doesn't matter
Much if we just shoot them down.
Our stockade is ditched and barbed,
And you will love
The violence of our passions,
If not at first."

James Fenton

The Pitt-Rivers Museum, Oxford

Is shut
22 hours a day and all day Sunday
And should not be confused
With its academic brother, full of fossils
And skeletons of bearded seals. Take
Your heart in your hand and go; it does not sport
Any of Ruskin's hothouse Venetian
And resembles rather, with its dusty girders,
A vast gymnasium or barracks—though
The resemblance ends there.

Entering
You will find yourself in a climate of nut castanets,
A musical whip
From the Torres Straits, from Mirzapur a sistrum
Called Jumka, "used by aboriginal
Tribes to attract small game
On dark nights", a mute violin,
Whistling arrows, coolie cigarettes
And a mask of Saagga, the Devil Doctor,
The eyelids worked by strings.

Outside,
All around you, there are students researching
With a soft electronic
Hum, but here, where heels clang
On iron grates, voices are at best
Disrespectful: "Please sir, where's the withered
Hand?" For teachers the thesis is salutary
And simple, a hierarchy of progress culminating
In the Entrance Hall, but children are naturally
Unaware of and unimpressed by this.

JAMES FENTON

Encountering
"A jay's feather worn as a charm
In Buckinghamshire, Stone",
We cannot either feel that we have come
Far or in any particular direction.
Item. A dowser's twig, used by Webb
For locating the spring, "an excellent one",
For Lord Pembroke's waterworks at Dinton
Village. "The violent twisting is shown
On both limbs of the fork."

Yes
You have come upon the fabled lands where myths
Go when they die,
But some, especially the Brummagem capitalist
Juju, have arrived prematurely. Idols
Cast there and sold to tribes for a huge
Price for human sacrifice do
(Though slightly hidden) actually exist
And we do well to bring large parties
Of Schoolchildren here to find them.

Outdated
Though the cultural anthropological system be
The lonely and unpopular
Might find the landscapes of their childhood marked out
Here, in the chaotic piles of souvenirs.
The claw of a condor, the jaw-bone of a dolphin,
These cleave the sky and the waves but they
Would trace from their windowseats the storm petrel's path
From Lindness or Naze to the North Cape,
Sheltered in the trough of the wave.

For the solitary,
The velveted only child who wrestled
With eagles for their feathers
And the young girl on the hill, who heard
The din on the causeway and saw the large

Hound with the strange pretercanine eyes
Herald the approach of her turbulent lover,
This boxroom of the forgotten or hardly possible
Is laid with the snares of privacy and fiction
And the dangerous third wish.

Beware.
You are entering the climate of a foreign logic
And are cursed by the hair
Of a witch, earth from the grave of a man
Killed by a tiger and a woman who died
In childbirth, 2 leaves from the tree
Azumü, which withers quickly, a nettle-leaf,
A leaf from the swiftly deciduous "Flame of the
Forest" and a piece of a giant taro,
A strong irritant if eaten.

Go
As a historian of ideas or a sex-offender,
For the primitive art,
As a dusty semiologist, equipped to unravel
The seven components of that witch's curse
Or the syntax of the mutilated teeth. Go
In groups to giggle at curious finds.
But do not step into the kingdom of your promises
To yourself, like a child entering the forbidden
Woods of his lonely playtime:

All day,
Watching the groundsman breaking the ice
From the stone trough,
The sun slanting across the lawns, the grass
Thawing, the stable-boy blowing on his fingers,
He had known what tortures the savages had prepared
For him there, as he calmly pushed open the gate
And entered the wood near the placard: "TAKE NOTICE
MEN-TRAPS AND SPRING-GUNS ARE SET ON THESE PREMISES."
For his father had protected his good estate.

Acknowledgements

For permission to reprint copyright material, the following acknowledgements are made:

For poems by Conrad Aiken, to the author, Charles Scribner's Sons and A. M. Heath & Co. Ltd.

Preludes for Memnon (Scribners) 1931.

For poems by John Ashbery, to the author, Carcanet Press Ltd and Wesleyan University Press.

The Tennis Court Oath (Wesleyan University Press) 1962.

Self-Portrait in a Convex Mirror (Carcanet Press) 1977. Copyright © 1961 by John Ashbery.

For poems by W. H. Auden, to the author, Faber & Faber Ltd and Curtis Brown Ltd.

Collected Shorter Poems (Faber) 1950.

Nones (Faber) 1952.

Collected Poems (Faber) 1976.

In *Collected Shorter Poems,* "Prologue" appears under the title of "Perhaps" and "Watch any day" under the title of "A Free One".

For poems by George Barker, to the author and Faber & Faber Ltd.

Collected Poems 1930–1955 (Faber) 1957.

In Memory of David Archer (Faber) 1973.

Dialogues (Faber) 1976.

For poems by Martin Bell, to Peter Porter his literary executor.

Collected Poems 1937–1966 (Macmillan) 1967.

For poems by John Berryman, to Faber & Faber Ltd and Farrar, Straus & Giroux, Inc.

77 Dream Songs (Faber) 1964; (Farrar, Straus & Giroux) 1959. Copyright © 1959, 1962, 1963, 1964 by John Berryman.

Berryman's Sonnets (Faber) 1968; (Farrar, Straus & Giroux) 1967. Copyright © 1952, 1967 by John Berryman.

His Toy, His Dream, His Rest (Faber) 1969; (Farrar, Straus &

Giroux) 1968. Copyright © 1965, 1966, 1967, 1968, 1969 by John Berryman.

For poems by Elizabeth Bishop, to Farrar, Straus & Giroux, Inc.

The Complete Poems (Farrar, Straus & Giroux) 1969. Copyright © 1947, 1955, 1969 by Elizabeth Bishop. Renewed Copyright © 1974 by Elizabeth Bishop.

For the poem by Alan Brownjohn, to the author and Secker and Warburg Ltd.

A Song of Good Life (Secker & Warburg) 1975.

For the poems by Basil Bunting, to the author and Oxford University Press.

Collected Poems (O.U.P.) 1978. Copyright © Basil Bunting 1978.

For poems by Hart Crane, to the poet's family and Mr Horace Liveright.

Collected Poems (Liveright) 1933.

For poems by E. E. Cummings, to his literary executors, Mr Horace Liveright, Granada Publishing Ltd and Harcourt Brace Jovanovich, Inc.

is 5 (Boni & Liveright) 1926.

Complete Poems 1936–1962 (Granada) 1981; (Harcourt Brace Jovanovich) 1963. Copyright © 1963 by Marion Morehouse Cummings.

For poems by H. D., to her literary executors, Mr Horace Liveright, Chatto & Windus Ltd and Mr John Schaffner.

Collected Poems (Boni & Liveright) 1925.

Red Roses for Bronze (Chatto & Windus) 1931.

For poems by Keith Douglas, to Mrs Marie Douglas and Oxford University Press.

Collected Poems (Editions Poetry London) 1951.

The Complete Poems of Keith Douglas, edited by Desmond Graham (O.U.P.) 1978. Copyright © Oxford University Press 1978.

For poems by Douglas Dunn, to the author and Faber & Faber Ltd.

Terry Street (Faber) 1969.

The Happier Life (Faber) 1972.

Love or Nothing (Faber) 1974.

For poems by Lawrence Durrell, to the author and Faber & Faber Ltd.

Collected Poems (Faber) 1980.

For poems by Richard Eberhart, to the author and Chatto & Windus Ltd.

Collected Poems 1930–1960 (Chatto & Windus) 1960.

For poems by T. S. Eliot, to Mrs Eliot and Faber & Faber Ltd.

Collected Poems 1909–1962 (Faber) 1963.

For poems by William Empson, to the author and Chatto & Windus Ltd.

Collected Poems (Chatto & Windus) 1962.

For poems by Gavin Ewart, to the author.

Pleasures of the Flesh (Alan Ross) 1966.

The Deceptive Grin of the Gravel Porters (London Magazine Editions) 1968.

For the poem by James Fenton, to the author and Secker & Warburg Ltd.

Terminal Moraine (Secker & Warburg) 1972.

For poems by Roy Fisher, to the author.

Collected Poems (Fulcrum Press) 1969.

For the poem by Roy Fuller, to the author and Andre Deutsch Ltd.

New Poems (Deutsch) 1968.

For poems by David Gascoyne, to the author.

"Landscape" appeared in *The Year's Poetry* (Bodley Head) 1934 and "In Defence of Humanism" in *A Little Treasury of Modern Poetry* (Scribners) 1950.

For poems by W. S. Graham, to the author.

Collected Poems (Faber) 1979.

For poems by Robert Graves, to the author, the Seizin Press, Cassell & Co. Ltd, A. P. Watt Ltd and International Authors N.V.

Collected Poems (Cassell) 1938.

Collected Poems (Cassell) 1959.

For poems by Thom Gunn, to the author and Faber & Faber Ltd.

The Sense of Movement (Faber) 1957.

My Sad Captains (Faber) 1961.
Jack Straw's Castle (Faber) 1976.

For poems by Seamus Heaney, to the author and Faber & Faber Ltd.

Door into the Dark (Faber) 1969.
Wintering Out (Faber) 1972.

For poems by Anthony Hecht, to the author and Oxford University Press and Atheneum Publishers, Inc.

The Hard Hours (O.U.P.) 1967; (Atheneum Publishers) 1967. Copyright © 1959, 1967 by Anthony Hecht.

For poems by Geoffrey Hill, to the author and Andre Deutsch Ltd.

King Log (Deutsch) 1970.
Mercian Hymns (Deutsch) 1975.

For poems by Ted Hughes, to the author and Faber & Faber Ltd.

Hawk in the Rain (Faber) 1957.
Lupercal (Faber) 1960.
Wodwo (Faber) 1967.

For poems by T. E. Hulme, to Mr Herbert Read and Routledge & Kegan Paul Ltd.

Speculations (Kegan Paul) 1924. Hulme's five poems had previously been published as an addendum to Ezra Pound's *Ripostes* (Elkin Mathews).

For extracts from the poem by David Jones, to the author and Faber & Faber Ltd.

In Parenthesis (Faber) 1937.

For poems by Philip Larkin, to the author and Faber & Faber Ltd.

The Whitsun Weddings (Faber) 1964.
High Windows (Faber) 1974.

For poems by C. Day Lewis, to the author, The Hogarth Press Ltd and Jonathan Cape Ltd.

Collected Poems (Hogarth Press) 1935.
A Time to Dance (Hogarth Press) 1935.
Overtures to Death (Cape) 1938.
Poems 1943–1947 (Cape) 1948.

For poems by Robert Lowell, to the author, Faber & Faber

Ltd, Harcourt Brace Jovanovich, Inc., and Farrar, Straus & Giroux, Inc.

Lord Weary's Castle (Harcourt Brace Jovanovich) 1946, Copyright © 1946, 1974 by Robert Lowell.

Poems 1938–1949 (Faber) 1950.

Life Studies (Faber) 1959; (Farrar, Straus & Giroux) 1956. Copyright © 1956, 1959 by Robert Lowell.

Near the Ocean (Faber) 1967; (Farrar, Straus & Giroux) 1963. Copyright © 1963, 1965, 1966, 1967 by Robert Lowell.

History (Faber) 1973; (Farrar, Straus & Giroux) 1967. Copyright © 1967, 1968, 1969, 1970, 1973 by Robert Lowell.

For poems by George MacBeth, to the author and Macmillan, London and Basingstoke.

Collected Poems (Macmillan) 1971.

For poems by Hugh MacDiarmid, to Mrs Valda Grieve and Martin Brian & O'Keefe Ltd.

Complete Poems (Martin Brian & O'Keefe) 1978.

For poems by Louis MacNeice, to Mrs MacNeice and Faber & Faber Ltd.

Collected Poems 1925–1948 (Faber) 1949.

Solstices (Faber) 1961.

Collected Poems (Faber) 1979.

For poems by Charles Madge, to the author and Faber & Faber Ltd.

The Disappearing Castle (Faber) 1937.

The Father Found (Faber) 1941.

"Blocking the Pass" appeared in *Poems of Tomorrow* (Chatto & Windus) 1935.

"Lusty Juventus" and "At War" appeared in *New Verse* (August and December 1934).

For poems by Christopher Middleton, to the author and Carcanet Press Ltd.

Torse Three (Longmans) 1962.

Carminalenia (Carcanet) 1980.

For the poem by Harold Monro, to Mrs Alida Monro and Mr Cobden-Sanderson.

Collected Poems (Cobden-Sanderson) 1933.

For poems by Marianne Moore, to the author and Faber & Faber Ltd.

Collected Poems (Faber) 1951. In *Collected Poems,* "Black Earth" appears under the title of "Melancthon".

For poems by Wilfred Owen, to his literary executors and Chatto & Windus Ltd.

Poems (Chatto & Windus) 1931.

For poems by Sylvia Plath, to Mr Ted Hughes.

Collected Poems (Faber) 1981.

For poems by Ezra Pound, to the author, Mr A. V. Moore and Faber & Faber Ltd.

Homage to Sextus Propertius (Faber) 1934.

Selected Poems (Faber) 1948.

The Cantos of Ezra Pound (Faber) 1964.

"Canto 115" appeared in No. 28 of the *Paris Review.*

For poems by John Crowe Ransom, to the author, Alfred A. Knopf, Inc., Eyre & Spottiswoode Ltd and Laurence Pollinger Ltd.

Selected Poems (Eyre & Spottiswoode) 1947.

For poems by Herbert Read, to the author and Faber & Faber Ltd.

Collected Poems (Faber) 1946.

For poems by Peter Redgrove, to the author and Routledge & Kegan Paul Ltd.

Dr Faust's Sea-Spiral Spirit (Routledge & Kegan Paul) 1972.

For poems by Isaac Rosenberg, to his literary executors and Chatto & Windus Ltd.

Collected Poems (Chatto & Windus) 1950.

For poems by Edith Sitwell, to her literary executors, Mr Basil Blackwell and Duckworth & Co. Ltd.

The Wooden Pegasus (Blackwell) 1920.

Collected Poems (Duckworth) 1930.

For poems by Stephen Spender, to the author and Faber & Faber Ltd.

Collected Poems (Faber) 1955.

For poems by Wallace Stevens, to his literary executors, Faber & Faber Ltd and Alfred A. Knopf, Inc.

Collected Poems of Wallace Stevens (Faber) 1955; (Knopf)

1954. Copyright © 1942, 1950, 1952, 1954 by Wallace Stevens.

Opus Posthumous (Faber) 1959; (Knopf) 1957. Copyright © 1957 by Elsie Stevens and Holly Stevens.

For poems by Allen Tate, to the author and Eyre & Spottiswoode Ltd.

Selected Poems (Eyre & Spottiswoode) 1947.

For poems by Dylan Thomas, to the Trustees for the Copyrights of the late Dylan Thomas and J. M. Dent & Sons Ltd.

Collected Poems 1934–1952 (Dent) 1952.

For poems by R. S. Thomas, to the author, Granada Publishing Ltd and Macmillan, London and Basingstoke, Ltd.

Selected Poems 1946–68 (Granada) 1973.

H'm (Macmillan) 1972.

Laboratories of the Spirit (Macmillan) 1975.

For poems by Charles Tomlinson, to the author and Oxford University Press.

The Way of a World (O.U.P.) 1969. Copyright © Oxford University Press 1969.

For poems by Richard Wilbur, to the author, Faber & Faber Ltd and Harcourt Brace Jovanovich, Inc.

Ceremony and Other Poems (Harcourt Brace Jovanovich) 1950. Copyright © 1950, 1978 by Richard Wilbur.

Advice to a Prophet and Other Poems (Faber) 1962; (Harcourt Brace Jovanovich) 1961. Copyright © 1960 by Richard Wilbur. "A Summer Morning" first published in the *New Yorker* magazine.

The Mind-Reader (Faber) 1977; (Harcourt Brace Jovanovich) 1972. Copyright © 1972 by Richard Wilbur.

For poems by William Carlos Williams, to New Directions, New York.

Collected Later Poems (New Directions) 1962; Copyright © 1944, 1948 by William Carlos Williams.

Pictures from Brueghel and Other Poems (New Directions) 1962; Copyright © 1954 by William Carlos Williams.

For poems by W. B. Yeats, to Michael and Anne Yeats and Macmillan London Ltd.

Collected Poems (Macmillan) 1950.